Sermons on the Gospels of the ecclesiastical year – Primary Source Edition

Sieck, Henry, 1850-1916

SERMONS

ON THE

GOSPELS OF THE ECCLESIASTICAL YEAR

BY

HENRY SIECK,

Pastor of Mount Olive Lutheran Church, Milwaukee, Wis.

PART FIRST.

. Louis, Mo.
CONCORDIA PUBLISHING HOUSE.
1902.

PREFACE.

Of the early Christians at Jerusalem we read that *they continued steadfastly in the apostles' doctrine,* and the apostles themselves spoke not as of themselves, but preached and propagated the doctrine committed to them by their Lord and confirmed to them by the Spirit whom He had sent from the Father. Thus did they, preachers and hearers, bear the first and foremost token of true discipleship, according to their Master's word, *If ye continue in my word, then are ye my disciples indeed.* Again, when Antichrist set up his throne in the church, the chief abominations in holy places were the false doctrines whereby the souls of men, instead of being made free by the truth of the gospel, were fettered and held in bondage and the thraldom of a worse than Babylonian captivity. And when, in the days of the Reformation, the bulwarks of Satan were laid low and Israel was set free, this wondrous work of God was performed by the restoration of the doctrine of Christ to the preachers and hearers of Christendom. Alas, then came a time when this kindly light of saving truth was again obscured, when rationalism was enthroned in the pulpits of what went under the name, but no longer fought under the standards, of the Lutheran church. It was then chiefly in the old books handed down from better days and read and reread at the firesides of humble people, whose libraries consisted of the Bible, the Hymnbook, the Catechism, and the family postils, that the pure doctrine of the grace of God in Christ Jesus was still the bread of life which nourished immortal souls unto life everlasting. God bless those old postils and those who read them, the old German postils, of which there are thousands also in this country, where they have contributed and still contribute not a little toward keeping preachers and hearers steadfastly in the apostles' doctrine. For though by the goodness and mercy of God the Lutheran church is no longer an unknown quantity in America, and its light of pure doctrine is not hidden under a bushel, but shines throughout the land from coast to coast, and to far distant shores beyond the seas, it must not be forgotten that this light of pure Scripture doctrine came to the restorers of sound Lutheranism in America largely through the quarto and folio volumes of the sixteenth and seventeenth centuries and was to a considerable extent exhibited and communicated to hearers and readers directly from these sources. Nor are the days of their usefulness now at an end. May their blessings never cease.

But here we have a new postil, not in the language of Luther and of the land of our fathers in the faith of the Lutheran church. And this should not be a cause of regret, but of grateful rejoicing. For here we have the same doctrine, pure and unalloyed, the same precious truth of God which the apostles and prophets set forth by divine inspiration, which was professed by the martyrs, was voiced forth in strains of spiritual song, was cherished by our fathers, is held in sacred esteem by ourselves, and is being, God grant it, handed down to our children and children's children, also in the language in which this volume speaks, and in which these sermons were preached. Every page of the book bears testimony that the preacher and his hearers continue steadfastly in the apostles' doctrine. May the same be said of its readers, and may their numbers be great and increasing. May the Lord, who blessed the old postils, abundantly bless this new one. And let those who love Zion say, Yea and Amen.

Pago Pago, Tutuila, April 2, 1902.

A. L. GRAEBNER.

CONTENTS.

FIRST SUNDAY IN ADVENT.

MATT 21, 1—9.

And when they drew nigh unto Jerusalem, and were come to Bethphage, unto the mount of Olives, then sent Jesus two disciples, saying unto them, Go into the village over against you, and straightway ye shall find an ass tied, and a colt with her· loose them, and bring them unto me   And if any man say ought unto you, ye shall say, The Lord hath need of them, and straightway he will send them   And this was done, that it might be fulfilled which was spoken by the prophet, saying, Tell ye the daughter of Sion, Behold, thy King cometh unto thee, meek, and sitting upon an ass, and a colt the foal of an ass   And the disciples went, and did as Jesus commanded them, and brought the ass, and the colt, and put on them their clothes, and they sat him thereon   And a very great multitude spread their garments in the way, others cut down branches from the trees, and strawed them in the way.   And the multitudes that went before, and that followed, cried, saying, Hosanna to the son of David· Blessed is he that cometh in the name of the Lord, Hosanna in the highest.

BELOVED FRIENDS IN CHRIST:

About three hundred years before the event occurred which is recorded in our Gospel — Christ entering the city of Jerusalem — there was an occurrence of a similar nature at the gates of that city. A great king, in command of a formidable army and surrounded with military splendor, halted his fiery steed before the walls and demanded of the sentinels that were stationed in the turrets an unconditional surrender.   There was consternation among the inhabitants.   While the king was making preparations to besiege the city of the Jews, the highpriest hurriedly called together the priests, and had them put on their white robes, and quickly escorted them to the gate where the king was issuing his orders for the assault.   The gate was opened, and the priests reverently bowed before the great king, and he was informed by the highpriest that the inhabitants would not offer resistance, but that they surrendered the city to him and his army.   All they asked of him was that he should show clemency and consider the Jews his loyal subjects   That king was Alexander the Great.

What a difference between that great monarch coming to the holy city in military attire, followed by grim warriors, and Jesus coming meek and lowly, surrounded by the joyful throng of his followers shouting as they moved along, "Hosanna to the Son of David· Blessed is He that cometh in the name of the Lord; Hosanna in the highest!" Not a welcome guest was Alexander the Great, though it is said that he kindly treated the Jews and even condescended to offer sacrifice in the temple according to Jewish rites. The Jews had just cause to fear the Macedonian king who on his conquering tour to the East laid waste the land, and burned the cities, and either slew or took captive and then sold as slaves all who dared to oppose him. But what cause did the Jews have to fear Jesus with whom the prophecy of Zechariah was being fulfilled: "Tell ye the daughter of Sion, Behold, thy king cometh unto thee, meek, and sitting upon an ass, and a colt the foal of an ass?" Gladly could all the inhabitants of Jerusalem welcome that king in their midst.

And now, my hearers, that King comes to this day. He comes invisibly in His word and in His holy sacraments. Every land, every city, every hamlet, every home where the gospel has found a place, is Jerusalem, and there is the daughter of Sion, and the promise given to her is being fulfilled: "Behold, thy King cometh unto thee." And since among us we have the Word of God taught in its purity and the sacraments administered according to the Lord's institution, that King is our King also, and He continually comes to us also in His word and sacraments. Hear me, therefore, proclaim to all of you this day the joyful message of Advent,

"BEHOLD, THY KING COMETH UNTO THEE!"

And we shall consider,

    I. *What manner of King cometh unto us,*
    II. *What is the purpose of His coming.*

I.

What comfort for us to know that our King cometh unto us: Jesus who came to Jerusalem. He has not forsaken us. Though He does withhold from us His visible presence, yet He is with us invisibly and enters our homes and our hearts! What comfort for us to know that our King does *visit* us on this earth, though He ascended into heaven and sits on the right hand of God the Father Almighty! And why is that so comforting? Because our King is the King of kings and the Lord of lords. He is more than Alexander the Great and all the powerful rulers on earth. He is a King under whose rule and guidance we shall neither fear nor want For how does our Gospel describe this King? What manner of King cometh unto us? He is an omniscient King who knows even the most secret thoughts in the hearts of men; He is an almighty King who can accomplish all He desires and with whom nothing is impossible; He is a meek King whose heart is full of kindness and tender mercies.

He is, first of all, an omniscient King We read, "*And when they drew nigh unto Jerusalem, and were come to Beth-phage, unto the mount of Olives, then sent Jesus two disciples, saying unto them, Go into the village over against you, and straightway ye shall find an ass tied, and a colt with her loose them and bring them unto me.*" We must know that the Lord had not been in the village where the beasts of burden were tied. He had not sent some one ahead to procure those animals and tie them there for His disciples to come and get them for Him. No; He came from the opposite direction, from Galilee, by the way of Jericho and Bethany. And yet He knew, as though Himself He had been there, that those animals were in waiting for Him. Now, how is that to be explained? There is but one explanation, and that is to concede His omniscience. O what comfort to be derived therefrom ! Behold, thy King cometh unto thee, an omniscient King! He knows everything and all, the past and the future. Nothing is hidden before Him He knows all our cares and troubles. Men may make light of our tribulations, while we are suffering to such an extent as almost to make us feel as though we could not bear our burden any longer; the Lord, our King, does not undervalue our agonies and our distress. He knows our difficulties and fully understands our groaning under those heavy burdens. He knows even the very thoughts in the hearts of men, and, if there are enemies plotting against us secretly, He knows all their designs; and He even knew them before they conceived such thoughts of wickedness. He is an omniscient King.

And, at the same time, an almighty King. We read, "*And if any man say ought unto you, ye shall say, The Lord hath need of them; and straightway he will send them.*" And again we read, "*The disciples went, and did as Jesus commanded them, and brought the ass, and the colt*" In the gospel according to St. Luke we find an account of this same occurrence, and there we are told, "And as they were loosing the colt, the owners thereof said unto them, Why loose ye the colt? And they said, The Lord hath need of him." How wonderful! The Lord would make use of a colt. He does not purchase the animal. He borrows it from a man who is apparently a perfect stranger to Him. He does not even ask for it, but directs His disciples to get it and moves the owner's heart not to interfere, but to let the disciples take the animal to their Master. He influences that man's will from afar off and makes him do exactly what He wants Him to do. Now, how is this to be explained? There is but one explanation, and that is to concede His omnipotence. O what comfort to be derived therefrom! Behold, thy King cometh unto thee, an almighty King, a King who is so powerful as even to rule the hearts of men and to make them perform and do His will! Art thou in want and bodily needs? Art thou tempted to say, "What shall we eat? what shall we drink? wherewithal shall we be clothed?" Behold, thy King cometh unto thee! He can furnish thee with the necessaries of life. Heaven and earth belong to Him. His resources will never give out. He is able to procure for you in some way all that you need. Art thou in ill health and suffering, coping with diseases that baffle medical skill? He is the Lord, thy Healer He can give thee health and strength and make all thy diseases disappear. Art thou in difficulties or perplexities of any kind, in sorrow, in trials and tribulations? He can deliver thee. He can lead thee out of thy troubles with His powerful hand. He is almighty. With Him nothing is impossible

But the most comforting point of our gospel is this: He is also a meek King. We read, "*All this was done, that it might be fulfilled which was spoken by the prophet, saying, Tell ye the daughter of Sion, Behold, thy King cometh unto thee, meek, and sitting upon an ass, and a colt, the foal of an ass.*" Woe unto us if that omniscient and omnipotent King came to us provoked and full of anger! For since He is omniscient, He certainly knows all our sins and manifold transgressions; and since He is almighty, He can severely punish our iniquities and pour out upon us the vials of His wrath. And what else have we deserved with our sins than to be doomed to eternal condemnation? But no; our King comes unto us not to mete out justice and to reward us according to our iniquities. He comes meek, in lovingkindness. No harm does He intend. He is full of compassion. His heart is filled with kindness and tender mercies. Art thou troubled on account of thy sins? Does thy conscience tell thee thou wert too great a sinner, thy sins could never be forgiven, thou hadst no right to grace, because thou didst not accept the Lord's grace at the time it was offered unto thee? Behold, thy King cometh unto thee, meek. He again offers unto thee His grace and assures to thee the full forgiveness of all thy sins. Art thou afflicted with some malady, with poverty, with want, with distress, with sorrow of any kind, or tribulation of any description? Behold, thy King cometh unto thee, meek. His desire is to lighten thy burden or to give thee strength patiently to bear what thou must bear in this life for thine own good, so as not to be deprived of the happiness of a future world. He will allay thy sorrows, comfort thee in distress, and wipe the tears from thine eyes.

Behold then, such is thy King who cometh unto thee in His word and sacraments, an omniscient King before whom nothing is concealed, an almighty King with whom nothing is impossible, a meek King who is kindly disposed to all, even the greatest of sinners.

II.

And now, in the second place, let us consider the purpose of His coming.

We read, "*And a very great multitude spread their garments in the way; others cut down branches from the trees, and strewed them in the way. And the multitudes that went before, and that followed, cried, saying, Hosanna to the Son of David: Blessed is He that cometh in the name of the Lord; Hosanna in the highest!*" What a grand spectacle! What a joyous gathering! The Lord is coming down the slope from mount Olivet, riding a beast of burden and advancing toward the city. His eyes are fixed on Jerusalem with its white shining walls, enclosing thousands of dwellings and gardens, and on that magnificent structure, the temple of Jehovah with its glittering pinnacles flashing in the sun His disciples form the escort A very great multitude gathers at the gate and conducts the Lord into the city The crowd swells more and more as they move along. Everybody is happy. Everybody is filled with joy. Branches are cut down from the trees and thrown in the way. Garments are spread out on the ground for the Lord to ride over them. With rejoicing, with singing and shouting, as if the king were coming home to his royal palace from some expedition, the procession passes along the streets up to the temple, where even the children join in the songs of praise and cry, "Hosanna to the Son of David."

Here, my friends, we find depicted the true purpose of the Lord's coming to us in His word and sacraments. His purpose is not merely to take away from us our sorrows, as the omniscient and almighty King. No, His purpose is to substitute joy for sorrow, to fill our hearts with gladness, to make us rejoice over our salvation At that time He came to Jerusalem to die for the sins of the world. Only a few days later He was taken before the tribunal of Pontius Pilate, condemned to death, nailed to the accursed tree, and for three days His lifeless corpse remained in the tomb and was then raised again from the dead. He paid the penalty for our sins and the ransom price for our souls. He performed the great work of the redemption, worked out the forgiveness of all our sins, and gained for each and every one of us eternal life. And now, when the Lord, our heavenly King, comes to us in His word and sacraments, He offers, gives and imparts to us these sublime treasures, procured with the high price of His own precious blood. Wherever His word is, there is Christ Himself; and the purpose of His coming to us is always to bring joy and happiness to our hearts and to fill our souls with the hope of eternal life

May the Lord, then, never come to us in vain! May we always receive Him cheerfully, as did the disciples and the multitudes in our Gospel, receive Him in true faith, and prove such faith not only with our lips, but also with our lives; not only singing His praises, but also doing Him service and leading a godly and holy life in uprightness and honesty. Then the purpose of His coming shall be accomplished. We shall be a happy people indeed. Joy shall reign supreme in our hearts and homes, and such joy as can never be compared to the joys and pleasures of this world. Anthems of praise shall fill the earth; and when the storm of life is past, we shall join the angel chorus and sing with them, "Blessed is He that cometh in the name of the Lord; Hosanna in the highest!" Amen.

SECOND SUNDAY IN ADVENT.

LUKE 21, 25—36.

And there shall be signs in the sun, and in the moon, and in the stars; and upon the earth distress of nations, with perplexity; the sea and the waves roaring; men's hearts failing them for fear, and for looking after those things which are coming on the earth: for the powers of heaven shall be shaken. And then shall they see the Son of man coming in a cloud with power and great glory. And when these things begin to come to pass, then look up, and lift up your heads: for your redemption draweth nigh. And he spake to them a parable: Behold the fig tree, and all the trees: when they now shoot forth, ye see and know of your own selves that summer is now nigh at hand. So likewise ye, when ye see these things come to pass, know ye that the kingdom of God is nigh at hand. Verily I say unto you, This generation shall not pass away, till all be fulfilled. Heaven and earth shall pass away: but my words shall not pass away. And take heed to yourselves, lest at any time your hearts be overcharged with surfeiting, and drunkenness, and cares of this life, and so that day come upon you unawares. For as a snare shall it come on all them that dwell on the face of the whole earth. Watch ye therefore, and pray always, that ye may be accounted worthy to escape all these things that shall come to pass, and to stand before the Son of man.

BELOVED IN CHRIST:

Our Gospel treats of a very serious matter, of the last day, or the day of judgment. Jesus tells us that this world shall not last forever, but come to a sudden, abrupt end; and that this end shall be attended by the most fearful signs in the planets above us, and upon the earth, and among the nations. He says, "*And there shall be signs in the sun, and in the moon, and in the stars; and upon the earth distress of nations, with perplexity; the sea*

2

and the waves roaring, men's hearts failing them for fear, and for looking after those things which are coming on the earth. for the powers of heaven shall be shaken   And then shall they see the Son of man coming in a cloud with power and great glory." And still more distinctly does He predict the end when He says in plain language, not to be misunderstood, "*Heaven and earth shall pass away*" Pass away, that is, be utterly destroyed, annihilated, be no more.

Now, is not this a terrible thing to think of, that heaven and earth shall pass away, pass away as surely as they were called into being, and that this catastrophe may come at any time, even to-day? That, as St Peter says, "The day of the Lord will come as a thief in the night; in the which the heavens shall pass away with a great noise, and the elements shall melt with fervent heat; the earth also and the works that are therein shall be burned up?" The children of this world can not bear to hear this. It is disagreeable to them   It is too fearful. And for this reason they oppose the doctrine of the day of judgment, ridicule it, and treat it with contempt   Yet this doctrine of the last day does not stand in contradiction to human reason. For even human reason must admit not merely the possibility, but even the probability that there will be an end of this world. "But human imagination finds it hard to picture to itself this tremendous collapse, this altogether unparalleled catastrophe, after the passage of centuries or ages during which the world has pursued its accustomed course. The imagination can not conceive, amid the well-ordered facts of our daily life, so sublime and terrific an interruption, so overwhelming a conclusion of all that we see and are conversant with "

The day of judgment, as described in the Holy Scriptures, must be viewed by all the children of this world with fear and trembling. It is to them a day of terror, a day depriving them at once of all their joys and pleasures and plunging them into the greatest imaginable misery   But what does Jesus say to His disciples, to the true Christians, about that day? Should they fear the day of judgment? No; He says, "*When these things begin to come to pass, then look up, and lift up your heads; for your redemption draweth nigh* " It is not a day of terror, but a day of joy for all the true followers of Christ. And this shall be the subject of our discourse, with the aid of God's Holy Spirit,

THE LAST DAY A DAY OF JOY FOR ALL TRUE CHRISTIANS.

Let us consider,

    I. *Why all true Christians look forward to the last day as a day of joy for them, and*

    II. *What they must do so as not to be deceived in their joyful expectation.*

I.

True Christians are often worried about the last day. The thought sometimes troubles them, How if that day should suddenly come upon you? How would you feel, if you should have to witness those terrible signs in heaven above and upon earth below? Would not your heart fail you for fear? And when the Supreme Judge appears in the clouds, can you face Him? Must you not hide your face in shame because you have sinned? Does not the word of God say, "The world passeth away, and the lust thereof: but he that doeth the will of God abideth for ever?" How then can you expect to abide forever while the earth is passing away? Are you not an unprofitable servant, a frivolous transgressor, who did almost everything else, but not the will of God?

These thoughts come to true Christians, I say. They are not entertained by godless people. These do not believe Christ's prediction, and when the thought of judgment day fastens upon their mind, they quickly dismiss that thought, thinking, What is the use of worrying over so uncertain a thing? When, therefore, at times you feel frightened about the last day, let it be because you are earnestly concerned about your eternal welfare. But you must get beyond such fear and fright. For Jesus says to all His followers, "*When these things begin to come to pass, then look up, and lift up your heads; for your redemption draweth nigh.*" You must look forward to the last day as a day of joy. Why? Because that day is the day of your redemption, as Jesus says, the day in which you shall be redeemed from each and every trouble, from everything that is hurtful to body and soul.

In the first place, why should you feel frightened when those "*signs occur in the sun, and in the moon, and in the stars; and when the sea and the waves are roaring, and the powers of heaven are shaken?*" For godless people, for the children of this world, these are indeed signs foreboding distress and misery, so that *"their hearts must be failing them for fear, and for looking after those things which are coming on the earth."* For godless people these terrible signs are the tolling of the bell of eternal death, the rap of the angry Judge at the door of the tottering world. But for the true Christians these signs are the melodious chimes of the eternal Sabbath, the gentle breezes of the everlasting spring. When they behold these signs, they must picture to their minds Jesus standing before them and saying, Fear not, my beloved children, I am here, I am come to destroy the prison in which you are being held, and to set you free. The Lord illustrates this by a beautiful parable. He says, *"Behold the fig tree, and all the trees; when they now shoot forth, ye see and know of your own selves that summer is now nigh at hand. So likewise ye, when ye see these things come to pass, know ye that the kingdom of God is nigh at hand."* Is the sprouting of the trees and the blooming of the flowers in spring something frightening? Does not the entire creation, and man above all, rejoice when the winter season is ended and beautiful spring is ushered in amid the songs of birds and the blooming of the flowers? Behold then, thus must those signs which are so terrible for the children of this world be viewed by the true Christians. They are not to be looked upon as dismal forebodings, but as the most pleasing indications of the coming of God's kingdom, which is peace, joy, happiness, bliss for ever and ever.

Furthermore, why should you feel frightened when you behold *"the Son of man coming in a cloud in power and great glory."* True, those who have not been waiting for the Lord and did not care for Him shall be terrified when most unexpectedly, like a flash of lightning in a clear sky, the Lord appears in the clouds. They shall perceive at once Him whom they pierced by their infidelity, and all their sins, especially their enmity against Jesus and His divine word, will come home to them, and fill them with unspeakable fear, so that in utter despair they will say to the mountains, Cover us, and to the hills, Fall on us. But what cause has a true Christian to be afraid of Jesus, even in that great moment when as the Judge of the world He shall descend from heaven? Jesus is his Friend, his best Friend, his truest Friend. Even if now he thinks that the sight of Jesus in the clouds will frighten him, he shall find it otherwise. Even the weakest believer who puts his trust in Christ shall find himself transformed in a moment, when Christ comes, and his heart filled with ineffable joy. For then his faith shall at once be changed into sight and all those weaknesses by which faith is hampered in this world shall be gone.

And also this is true that the destruction of this visible world shall be a terrible thing for those that love the world, and the things of this world, and know of no other joy than earthly joy and earthly pleasure. For Jesus says, *"Heaven and earth shall pass away."* But what does He add? He says, *"But my words shall not pass away."* Why does Jesus add this? He obviously means to say, Fear not, my beloved Christians; let the visible world pass away, my words shall come true. Did I not promise you a new heaven and a new earth wherein dwelleth righteousness? If then you believe my words, you shall find a new creation coming forth, immediately after this world has been consumed by fire; and triumphantly you shall enter into life eternal.

O, my friends, what a joyful day, then, must the last day of this world be for every true Christian! It is the day of perfect redemption, the day in which we shall be made rid of our sins, our frailties, our natural depravity, our fears, our sobs, our tears, our pains, our misfortunes, our anxieties, and all our crosses, and tribulations. It is the day in which the gates of Paradise shall be opened unto us, and in our flesh we shall behold God, and in Him be ineffably happy, experiencing those things which eye hath not seen, nor ear heard, neither have entered into the hearts of men; but which God has prepared for them that love Him. O, let us not wish for that day to be long coming and far away, but beseech our divine Lord to come, to come soon, and to redeem us from this vain world by His glorious advent in the clouds.

II.

And now, in the second place, let us consider what we must do, so as not to be deceived in our joyful anticipation.

Saint John says in his first epistle, "Little children, abide in Him, that, when He shall appear, we may have confidence, and not be ashamed before Him in His coming." So the one and only thing we must do, not to be deceived in our joyful anticipation, is to abide with Jesus, that is, to remain with Him in true faith, not to leave Him, and always to come back to Him when we have gone astray.

And what must we do to remain with Jesus? He says, "*Take heed to yourselves, lest at any time your hearts be overcharged with surfeiting, and drunkenness, and cares of this life, and so that day come upon you unawares. For as a snare shall it come on all them that dwell on the face of the whole earth*" Surfeiting and drunkenness are not human, they are worse than beastly. The greediest beast knows when it has enough and will stop eating and drinking when the craving of its appetite has been satisfied. Debaucheries and drunken carousals are unmanly wrongs even from a heathen's moral point of view, how much the more from the Christian's moral standpoint. Does not God say distinctly, "The drunkards shall not inherit the kingdom of God?" A drunkard is not a Christian, no matter how much he goes to church or how religiously he deports himself otherwise. Must he not himself admit that he could not face the Lord Jesus in one of his drunken revelries? Take heed then, this is the Lord's warning, "*take heed, lest at any time your hearts be overcharged with surfeiting and drunkenness*"—And the cares of this life are not less dangerous than surfeiting and drunkenness. How shall a man be duly prepared to meet his God when his thoughts are never with God, when he never sets his affection on things above, when he never seeks the kingdom of God and His righteousness, but has his mind fixed on this world and nothing but this world, when the craving for and hankering after wealth, earthly goods, earthly pleasures and enjoyments is the one sole aim and object of his earthly existence? Here is where many make a grave mistake They make a pretense of religion. They run along with the true followers of Christ They do as if they were striving for heaven. But their religion is nothing more than a show and a sham. It is not heaven they are after, but the earth. Their hearts are overcharged with the cares of life, and this they show by their neglect to come up to the duties of a Christian, by shunning the house of God and neglecting prayer. O, how can you expect Jesus to confess you before His Father in heaven when suddenly He shall come, if you refuse to confess Him before men? How can you expect to be received into heaven, if your heart clings to this world and you do not sincerely seek the kingdom of God? Take heed then, beware of the cares of this life, do not let these take possession of your soul and lead you away from Jesus, and on the last day you shall not be deceived in the joyful anticipation of true Christians.

Finally Jesus says, " *Watch ye therefore, and pray always, that ye may be accounted worthy to escape all these things that shall come to pass, and to stand before the Son of man.*" Behold then, if you would not be deceived in your joyful anticipation on the last day, if you would remain in the faith and be duly prepared to meet Christ when He comes to judge the quick and the dead, you must also watch and pray. We must watch our sinful heart, which is always prone to evil, watch our thoughts, which easily become vain, watch our words that our lips speak no guile, watch our walk and conversation that we always remain in the path of true Christians and that we take as our rule and guide the word of God, watch all the foes of our eternal salvation, the devil, the world and our own flesh, that they may not lead us into misbelief, despair, and other great shame and vice.

And to watchfulness we must add prayer. For "with might of ours can nought be done." All that *we* do is utterly useless and will accomplish nothing. God must do everything and all. Therefore we must pray without ceasing and call upon God, saying, Lord, I admit that I am a damnable sinner, not worthy to stand before Thee. But Thy grace is from everlasting to everlasting upon them that fear Thee. Thou hast given me Thine only begotten Son and He has atoned for all my sins and made me acceptable in Thy sight. O, keep me in the blessed faith of Thy dear Son. Take not Thy Holy Spirit from me. Let me remain Thy dear child, and endure to the end, and receive the crown of life.

O, blessed is he who thus entrusts himself to the grace and mercy of God in Jesus the Savior! Let death come, or let the last day come, he shall not be deceived, he shall be found worthy to stand before the Son of man and enter into eternal glory. Amen.

THIRD SUNDAY IN ADVENT.

Matt 11, 2—10

Now when John had heard in the prison the works of Christ, he sent two of his disciples, and said unto him, Art thou he that should come, or do we look for another? Jesus answered and said unto them, Go and shew John again those things which ye do hear and see The blind receive their sight, and the lame walk, the lepers are cleansed, and the deaf hear, the dead are raised up, and the poor have the gospel preached to them And blessed is he, whosoever shall not be offended in me And as they departed, Jesus began to say unto the multitudes concerning John, What went ye out into the wilderness to see? A reed shaken with the wind? But what went ye out for to see? A man clothed in soft raiment? behold, they that wear soft clothing are in kings' houses But what went ye out for to see? A prophet? yea, I say unto you, and more than a prophet For this is he, of whom it is written, Behold, I send my messenger before thy face, which shall prepare thy way before thee

BELOVED FRIENDS IN CHRIST

"*Art Thou He that should come, or do we look for another?*" That is the question which John the Baptist has two of his disciples ask Christ The purport of this question was to ascertain whether Jesus was the promised Messiah. But why did John the Baptist have his disciples ask Jesus that question? Did he himself doubt whether Jesus is the Messiah? Many commentators offer this explanation. They say, When John the Baptist was brooding in his gloomy prison cell, when he found that his earthly career was drawing to a close, when Jesus did not come to his rescue, his faith was shaken, he began to doubt whether he had not made the greatest mistake of his life when at the river Jordan he testified that Jesus of Nazareth is the promised Messiah and pointed at Him with his finger, saying, "Behold the Lamb of God, which taketh away the sin of the world " But such a thing is hardly credible that God's appointed fore-runner of the Messiah should so utterly fail in his mission as to doubt the truth of what God Himself had told him to say. And does not Christ say in our gospel that John the Baptist is not a reed shaken with the wind? What does that mean but that he is not a man given to doubts and wavering opinions? We therefore accept Luther's explanation. Luther says, "It is certain that John has Christ asked for the sake of his disciples." Not because he himself doubted, but because his disciples doubted, did John put this question to

Christ. This explanation also conforms to what we are told of John's disciples in the third chapter of the Gospel according to St. John. There they are reported as coming to John the Baptist and saying, "Rabbi, He that was with thee beyond Jordan, to whom thou bearest witness, behold, the same baptizeth, and all men come to him." They did not seem to like it that all men went to Jesus. They had heard John bearing witness of Jesus, but as yet did not have the confidence in Jesus which they should have had.

To this day there are people who either do not at all believe in Christ Jesus as the promised Messiah, or doubt whether Jesus is He that should come. The first class, who openly *reject* Christ, are the Jews and infidels. The Jews are to this day expecting the promised Messiah to come, and the infidels discredit the clearest Bible statements concerning Christ. The second class, those who *doubt* whether Jesus Christ is the promised Messiah, are such as claim to be Christians, but are not made divinely certain in the faith. They do not openly reject Christ as do the Jews and infidels. They hear the Gospel like the disciples of John the Baptist. But they are as the reed shaken with the wind. When any supposed arguments and proofs against the Gospel are placed before them, their faith is shocked and they begin to doubt. Let me explain to you with the aid of God's Holy Spirit,

THAT JESUS CHRIST IS TRULY THE MESSIAH WHO SHOULD COME.

  I. *Because His person exactly answers to the description of the promised Messiah,*
 II. *Because His deeds exactly correspond to the deeds the Messiah was to perform,*
III. *Because He was preceded by the fore-runner who was to go before the Messiah.*

I.

What was Jesus' answer when John's disciples had asked Him, "*Art Thou He that should come, or do we look for another?*" Does He say, No, I am not He, John the Baptist ought not to have sent you to Me? No! He silently admits that He is the promised Messiah and says to these two men, "*Go and shew John again those things which ye do hear and see.*"

Jesus Christ is truly the Messiah, who should come, and that is attested, in the first place, by the fact that His person exactly answers to the description of the promised Messiah   In the Old Testament God has given a full description of the Messiah's person, and so perfectly does that description correspond with Jesus' person. that nobody can look for another, if he sincerely accepts and believes the clear words of Scripture.   In the Old Testament God has so perfectly portrayed the Messiah that everybody should have known Him when He came   In the Old Testament God stated the time when the Messiah should come, the place where He should be born, and the family and people from whom He was to descend.   And who is it that answers to this description exactly, in every detail?   Nobody in this world excepting Jesus Christ.

As to the *time* when the Messiah was to come, had not Jacob, the patriarch, spoken the prophecy, "The sceptre shall not depart from Judah, nor a lawgiver from between his feet, until Shiloh come?"   And had not the sceptre departed from Judah, had not the Jews ceased to be an independent people, had not the Romans conquered and subdued them and made of Judaea a Roman province when Jesus came?   Furthermore, had not Daniel given the prophecy; "Seventy weeks are determined upon Thy people and upon Thy holy city . . . to anoint the Most Holy?"   And what did Daniel mean to say?   As the context shows, he meant to say that in seventy weeks, not of days, but of years, that is, in 490 years, counting from the rebuilding of the temple after the Babylonian captivity, the Holy One in Israel, the Messiah, should appear. And what do we read in the books of history? How long after the reconstruction of the temple was it when Jesus came? It was about 490 years, as everybody can ascertain for himself.

And as to the *place* where the Messiah was to be born, had not Micah prophesied, "And thou, Bethlehem in the land of Judah, art not the least among the princes of Judah, for out of thee shall come a Governor that shall rule my people Israel?" And was not Jesus born in Bethlehem?   But there were two villages called Bethlehem   One was in the land occupied by the tribe of Sebulon and the other in Judah. Now, that there might not be a mistake, the prophet points out Bethlehem in the land of Judah; and was not Jesus born in that selfsame Bethlehem?

And, finally, as to the *family* and people from whom the Messiah was to descend, had not the prophets announced that the Messiah should descend from king David? Did not Isaiah, for instance, say, "And there shall come forth a rod out of the stem of Jesse, and a Branch shall grow out of his roots: and the Spirit of the Lord shall rest upon Him?" Now, Jesse was king David's father. And did not Jesus Christ descend from the house and lineage of David? But at the time of Christ there were many others that descended from king David, and to avoid mistakes God added another prophecy to point out the very person among those descendants. He had His prophet Isaiah exclaim, "Behold, a virgin shall conceive, and bear a Son, and shall call Him Immanuel." And do not the holy evangelists inform us that Jesus was born of the Virgin Mary? And since He was conceived by the Holy Ghost and born of the Virgin Mary, is He not Immanuel, that is, God and man in one person?

We see, Christ's person exactly answers to the description of the promised Messiah. He is the Messiah, and none other.

II.

The second reason upon which we base our faith in Jesus Christ as the Messiah who is to come, is, because His deeds exactly correspond to the deeds which the Messiah was to perform.

What deeds was the Messiah to perform according to the prophecies of the Old Testament? In the first place, He was to perform the greatest miracles which the earth had ever seen. In the thirty-fifth chapter of his prophecies Isaiah says of the Messiah and of His time, "Then the eyes of the blind shall be opened, and the ears of the deaf shall be unstopped. Then shall the lame man leap as an hart, and the tongue of the dumb sing." Jesus evidently refers to this very prophecy when He gives answer to John's disciples, saying, "*The blind receive their sight, and the lame walk, the lepers are cleansed, and the deaf hear, the dead are raised up.*" Jesus means to say, How can you doubt whether I am He that should come? Do you not see that I am performing exactly those deeds which the Messiah is to perform? And to this day Christians can challenge the world to show them a man in the entire history of the world who so perfectly came up to all the requirements of the promised Messiah as did Jesus of Nazareth.

Let unbelievers search the books of history and point out a man
who did the miracles that Christ performed. It is folly to dispute
those miracles.   They are recorded not only in the New Testament; an account of some of these miracles is to be found even
in contemporaneous writings of the enemies of Christianity   But
not another man did the world produce who in his own name and
by his own authority healed thousands of the sick by means of
his simple word and will, opened the eyes of the blind, restored
unto the deaf the power of hearing, gave unto the dumb the power
of speach, and unto the lame the use of their limbs, and even
called back into the land of the living those that were entombed.
The four Gospels of the New Testament are almost one continual
narrative of divine miracles wrought by Jesus Christ, and, as
St. John informs us, "These are written that ye might believe
that Jesus is the Christ, the Son of God, and that believing ye
might have life through His name."

According to the prophecies of the Old Testament the Messiah was to perform another great work. He was to proclaim the
Gospel, the glad tidings of the forgiveness of sins   In Isaiah,
chapter 61, we read, the Messiah Himself being the speaker.
"The Spirit of the Lord God is upon me; because the Lord hath
anointed me to preach good tidings unto the meek; He hath sent
me to bind up the broken-hearted, to proclaim liberty to the captives, and the opening of the prison to them that are bound "
Christ evidently refers to this passage of the Old Testament when
He adds, "*And the poor have the Gospel preached to them.*" Christ
means to say, Do you not hear that I am preaching the Gospel,
the glad tidings, which the Messiah is to proclaim? And if we
examine the records of the New Testament, we find that Jesus
was almost constantly surrounded by the meek, and the broken-
hearted, and distressed, proclaiming to them the Gospel, speaking words of eternal life.   And did not Christ Himself perform
the great work of the redemption which the Messiah was to perform and upon which He was to base His proclamation of liberty
to the captives? Read the 22d Psalm and the 53d chapter of Isaiah,
where the Messiah's suffering, death and resurrection are described, and compare the history of Jesus' holy passion ! See
how these prophecies in their minutest details were fulfilled in
Christ Jesus ! Nothing is missing. Jesus' deeds exactly corre-

spond to the deeds which the Messiah was to perform. Christ therefore says, "*And blessed is he, whosoever shall not be offended in me.*" Blessed is he that is not offended in Christ's lowliness and humiliation! Blessed is he that receives Christ as the promised Messiah who should come, as the heavenly Prophet who proclaimed to us lost and condemned sinners the Gospel, as the great High-priest who upon the altar of the cross brought the great sacrifice of His life for our sins, as the King of kings and Lord of lords!

III.

The third reason upon which we base our faith in Jesus Christ as the promised Messiah is, because He was preceded by the same fore-runner who was to go before the Messiah.

God had arranged that a fore-runner should precede the Messiah, a man who should prepare for Him the way, call attention to Him, and point Him out to the people as the promised Messiah. Isaiah speaks of that fore-runner when he says in the 40th chapter, "The voice of him that crieth in the wilderness, Prepare ye the way of the Lord, make straight in the desert a highway for our God." And Malachi, the last of the prophets, alludes to that fore-runner, saying, "Behold, I will send my messenger, and he shall prepare the way before me, and the Lord whom ye seek shall suddenly come to His temple, even the Messenger of the Covenant whom ye delight in; behold, He shall come, saith the Lord of hosts." And at the end of his prophecies the same prophet says, "Behold, I will send you Elijah, the prophet, before the coming of the great and dreadful day of the Lord."

Did not such a fore-runner as the one described by the prophets precede the coming of the Lord Jesus Christ? Who was that fore-runner? It was John the Baptist. We, therefore, read in our Gospel, "*And as they departed, Jesus began to say unto the multitudes concerning John, What went ye out into the wilderness to see? A reed shaken with the wind? But what went ye out for to see? A man clothed in soft raiment? behold, they that wear soft clothing are in kings' houses. But what went ye out for to see? A prophet? yea, I say unto you, and more than a prophet. For this is He of whom it is written, Behold, I send my messenger before Thy face, which shall prepare Thy way before Thee.*" After the departure of those two disciples of John who had asked Him whether He was the promised Messiah, Jesus addresses the people concerning John and tells them, You must not think that John no longer takes me for the Messiah. No; he is not a reed shaken with the wind. He does not revoke his testimony concerning me. Neither must you think that John would come out a changed man in speech and appearance were he to be pardoned by king Herod and leave the prison No; he is not a man in soft clothing as worn by those who are in kings' houses. He remains the same preacher of repentance, clad in a robe of camel's hair. Nor must you think that John is but a common prophet. He is more than a prophet. He is the second Elijah promised to come. He is the man of whom the prophet wrote that he should prepare the way before me. He is the Messiah's fore-runner

How, then, can anyone doubt whether Jesus Christ is really the promised Messiah? Did not the promised fore-runner go before Him? Did not John the Baptist precede Him in the spirit and power of Elias and do exactly what the Messiah's fore-runner was to do? Did he not prepare before Him the way, declaring, "He it is, who coming after me is preferred before me, whose shoe's latchet I am not worthy to unloose?" Did he not bear record that Jesus is the Son of God?

Let all the Jews and infidels and all the enemies of Christ say what they may Their arguments against Christ are illusions. Jesus Christ is truly the Messiah who should come. As we have seen, His person exactly answers to the description of the Messiah given in the Old Testament, His deeds exactly correspond to those deeds which the Messiah was to perform, and He was preceded by the fore-runner who was to go before the Messiah Let us, therefore, lift up our heads in triumph and rejoice in our faith which is so well founded that even the gates of hell shall not prevail against it, and sing praises to our beloved Savior and King, in whom all the promises of God are yea and amen to the glory of our God Amen.

FOURTH SUNDAY IN ADVENT.

JOHN 1, 19—28.

And this is the record of John, when the Jews sent priests and Levites from Jerusalem to ask him, Who art thou? And he confessed, and denied not; but confessed, I am not the Christ. And they asked him, What then? Art thou Elias? And he saith, I am not. Art thou that prophet? And he answered, No. Then said they unto him, Who art thou? that we may give an answer to them that sent us. What sayest thou of thyself? He said, I am the voice of one crying in the wilderness, Make straight the way of the Lord, as said the prophet Esaias. And they which were sent were of the Pharisees. And they asked him, and said unto him, Why baptizest thou then, if thou be not that Christ, nor Elias, neither that prophet? John answered them, saying, I baptize with water: but there standeth one among you, whom ye know not; he it is, who coming after me is preferred before me, whose shoe's latchet I am not worthy to unloose. These things were done in Bethabara beyond Jordan, where John was baptizing.

BELOVED FRIENDS IN CHRIST:

In those days when John the Baptist preached in the wilderness, the longing and waiting for the promised Messiah had reached its highest pitch in Israel. The time was fulfilled, the seventy weeks of Daniel were accomplished, Judah had lost its sceptre. Now the Messiah had to be expected. When, therefore, John arose and deported himself like an ancient prophet, living the life of a hermit in the wilderness, clothed in camel's hair, feeding on locusts and wild honey, and preaching with great power that the Kingdom of heaven was nigh at hand, the whole country round about was wild with excitement. We are told that Jerusalem, and all Judaea, and all the region round about Jordan went out to him. The people heard his thundering sermons, bidding them to repent of their sins. They were baptized and confessed their wrongs. And not only did they regard John as a great prophet, but day by day the conviction grew that he must be the very Christ himself, the Messiah for whom they had been waiting so long.

Even the Sanhedrim in Jerusalem became alarmed. The Sanhedrim, composed of seventy-one men, was the ecclesiastical court. Upon these men devolved the duty to settle all religious questions that disturbed the public mind. So they sent to John a delegation consisting of priests and Levites, highly respected men belonging to the order of the Pharisees, to ask him formally whether he himself laid claim to being the promised Messiah.

This delegation faithfully performed its mission and received a straight-forward answer from John. John disclaimed all honor. "*He confessed, I am not the Christ.*" And when "*they asked him, What then? art thou Elias? he saith, I am not. Art thou that prophet? he answered, No.*" And when they pressed him to tell them who he was, that they might give answer to them that sent them, and to state why he was baptizing, though he is neither the Christ, nor Elias, nor that prophet, he made a noble confession concerning Jesus, a model confession, to be imitated by every Christian. Accordingly, let us consider with the aid of God's Holy Spirit,

THE CHRISTIAN'S CONFESSION CONCERNING JESUS,

and see,

    I. *What a Christian must confess concerning Jesus,* and

   II. *In what manner this confession is to be made.*

I.

By his example John the Baptist plainly teaches what Christians must confess concerning Jesus. When pressed to make a confession concerning the Christ, what did he say? He referred to Jesus and said, "*He it is, who coming after me is preferred before me, whose shoe's latchet I am not worthy to unloose.*" What curious language, "coming after me and preferred before me!" For the latter words do not merely mean that Jesus ranks higher than John, but that He was, that He existed before him. John himself renders this explanation when shortly afterwards he says, "This is He of whom I said, After me cometh a man which is preferred before me: for He *was* before me." Was not John older than Jesus and therefore before Jesus? How can he say that Jesus existed before him? John evidently testified to Christ's divinity. He meant to say that Jesus is the eternal Son of God, the Word which in the beginning was with God and by whom all things are made. But John confesses more concerning Jesus. He says, "*I am the voice of one crying in the wilderness, Make straight the way of the Lord, as said the prophet Esaias.*" The Lord whose way should be made straight and of whom Esaias speaks, is the Messiah, is Jesus. What, then, does John confess here concerning Jesus? He confesses that Jesus is the Lord, Jehovah who was to come into the flesh, the Savior of the world. Behold, then, the noble confession of John the Baptist concerning Jesus. He confesses two distinct things concerning Jesus. He confesses that Jesus is before him, that He is true God, and that He is the Jehovah to come, the promised Savior and Deliverer.

The very same two things must Christians confess to this day concerning Jesus. They must make a true confession concerning the person and the office of Jesus Christ.

The main reason why Christians must confess Jesus before men is, because to this day the world knoweth Him not. By the Christian's testimony Christ should be made known and honored among men. Now, it is a historical fact that there was a man living in the land of Judaea almost 1900 years ago, whose name was Jesus. No sane person will deny that. Neither will the children of this world deny that Jesus was the founder of the Christian religion. Jesus was true man. His humanity is undisputed. But this is what the world will not believe that this despised man Jesus, who was laid in the manger, who had not where to lay His head, who shamefully died on the cross, should be the Lord of glory, the true and everlasting God. This is what the children of this world will not believe, that Jesus came into this world to redeem us from sin and death by His innocent suffering and painful death on the cross, and that we are saved by faith in Christ Jesus, and not in any other way. These are the two principal points of dispute between the Christians and the children of this world, Christ's divinity and His redemption. And here we must confess and declare openly before all men that Jesus is more than mortal man, more than an angel and archangel, that He is Jehovah, the Lord, before whom John the Baptist made straight the way, the eternal One who was preferred before all, who was and existed before any one was born, before whom all men must bow, even the prophets, even he who was more than a prophet, John, who was the greatest man in his day, but had to deem himself unworthy to perform upon Jesus the work of a slave and to unloose his shoe's latchet. This is the principal part of our Christian confession before the world that we assert and defend Christ's divinity. Then we must also declare the truth of His miracles, of His resurrection and ascension into heaven, His enthronement at the right hand of God the Father Almighty, and His coming to judge the quick and

3

the dead. We must confess our faith that "there is no salvation in any other, that there is none other name under heaven given among men whereby we must be saved," but the sweet name of Jesus. We must confess that Jesus receives sinners, that He welcomes all who come to Him, that His grace is boundless as the sea in its wide expanse, that He yearns and longs to save all and would not have a single soul eternally lost. We must confess our own experience with Jesus, how in Him we found forgiveness of sins, peace with God, life and salvation, and thus bear witness unto the world that the Christian faith is not a delusion, but a real thing and a precious thing, a thing which will make man truly happy both in this life and in the world to come.

O my friends, must we not say that perhaps many an unbeliever would have been won over to Christ, if those Christians with whom he came in contact in the world had not been so shy and backward in confessing Christ? Must we not say that many Christians dare not open their mouths to confess the faith when they should speak? that in their dealings with the children of this world they never seek an opportunity to plead for Christ and for his cause? aye, that sometimes they act in the presence of unbelievers as if they were ashamed of Christ and of the religion which they profess? O let us all remember that we must confess Jesus, that this duty devolves upon every Christian, and that Jesus says, "Whosoever shall confess me before men, him will I confess also before my Father which is in heaven. But whosoever shall deny me before men, him will I also deny before my Father which is in heaven."

II.

And now, in the second place, let us consider in what manner this confession is to be made.

A striking feature in John's record is his deep humility, his remarkable modesty. He claimed to be nothing more than a message, a voice rather than a person, a man whose highest work and glory it was to forget his miserable self in the surpassing greatness of his commission from heaven. *"He said, I am the voice of one crying in the wilderness."* And when they asked him and said unto him, *"Why baptizest thou then, if thou be not that Christ, nor Elias, neither that prophet? John answered them, saying, I baptize with water.*" He would say, I am not the Master, but the servant, I simply baptize with water, but there is another who gives unto this sacrament its efficacy, its wonderful power to work forgiveness of sins, to deliver from death and the devil, and to give eternal salvation; and that man is Jesus, "*whose shoe's latchet I am not worthy to unloose.*"

Behold then, in such manner must we also confess Jesus before men, with sincere humility, with a deep conviction of our own unworthiness. It is not the true Christian spirit to think a great deal of yourself, to have and hold a high opinion of your own person, to compare yourself with others, and then to find yourself much better, and to boast of your virtues and own righteousness. That is the spirit of the Pharisee who went into the temple and prayed, saying, "God, I thank Thee, that I am not as other men are, extortioners, unjust, adulterers, or even as this publican. I fast twice in the week, I give tithes of all that I possess." That is the spirit of the hypocrite who seeks to extract the mote in another's eye and does not perceive the beam in his own eye. Christians must admit always, admit also before the children of this world, while confessing Jesus, that they are damnable sinners, that they sin daily and deserve nothing but punishment, that in themselves they are not any better than the rest of the children of men, and that, if God should deal with them after their sins and reward them according to their iniquities, they would be eternally lost. And that they *are* Christians, that they *have* been converted to Christ Jesus, that they *are* walking in the narrow way that leads to eternal life, that they stand in God's grace and favor, that they *have* the forgiveness of their sins and *are* made heirs of eternal life, this they must not credit to themselves, as if they were the authors of their own salvation, but to the grace and mercy of the Almighty, and say, "I did not by my own reason or strength come to Jesus, but the Holy Ghost called me by the Gospel, enlightened me with His gifts, sanctifies and keeps me in the true faith." Not in an overbearing spirit, but in sincere humility must a Christian confess Jesus before men.

Another feature in John's record is his courage, his fearlessness in confessing Christ. The delegation sent to him by the Sanhedrim was composed of priests and Levites. They were the men who sat in Moses' seat, the rightful teachers of the people.

Yet John is bold enough to say to them, "*There standeth one among you, whom ye know not*" These words implied a censure. They should have known Jesus, known that He is the Christ. Did not the wise men come to Jerusalem from the East seeking the new-born King of the Jews? and did they not direct these wise men to Bethlehem? Did not God show them plainly by these wise men that the Messiah was come? Did not old Simeon in the temple take up the child Jesus in his arms and say, "Lord, now lettest Thou Thy servant depart in peace, according to Thy word: for mine eyes have seen Thy salvation?" And did they not converse with Jesus in the temple, when He was twelve years old, and admire His understanding and His answers? Why did they not watch and interest themselves in this wonderful child? John, therefore, boldly censures them for their negligence and confesses that Jesus, whom they do not know, is the Christ, let them say and do what they will about it.

Behold then, in such manner must we also confess Jesus before men, with boldness and undaunted courage It is not an easy thing to confess Jesus in our days. If you confess Jesus, you are very apt to be persecuted You may be injured in your profession, business or trade, lose your customers or work You may be ridiculed and looked down upon as out of touch with the progress of the age. You may be laughed to scorn and sneered at as a hypocrite and a coward when you refuse to walk in the counsel of the ungodly, and to stand in the way of sinners, and to sit in the seat of the scornful, and say that your delight is in the law of the Lord It takes courage to confess Christ

Let us not be afraid to face those who can not bear to hear the name of Jesus professed before them as the Lord and Savior Let us not be afraid to suffer the consequences which the confession of that blessed name may bring upon us. What is this world to us, and what are the things of this world to us? The world shall pass away and the lust thereof but he that doeth the will of God abideth for ever. Let us fearlessly confess our divine Lord like John the Baptist did And when the storm of life is passed and our confession is ended, we shall find in our beloved Savior Jesus an Advocate with the Father, saying to Him, Let these enter into the glory they have confessed me before men and endured to the end; they shall live before me for ever and ever. Amen.

GOSPEL ON CHRISTMAS DAY.

LUKE 2, 1—14.

And it came to pass in those days, that there went out a decree from Cæsar Augustus, that all the world should be taxed. (And this taxing was first made when Cyrenius was governor of Syria.) And all went to be taxed, every one into his own city. And Joseph also went up from Galilee, out of the city of Nazareth, into Judaea, unto the city of David, which is called Bethlehem; (because he was of the house and lineage of David:) to be taxed with Mary his espoused wife, being great with child. And so it was, that, while they were there, the days were accomplished that she should be delivered. And she brought forth her first-born son, and wrapped him in swaddling clothes, and laid him in a manger; because there was no room for them in the inn. And there were in the same country shepherds abiding in the field, keeping watch over their flock by night. And, lo, the angel of the Lord came upon them, and the glory of the Lord shone round about them: and they were sore afraid. And the angel said unto them, Fear not: for, behold, I bring you good tidings of great joy, which shall be to all people. For unto you is born this day in the city of David a Savior, which is Christ the Lord. And this shall be a sign unto you; Ye shall find the babe wrapped in swaddling clothes, lying in a manger. And suddenly there was with the angel a multitude of the heavenly host praising God, and saying, Glory to God in the highest, and on earth peace, good will toward men.

BELOVED FRIENDS IN THE NEW-BORN SAVIOR:

"Behold, I bring you good tidings of great joy." This was the angel's introduction as he delivered his great message from heaven on Christmas day, the first Christmas that dawned upon the world. Christmas was intended to be a day of joy, of universal joy. Not another day in the year is hailed with such delight by both young and old as Christmas day. Not another festival of the Christian Church causes so much gladness as does this glorious festival, which, by the grace of God, we have again been permitted to celebrate to-day. To-day the whole world round about us seems turned into a sea of gladness. Faces beaming with joy are seen everywhere. Man for once seems to forget his own precious self and to find pleasure in making others happy. Tokens of love are exchanged among friends. Parents desire to see their children happier on this day, and children desire to see their parents joyful. Brothers and sisters under the Christmas tree more than on any other occasion are made to feel that they are members of the same family. Thus has Christmas come to be a day of joy, a day of prevailing happiness, a day in which almost everybody feels that he should be happy and make others happy.

But this time-honored custom of bestowing and receiving gifts, though laudable in itself, is not the foundation nor everywhere a token, of that joy whereof the angel speaks. The angel does not say, I bring you good tidings of great joy, for henceforth this day shall be among men a day of showing love and kindness. No, he says, "*For unto you is born this day in the city of David a Savior, which is Christ the Lord.*" The true reason for joy on Christmas day is to be sought in the fact that a Savior was born unto us this day. This is the great message of the day. Let us consider then, with the aid of God's Holy Spirit,

THE ANGEL'S MESSAGE: UNTO YOU IS BORN THIS DAY A SAVIOR.

Every word of this message is of utmost importance We shall, therefore, analyze it and consider its four component parts, namely,

I. *The Savior*, II. *Is born*, III. *Unto you*, and IV. *This day*

I.

"*A Savior*," says the angel —Could the culprit on the scaffold receive better news than to be informed that the governor's messenger has arrived with a pardon? Could the shipwrecked man who is about to sink into the depths of the sea receive better aid than to be grasped by a strong hand and lifted into the boat? Now, we are all as the culprit and the drowning man. We are sinners and as such we are lost and condemned. By the fall of Adam and Eve in the garden of Eden the whole human family was corrupted with the filth of sin and made odious in the sight of God, who is a consuming fire to evil-doers Hell and damnation is our inevitable doom because we have sinned. Why were the shepherds sore afraid when, as we are told, "*the angel of the Lord came upon them, and the glory of the Lord shone round about them?*" They were afraid because they were sinners. Nothing in heaven or on earth could frighten man if he were sinless But now we have a Savior, a Savior by divine assurance, a Savior to deliver us from everlasting death. O my friends, could we receive better news than that? Do we value the benefactor who saves our life and rescues us from temporal death? But here is the Savior from greater perils than all the dangers upon earth, the Savior from hell. O how we should rejoice, how we should thank our God for that Savior, who is God Himself, who could never save us from eternal death if He were not God.

Or do you doubt that the Babe of Bethlehem is the Savior that came down from heaven? Look into our Christmas Gospel and all doubts must disappear. We read, *"And it came to pass in those days, that there went out a decree from Caesar Augustus, that all the world should be taxed. And this taxing was first made when Cyrenius was governor of Syria. And all went to be taxed, every one into his own city. And Joseph also went up from Galilee, out of the city of Nazareth, into Judaea, unto the city of David, which is called Bethlehem; because he was of the house and lineage of David: to be taxed with Mary his espoused wife, being great with child."* O what a wonderful child! For the sake of this child the whole world is set in commotion. God puts into the heart of the greatest living ruler, Caesar Augustus, to issue a decree of taxation which affects the whole world. In every land under the Roman rule the inhabitants must repair to the city or place of their birth to be taxed. And why all this? That Mary and Joseph should go to Bethlehem and that the child Jesus should be born in the city of David. Aye, what a wonderful child! Not only the world, even the heavens are set in commotion for the sake of this child. The angel of the Lord appeared unto the shepherds on the plains of Bethlehem to bring them the good tidings of the Savior's birth; and *"suddenly there was with the angel a multitude of the heavenly host praising God, and saying, Glory to God in the highest, and on earth peace, good will toward men."* What more evidence do we want that this child is the Savior? Could God do more than to set heaven and earth in commotion to make us understand the importance of the great event in the holy night?

II.

But let us continue and look at the next word in the angel's message. He says, *"Born,"* born is a Savior, and the following account is given of His birth: *"And so it was, that, while they were there, the days were accomplished that she should be delivered. And she brought forth her first-born Son, and wrapped Him in swaddling clothes, and laid Him in a manger; because there was no room for them in the inn."* The Savior of the world was born in extreme poverty. There was no bed or cradle for Him; He was laid in a manger. And the fact that He was laid in a manger also discloses the place of His birth. He must have been born in a stable, where mangers are kept and beasts are fed. He was born; the Savior of the world was born! What joy and happiness is contained for us in that little word! Suppose God had come down from heaven in His glorious majesty to deal with us fallen creatures, could we stand before Him? No; we would have to cry for the mountains to fall upon us, and for the hills to cover us. But now God is born; the Word is made flesh; God is become man; God has taken upon Himself our human nature; God is become our brother. Could there be a greater evidence of God's love to man? Could God show more plainly that He desires our eternal happiness than by giving us His own Son, in our own likeness, in the form of man, in all respects the same as we with the exception of sin? For what was the purpose of all this? Why did God become man? That he might work out that righteousness which God requires of man and which no man can show forth, that in our stead, as our substitute, He might fulfill the commandments and atone for all our transgressions by a painful suffering and bitter death. The Babe of Bethlehem is our Redeemer, who reconciled us to God, in whom God has manifested His great love to the sinful creature. "God so loved the world that He gave His only begotten Son, that whosoever believeth in Him should not perish, but have everlasting life." No better illustration could be given of this great Word of God than the birth of Jesus in Bethlehem.

III.

But the great trouble is that so many do not believe in Him. The sinner who is conscious of the greatness of his guilt will say, There is surely no help for me. Others may rejoice in the Savior and joyfully kneel at the manger of the heavenly child. As for me, I have no right there, I must stay away. But what does the angel say in his message? He says, "*Unto you* is born this day a Savior." Whom does he mean? He was addressing the shepherds. Did he mean the shepherds alone? Or, since the shepherds were members of God's chosen people, of the Jewish nation, did he mean to say that unto the Jews alone a

Savior was born? No, my friends, the angel himself explains these two little words, "unto you," when he says, "*Fear not: for, behold, I bring you good tidings of great joy, which shall be to all people.*" Unto whom, then, is the Savior born? O joyful message, unto all people! Do you hear it, O sinner? Unto all people, that is, unto all that ever lived on the face of the earth from the first man, Adam, unto the last man that shall be born before the coming of the day of judgment, unto Jews and Gentiles, Christians and non-Christians, saints and sinners. You have a claim upon this child and if you were ever so great a sinner. Let your sins be as many as the sands on the sea-shore and as black as night, the Babe of Bethlehem extends also to you His little hands and bids you rejoice in the full forgiveness of your foul deeds. You have as much right to this heavenly child as the greatest saint. For this child is the Son of man, who came to seek and to save that which was lost. He is the Lamb of God that taketh away the sins of the world. He is the propitiation for our sins, and not for ours only, but for the sins of the whole world. And if you had done ever so many wrongs and had shown yourself ever so unworthy of God's love, come, let not the greatness or the multitude of your sins keep you away; come and say, O Thou heavenly Child, I can hardly believe it, but it is true, yes, it is true and certain, Thou art mine also, my brother, my God, my Savior, for thou wast born also unto me.

IV.

There is but one more expression in the angel's message: "*This day,*" "this day is born unto you a Savior." What does that mean "this day?" The angel obviously meant to say nothing more than that now was the hour of fulfillment of all those divine prophecies concerning the coming Savior from the beginning of the world. That promised Deliverer did not come some time ago and remain unknown, nor was He to be expected in some future day, but now, this very day, He came. To convince the shepherds the angel gave them a special sign. He said, "*And this shall be a sign unto you; Ye shall find the Babe wrapped in swaddling clothes, lying in a manger.*" This was indeed a sign by which the shepherds could not be misled. That a new-born infant should be cradled in a manger was a most extraordinary thing, and if that night some other child was born in Bethlehem it was surely bedded more comfortably than Mary's son.

"This day is born unto you a Savior." It is this day alway for those who believe in Him. The moment the sinner believes in Jesus, the Savior is his and all the blessings of the Savior are conferred upon him. Melanchthon was once asked by a learned man why we still say, "This day Christ is born," notwithstanding the fact that Jesus was born so many hundreds of years ago. Melanchthon answered, "Are you not in need of a Savior this day? Because every day we must have a Savior we still say, This day He is born."

Let this day then be for you the day of Christ's birth, the day in which Christ is born anew in your heart. This day, when you hear His voice, harden not your heart. Let this day be unto you a day of rejoicing in the Savior. And when no more we can say "This day," there will be an endless day, a day of glory, of happiness and bliss, a day in which we shall unite with the angels and sing glory to our God and Savior for ever and ever. Amen.

GOSPEL ON SECOND CHRISTMAS DAY.

LUKE 2, 15—20.

And it came to pass, as the angels were gone away from them into heaven, the shepherds said one to another, Let us now go even unto Bethlehem, and see this thing which is come to pass, which the Lord hath made known unto us. And they came with haste, and found Mary, and Joseph, and the babe lying in a manger. And when they had seen it, they made known abroad the saying which was told them concerning this child. And all they that heard it wondered at those things which were told them by the shepherds. But Mary kept all these things, and pondered them in her heart. And the shepherds returned, glorifying and praising God for all the things that they had heard and seen, as it was told unto them.

DEARLY BELOVED FRIENDS:

Shepherds on the plains of Bethlehem were the first to be notified that the Savior is born. God did not send His angel to the great men of the Jewish nation, to the scribes and chief priests in Jerusalem, to let them know that now the time was fulfilled and

GOSPEL ON SECOND CHRISTMAS DAY.

the Savior was come. No; the first to receive the good tidings of the Savior's birth were plain shepherds keeping watch over their flocks by night. This is significant. It is in full accordance with what St. Paul says in his first epistle to the Corinthians, "For ye see your calling, brethren, how that not many wise men after the flesh, not many mighty, not many noble, are called: but God hath chosen the foolish things of the world to confound the wise." It is not very likely that the great men of Jerusalem, which was only a short distance, only six miles, from Bethlehem, would have received the angel's message with such an humble faith as did the shepherds, these plain and unpretentious men. These shepherds of the city of David must have been devout Israelites, waiting for the consolation of Israel, believing sincerely in the promised Messiah. At the end of our Gospel we are told that *"the shepherds returned, glorifying and praising God for all the things that they had heard and seen, as it was told unto them."* This plainly shows the piety of these men. They appreciated what God had revealed unto them. Their hearts were filled with thanks and their lips with praise when they returned from their visit to the village and went back to their flocks which they had left on the plains. And the same state of mind they displayed when the angel suddenly appeared and when in Bethlehem they beheld the Child in the manger. The most prominent characteristic of these shepherds is their faith. The subject of our discourse shall be, with the aid of God's Holy Spirit,

THE FAITH OF THE SHEPHERDS.

I. *The nature of their faith.*
II. *The fruit of their faith.*

I.

We read, *"And it came to pass, as the angels were gone away from them into heaven, the shepherds said one to another, Let us now go even unto Bethlehem, and see this thing which is come to pass, which the Lord hath made known unto us."* Note well, the shepherds do not say, Let us go and see whether this be true which the angel of the Lord hath said. They do not speak as if in the least they doubted the angel's statement. They are fully persuaded, they are sure that all must be so. They believe firmly

and steadfastly   And on what do they base their faith?   On the
word alone.   The angel had spoken to them.   The angel of the
Lord had brought down to them from heaven the joyful message
that the Savior is born   This message they do not receive as coming from the angel, but as coming from the Lord God, as they
themselves say, "*The Lord hath made it known unto us*"   Their
faith rests upon the foundation of the word of God alone and they
are made so sure and certain about these things because they are
fully aware that God Himself has told them, God who is true, and
whose word is absolutely reliable.

Behold, then, here we have the true nature of faith.   True
faith is not a thing which is uncertain in itself   If you are a true
believer you will not be in a doubting, wavering state of mind,
thinking that possibly the things that are recorded in the Bible
might be true, but not sure and certain about them.   No; as
Luther says in his preface to his explanation of St. Paul's epistle
to the Romans, "Faith is a living and solid confidence in the grace
and mercy of God and is so certain that a man would rather die a
thousand times than suffer such confidence to be taken away from
him"   If you are a true believer you will base your faith on the
word of God alone, on the word which is written in the Bible.
You will believe that God is merciful to you, a lost and condemned
sinner, that your sins are all forgiven, and that you have been pardoned for the sake of His beloved Son Jesus Christ, who died for
your sins on the cross, that heaven is your eternal home, and that
finally you will be received into the celestial mansions   You will
believe these things, not because any man has told you or because
your heart desires them, but because God says so.   And what is
more truthful, what can we rely upon more firmly, what is more
sure and certain than the word of God?   Such is the nature of
faith.   It is unwavering reliance in the word of God

But we learn more of faith.   Behold the shepherds!   At first
they were sore afraid when the glory of the Lord shone round
about them.   Being sinners the glory of the Lord struck terror to
their hearts.   But the moment they received the angel's message,
the moment they believed the word, all their fear vanished like
the mist before the sun, and they rejoiced in what the Lord had
made known unto them   Joyfully they hastened to Bethlehem to
behold the new-born Savior.   We read: "*And they came with*

haste, and found Mary, and Joseph, and the babe lying in a manger.' They came with haste. Why with haste? Were they afraid to leave their flocks and were they in a hurry to return as quickly as possible to their folds? No; they were overjoyed to know that now, at last, the Savior was come whom Israel had been expecting so long. They had been longing for Him, praying for Him, who should redeem Israel. And now He was come. Their most fervent desire was gratified. The state of their mind was like that of Simeon in the temple when he took the child Jesus up in his arms and exclaimed with rapture, "Lord, now lettest Thou Thy servant depart in peace, according to Thy word· for mine eyes have seen Thy salvation." The child in the manger was Christ the Lord, *born in the city of David, a Savior.* They knew that they were sinners, coming short of the glory of God. But they also knew that their Redeemer lived, that the child born at Bethlehem was the Savior of their souls, and in Him they reposed their trust and confidence; in Him they found true and enduring comfort; in Him they rejoiced as in the God of their salvation. Such is faith.

There is not a happier man on earth than a true Christian. Believing in Christ his Savior, he, and he only, has true comfort. In all the vicissitudes of life in this vale of tears, in the consciousness of his sinfulness, in view of the righteous wrath of God as revealed on Sinai, he hastens to the manger of Bethlehem and with the shepherds finds comfort and celestial joy in the Son of God and Mary's son, his brother and kinsman who was born in the city of David a Savior, poor that we should be made rich, despised and rejected of men that we might be received into grace and glory, the Lord our righteousness. Such is the nature of faith, firm reliance in the word of our salvation and trustful confidence in Him who is set forth in that word as the Savior of sinners, Christ the Lord.

And such faith is also sure to bear its fruit.

II.

We read in our text: "*And when they had seen it, they made known abroad the saying which was told them concerning this child. And all they that heard it wondered at those things which were told them by the shepherds. But Mary kept all these things, and pondered them in her heart.*"   The desire of the shepherds was to have others share their happiness and so rejoice with them.   Their hearts were filled to overflowing and they could not but speak   The first whom they told of the angel's appearance and joyful message, were Mary and Joseph; for of Mary we are told that she "*kept all these things, and pondered them in her heart.*"   We are, doubtless, indebted to Mary for the entire account of the Savior's birth which she communicated to Luke the Evangelist, who recorded it in his Gospel.   And when the shepherds had told Mary and Joseph they went to their friends and acquaintances   They were the first Christian missionaries, the first to make known the Gospel, the good tidings that the Savior was come   Their faith would not let them rest; they had to go forth and be witnesses of all that they themselves had heard and seen.

Behold, then, my friends, one of the first fruits of faith, love of the neighbor, a desire to see others rejoicing and happy. And which is the greatest blessing that we can bestow upon our neighbor?   It is to make known to him Jesus his Savior.   Jesus alone can make him truly happy.   Jesus alone can rid him of the guilt of his sin and lead him to eternal life.   Jesus alone can turn his griefs and sorrows into joy   True faith will induce you to attend also to the bodily needs of your neighbor, to feed the hungred and thirsty, clothe the naked, give shelter to the homeless, visit the sick, and to show sympathy to all.   But if your faith is true it will induce you to seek, above all things, the welfare of your neighbor's immortal soul.   David says, "I believe, therefore have I spoken," and so every Christian must say, I believe, therefore I speak, I believe, therefore I bear witness to the truth   I proclaim the great things which God hath shown unto me.   I praise the name of the Lord to those who still dwell in ignorance and in the shadow of death.

And now let us note the closing words of our text   "*And the shepherds returned,*" says the Evangelist.   Whither did they return?   To their herds and daily occupation.   They had found Christ the Lord, and to serve Him in true faith was henceforth the task of their lives   But it was in their humble walks that they sought and found the opportunities for serving the King of Glory, whose praises angels and archangels had voiced to their wondering ears, and in whose service the heavenly host find ineffable bliss. We too have been, in the spirit, at Bethlehem, and have heard the good tidings of great joy, and our hearts are filled and overflowing with the gladness of another world. How, then, are we to manifest our thanks and magnify the praises of the Father who has so loved us that He gave us His only begotten Son, and of the Son who for our sakes became poor that we through His poverty might be rich? Let us follow the shepherds' example, and return to our various occupations with hearts and hands ready to serve Him all the days of our lives in true godliness, until the Lord will send his holy angel and call us hence from all our earthly toil to our heavenly home, where we, too, shall see our Savior, not at Bethlehem, the city of David, but in Jerusalem on high, the city of our God, and voice forth His perfect praises for ever and ever. Amen.

SUNDAY AFTER CHRISTMAS.

LUKE 2, 33—40.

And Joseph and his mother marveled at those things which were spoken of him. And Simeon blessed them, and said unto Mary his mother, Behold, this child is set for the fall and rising again of many in Israel, and for a sign which shall be spoken against; (yea, a sword shall pierce through thy own soul also,) that the thoughts of many hearts may be revealed. And there was one Anna, a prophetess, the daughter of Phanuel, of the tribe of Aser: she was of a great age, and had lived with an husband seven years from her virginity; and she was a widow of about fourscore and four years, which departed not from the temple, but served God with fastings and prayers night and day. And she coming in that instant gave thanks likewise unto the Lord, and spake of him to all them that looked for redemption in Jerusalem. And when they had performed all things according to the law of the Lord, they returned into Galilee, to their own city Nazareth. And the child grew, and waxed strong in spirit, filled with wisdom: and the grace of God was upon him.

BELOVED FRIENDS IN CHRIST.

This is the last Sunday in the year, and our Gospel is a very suitable text for the occasion. The principal characters in our Gospel, aside from the Lord Jesus who is always the center of all, are an old man and an old woman, both far advanced in years, having arrived at a ripe old age and reminding us of life's eve and the end of our earthly pilgrimage. There is old Simeon, who had taken the child Jesus up in his arms and had said, "Lord, now lettest Thou Thy servant depart in peace, according to Thy word: for mine eyes have seen Thy salvation." There is the aged Anna, who was a regular attendant at the temple, and was full of rejoicing when she beheld the heavenly child Jesus, and spake of Him to all them that looked for redemption in Jerusalem.

These old Simeons and Annas have not died out. There is to this day many an old man, bent with years, his eyes dimmed and his feet tottering, but his tongue filled with the praise of Him who came to seek and to save that which was lost. There is to this day many a venerable matron in silvery hair, having braved the storms and tempests of many a year, but her soul's delight is to visit the Lord's temple; and with the Psalmist she says, "Lord, I love the habitation of Thy house, and the place where Thine honor dwelleth."

O, blessed be these old people that frequent the house of the Lord, though it is with faltering steps they must approach! Blessed be these old people that do not depart from the temple, do not keep away from the house of God, unless God Himself bids them stay at home! Blessed be these old people that remain steadfast in the faith unto the end, until their eyelids close in death and they are stretched on the bier, the expression of Christian joy and inward contentedness still remaining on their pallid features and silently proclaiming to those who gaze on these features, "I have fought a good fight, I have finished my course, I have kept the faith: henceforth there is laid up for me a crown of righteousness."

Simeon and Anna, both far advanced in years, both not far from the grave, and with them—what a contrast!—the child Jesus who had just entered upon life's pathway. This is what our Gospel presents to us on the last Sunday in the year. Let us inquire more into this and consider with the aid of God's Holy Spirit.

WHAT OUR GOSPEL PROPOSES TO US FOR THE LAST SUNDAY IN THE YEAR.

Two things, I. *A question,* II. *A lesson.*

I.

Our Gospel proposes to us for the last Sunday in the year, in the first place, a question. What question? Let us examine the beginning of our text, and we shall see. We read, "*And Joseph and His mother marveled at those things which were spoken of Him. And Simeon blessed them, and said unto Mary His mother, Behold, this child is set for the fall and rising again of many in Israel; and for a sign which shall be spoken against; yea, a sword shall pierce through thy own soul also, that the thoughts of many hearts may be revealed.*" The question involved here is this: What did you make of the child Jesus in the year now drawing to its close? Was He set for your fall or for your rising again? Or, in other words, did you cling to the Rock of ages, to the Lord Jesus, did you remain in the faith, and progress in the faith, and thus improve in your Christian walk and conversation? Or did you begin to lose faith in the Lord Jesus, to drop off, to leave that solid Rock, and float away upon the sea of this world and drown in despair or in the pleasures of this life?

My friends, there are only two ways, a narrow and a broad way, one leading to life eternal and the other to eternal damnation; and there are only two relations of men to the Lord Jesus Either He is set for their rising or for their fall. It is not God's will and purpose that anyone should fall. He wants all men to be saved But this is the outcome: Some rise at this Rock, and some fall. At this Rock the whole human race is split, is divided into two parts. The one part believe on the Lord Jesus and are saved by Him, and unto these He is set for their rising. The other part do not believe on Him, are offended in Him, reject Him, and unto these He is set for their fall. There is not another person in the world about whom there is so much controversy as the Lord Jesus. He is the sign spoken against. Some are for Him, some against Him. The message of the cross is unto some foolishness, unto others it is the power of God. The Gospel is unto some a savor of life unto life, unto others a savor of death unto death. And I beg you observe that the unfortunate class of those unto whom Christ is set for their fall does not consist of such only as are His declared and outspoken enemies, but also of those who neither openly deny, nor

4

publicly confess the Lord Jesus.   For what does the Lord say?
He says, "He that is not with me is against me."   There is no
neutrality in this question. Whosoever does not publicly deny
Christ, so as not to hurt the feelings of true Christians, and, at
the same time, refuses openly to confess Christ before men, so
as to be on good terms with the Lord's enemies also, is by no
means neutral, no, he belongs to those unto whom Christ is set
for their fall.

How is it with you, then, my friend?   Was Jesus set for
your fall or for your rising in the past year?   This is a grave
question, so much the more because with such as have been
brought up in the nurture and admonition of the Lord and are
accustomed to the preaching of God's holy Word, the fall generally does not come precipitately, but slowly and gradually.
When a huge stone is started from the top of a hill to roll downward, it will, at first, move slowly, but gradually its velocity
will increase, and finally it will tear along with frightful rapidity,
until with a crash it reaches the abyss below.   And thus it is
with many of those unto whom Christ is set for their fall.   The
first symptom of their fall is a certain indifference, a lack of zeal
for heavenly things, which takes possession of their souls.   They
are not interested in God's kingdom as much as they formerly
have been.   They do not care as much for the Gospel as they did
before.   If they can only find some trivial reason to stay at home
on Sunday and not go to church they are glad to do so.   They do
not listen to the sermon with devout attention and with a desire
to hear God's message.   And if something is said in the sermon
that stings and disturbs them they object inwardly and harden
their hearts against the divine Word.   And if there is no halt in
this downward course, still graver symptoms will appear.   They
will not read the Scriptures.   They will not come to the Lord's
Supper.   They will cease to pray.   They will shun the company
of Christians and seek their most intimate friends among the
children of this world.   They will commit gross sins and not
repent, and thus keep on like the rolling stone in its downward
course.

O, what a grave question, then, for all of us at the end of
the year, the question: Was the child Jesus set for your rising
or for your fall?   O, blessed is he unto whom Jesus was set for

a rising! Blessed is he who firmly clings to the Rock of ages, whose faith did increase, whose love to the Lord Jesus became only the more fervent! Blessed is he who did not waver amid all the trials and temptations that did beset him during the past year in this vale of tears, but who stood firm and sought comfort in Christ's words! Blessed is he whose walk and conversation was in conformity with his Christian calling! In short, blessed is he who came nearer to Jesus during the past year!

But how, my friend, if this were not the case with you? How, if you had started already on the downward course? Your own heart and conscience will tell you whether Jesus was set for your fall. But if that should be the case with you, sad as it is, let me tell you, there is still hope for you. The Lord God does not want to see you lost. Even now Jesus extends to you His powerful and merciful hand O come, believe on Him, trust in Him to give you strength, and you shall not perish, but have everlasting life.

II.

And to show what we must do in order to remain on the path that leads to eternal life and not to go astray, our Gospel proposes to us, for the end of the year, a threefold lesson

The first lesson we may take from Simeon's and Anna's good old age. Simeon had attained to an age reached by probably one among a hundred. He had been anxious to behold with his own eyes the promised Savior and then to depart in peace. An old tradition has it that this was his last visit at the temple, that he fell down and expired on the floor of the temple when he had finished his hymn to the Savior And of Anna we are told, "*She was a widow of about fourscore and four years*" Such a good old age is awarded to but few among the living. What lesson are we taught thereby? We are taught not to put off repentance, and wait for old age to come, and then to prepare to meet our God. You do not know how quickly and how suddenly you may be summoned to appear before the tribunal of your Maker Another year of your earthly pilgrimage is drawing to a close and so much nearer are you come to the grave Therefore fix your account with God, so as to be ready at any moment to depart in peace.

The next lesson we may take from Simeon's and Anna's piety and faithfulness in their attendance at the temple. Of Simeon we are told in the passage preceding our text that "he was just and devout, waiting for the consolation of Israel: and the Holy Ghost was upon him." And of Anna we read, "*She departed not from the temple, but served God with fastings and prayers night and day*" Seven years had she lived with her husband from her virginity. Then came the lone days of widowhood. But there is a guiding star by which she is directed on life's pathway, and that is the redemption through the Messiah, whom she expects to see before death comes. Having pondered over the promises and prophecies of the Old Testament, she knew that now the time was fulfilled and that the long expected Redeemer was to come. She is old and feeble, but there is an occupation to which she clings and from which she can not desist, and that is to serve God with fastings and prayers night and day. She is a widow indeed, as described by St Paul, "a widow who is desolate, trusteth in God and continueth in supplications and prayers day and night." Now, what lesson does that teach us? It teaches us to lead a pious life and faithfully to serve the Lord our God, not only privately in our homes by a diligent use of the word of God and by prayer, but also publicly by attending the house of worship, by taking an active part in the divine service, and by hearing with devout attention the preaching of the divine Word. Do not fail, then, in the coming year, diligently to provide for the wants of your immortal soul, and to be fed with the bread of eternal life.

Then, my friends, the coming year will be unto you a year of blessing. Even if dire calamities should be in store for you, it will be a year of blessing. We read in our Gospel, "*And when they had performed all things according to the law of the Lord, they returned into Galilee, to their own city Nazareth*" But something intervened before they reached Nazareth. King Herod sought to destroy the child, and they had to flee to the land of Egypt. This, most likely, was the first occasion for a sword to pierce through Mary's soul, to think that her child was the Son of God and that He must flee from a tyrant. But soon was this tribulation overcome, and at the end of our Gospel we read, "*And the child grew, and waxed strong in spirit, filled with wisdom· and the grace of God was upon Him.''* Now what lesson does that teach us? It teaches us not to fear for the child Jesus, not to fear for the spreading of His kingdom and for the future welfare of the church. Let the enemies of Christianity be ever so bold and use all their craftiness and power to destroy what God has built, they shall succeed as little as did King Herod. The Christ Child shall grow and wax stronger, and no power in heaven or on earth shall be able to stem the progress of His church and the coming of His kingdom. And if at times it should seem as if we must cry, ''Lord, help us, we perish!'' the Lord will always be with us, His little flock; He will not forsake us, He will help us with His powerful hand in all times of need and distress, and will finally conduct us to the realm of glory, where we shall sing His praise forever. Amen.

NEW YEAR'S DAY.

LUKE 2, 21.

And when eight days were accomplished for the circumcising of the child, his name was called JESUS, which was so named of the angel before he was conceived in the womb.

BELOVED FRIENDS IN CHRIST:

''*And when eight days were accomplished,*'' says our text. Eight days since when? Since the birth of Jesus. And this is the eighth day after the joyous festival of Christ's birth. So the reason why this Gospel was placed on the church calendar for the day is, because the occurrence corresponds with the date.

And what date is this? It is the first day in a new secular year, New Year's Day, a day of joy and mirth, a day greeted with delight and hailed with gladness by Christians and non-Christians. It will certainly interest us all to know that there was a time when this day was not celebrated in the Christian church as a festival. In the first centuries of the Christian era the Christians observed this day as a day of fasting. On this day the heathen had a great celebration in their way, offering great sacrifices to their gods, eating, drinking, dancing, and being merry. And the Christians were careful not to appear as if they took a

part in those festivities of the heathen   Augustine, who lived in
the latter part of the fourth and in the beginning of the fifth
century, says, "On this day we Christians fast and sigh for the
heathen who are joyful."   But when in the course of time
heathenism was dethroned and Christianity was made the religion
of the state, the Christians made a festival of the day which
formerly had been a day of fasting   It is not more than about
seven hundred years that New Year's Day is celebrated in the
church as a joyful festival   And why do Christians hail this day
with joy and gladness? Because, as we are informed in our Gospel,
the Lord God did for us a great thing on this day.   He conferred
upon us a great gift, a priceless treasure   And the solemn importance of the day reminds us that we should consecrate ourselves to God and thus present also to Him a gift on this memo-
rable day of our earthly lives.   Accordingly, the subject of our
discourse shall be with the aid of God's Holy Spirit,

TWO NEW YEAR'S GIFTS.

I   *A great gift which God presents to us*, and
II *A small gift which we should present to God*

I.

While with the children of men Christmas Day is the day of
gifts, New Year's Day is with them the day of good wishes and
congratulations.   And there is a New Year's wish for us all, written
by God and extended to us in His divine word.   That New Year's
wish is our simple and brief Gospel which reads, "*And when
eight days were accomplished for the circumcising of the child,
His name was called Jesus, which was so named of the angel
before He was conceived in the womb.*"   Now we must know that
God's wishes are not like the wishes of men, not simply cheering
words and hopeful expressions.   When God wishes us anything,
He, at the same time, imparts, presents to us that which He wishes.
David, therefore, says, "For Thou blessest, O Lord, and it shall
be blessed forever"   The fact is that God on this day had His
beloved Son shed the first drops of His precious blood to assure
us of the forgiveness of our sins, and that in the darkness before
us, in the dim future, which our eyes can not penetrate, He writes
the sweet name of Jesus in flaming letters to dispel all the darkness and to illumine our path.

In the first place, let us note that Jesus was circumcised on this day. Now that seems to be a very foolish thing in the eyes of man, that Jesus should submit to this old Israelitish rite and sacrament. But such are God's institutions, foolish in the eyes of man. It is the same with Baptism, which in the New Testament has followed in the wake of Circumcision. And why did Jesus submit to Circumcision? Did He have to do that? or did He do that for His own sake? No; Jesus was not under the Law. He is Lord of all. And yet He placed Himself under the Law and was obedient to the Law for our sakes, because by the Law we were all condemned. We are all sinners, and eternal condemnation is our doom, because we do not fulfill the commandments. However, Jesus came to fulfill the commandments in our stead and to pay the penalty for our transgressions. And on this day He made the beginning to atone for us by His precious blood. This day He shed the first drops of His blood, to be followed by His holy sacrificial offering on the cross, when as the Lamb of God He bled and died for us all. This day, the first day of the year, God extends to us in His New Year's wish a general pardon for all our transgressions, for all our sins in the past year and for all the sins of the new year: a general pardon by the blood and righteousness of His beloved Son.

And to this grand New Year's gift God adds something more. As in Baptism the child receives a name, so did the Son of God receive a name in Circumcision. And what is that name? Jesus. Why the name Jesus? Because "*He was so named of the angel before He was conceived in the womb.*" And what is the meaning of this name? The angel said to Joseph, "Thou shalt call His name Jesus, for He shall save His people from their sins." Jesus means Savior, Redeemer. Now in His great New Year's wish God presents to us the name of Jesus, and that is not an empty name. In the dark future before us, the name of Jesus boldly stands forth in shining letters, more bright than gold, and silver, and sparkling diamonds. Jesus will guide our way and illumine our path. Jesus will be with us in the new year, as He has been in the old. Jesus will be in our hearts, in our homes, in our humble little church, in our assembly. His grace will not depart from us, nor will the covenant of His peace be removed. His love will be the same, His mercy the same, His comfort the same. No matter what may be in store for us, in days of joy and in days of sorrow, Jesus will be with us. Let the dreary days come, let times of sorrowing come, let our best friends desert us, Jesus will not leave us. He will be with us alway, even unto the end of the world.

Tell me, my friends, is not this a grand wish and gift for the new year? O how happy, how fortunate are we, how rich, how blessed to have the sweet name of Jesus! God is the almighty Owner of the earth. If He wished, He could give us all the gold and silver in the world. But what should we be benefited if, at the same time, we did not possess the Gospel of His grace? We would be poor and miserable; for in death we must leave all, and all the riches of this earth can not purchase the kingdom of heaven. God could also give us the promise and make true the promise that during the year no illness should visit our homes, no sorrow should come into our hearts, no want should knock at our doors, that all our days should be joyful and happy on this earth. But how do we know that such continuous joy would be for our own good? What are all the joys of life without the grace of God? Must we not all die? And what is more terrible than the fate of the rich man who found himself in hell and torment, after he had fared sumptuously every day and had received his good things in his life-time?—Indeed, the grace of God imparted to us with the sweet name of Jesus is the grandest gift that God could bestow upon us.

II.

Having shown you the great gift which God bestows on us this New Year's Day, let me, in the second place, call your attention to a small gift which we should present to God.

Our Gospel says that Jesus "was so named of the angel before He was conceived in the womb." And, as we have heard before, the angel said to Joseph, "Thou shalt call His name Jesus, for He shall save His people from their sins." So the very name of Jesus reminds us of the fact that we are sinners, who are in need of a Savior.

And now what can we give to God as a New Year's gift since we are sinners? Shall we give Him our property, our earthly possessions? Ah, I am afraid that perhaps many a Christian would be unwilling to do that. How do some people grumble and complain when they are called upon to do something for God, to give for the church! They can spend money very lavishly for their own amusement and pleasure, but even a small amount for the church is too much for them. And yet Christ says, "Whosoever forsaketh not all that he hath he can not be my disciple." A true Christian should not only be willing to give freely for God's kingdom, but should do so without grumbling, should find pleasure in so doing, and thank the Lord when he is able to aid by earthly means in the establishment of God's kingdom. Still, if we should sacrifice all our possessions for Christ's sake, can we really say that we have given God anything? Is not God the real Owner? Does not heaven and earth belong to Him? Are we more than stewards who must give account to God how we dealt with those goods which He placed in our hands on this earth?

What else, then, can we give God as a New Year's gift? Shall we give Him our clothing, when in the shape of a beggar He appeals to us to give Him protection and shelter? Shall we give Him food and drink when to the poor that are starving, because they can not procure the necessaries of life, we give nourishment? All this we are required to do as Christians, and Jesus distinctly says of such deeds done in the faith, "Inasmuch as ye have done it unto one of the least of these my brethren, ye have done it unto Me." Still, can we really say that we have given God anything when we have ministered to the wants of those that are in need? Is not God the real Owner of all that we possess, also of our food and raiment?

Yet, my friends, there is one thing we have, and which we can really give God as a New Year's gift. It is very small indeed, insignificant compared with the great New Year's gift of our God; but God will gladly accept it, aye, He begs for it, as it were, He asks and demands of us that we should give Him that gift. In the book of Proverbs He says, "My son, give Me thy heart, and let thine eyes observe My ways."

O let us give God our hearts. Let this be our New Year's gift. And how shall we do that? The heart is the seat of our affection, the seat of love. To give God our hearts is to love Him. By nature our hearts are alienated from God. By nature our hearts do not cling to God, but to sin, to the world and its

evil lusts We must, therefore, tear away our heart from the
world and from sin and give it to Him who made it, to God.
This we can never do of our own natural power, but only in the
power of God And, therefore, we must call upon God to give
us strength from on high. We must be so minded that every
day of the year we say in our hearts, I do not covet the riches of
this earth, if only I am made rich in God; I do not care for the
pleasures of this world, if only I am made sure of the pleasures of
heaven; I do not desire earthly glory, if only I shall be honored
as a child of God. Our motto must be for the New Year, "Lord,
whom have I in heaven but Thee? And there is none upon earth
that I desire beside Thee." Behold, then, if this we do, then we
have given God our heart, and not a better New Year's gift does
He desire.

Let us love Him, then, for He hath first loved us. If we
remain in this love, we shall also remain in the faith, and if we
remain in the faith, the New Year shall be unto us a year of grace
and blessing May the Lord grant us this for the sake of Jesus,
His beloved Son, our Lord, unto whom be praise and glory forever and ever Amen.

SUNDAY AFTER NEW YEAR.

MATT 2, 13—23

And when they were departed, behold, the angel of the Lord appeareth to
Joseph in a dream, saying, Arise, and take the young child and his mother, and
flee into Egypt, and be thou there until I bring thee word for Herod will seek
the young child to destroy him. When he arose, he took the young child and
his mother by night, and departed into Egypt and was there until the death of
Herod that it might be fulfilled which was spoken of the Lord by the prophet,
saying, Out of Egypt have I called my son Then Herod, when he saw that he
was mocked of the wise men, was exceeding wroth, and sent forth, and slew all
the children that were in Bethlehem, and in all the coasts thereof, from two
years old and under, according to the time which he had diligently enquired of
the wise men Then was fulfilled that which was spoken by Jeremy the prophet,
saying, In Rama was there a voice heard, lamentation, and weeping, and great
mourning, Rachel weeping for her children and would not be comforted, because they are not But when Herod was dead, behold, an angel of the Lord
appeareth in a dream to Joseph in Egypt, saying, Arise, and take the young
child and his mother, and go into the land of Israel for they are dead, which
sought the young child's life And he arose, and took the young child and his

mother, and came into the land of Israel. But when he heard that Archelaus did reign in Judæa in the room of his father Herod, he was afraid to go thither: notwithstanding, being warned of God in a dream, he turned aside into the parts of Galilee: and he came and dwelt in a city called Nazareth: that it might be fulfilled which was spoken by the prophets, He shall be called a Nazarene.

BELOVED FRIENDS IN CHRIST:

King Herod was an enemy of Christ, though he pretended to be a friend of Christ when he said to the wise men from the East, *"Go and search diligently for the young Child, and when ye have found Him, bring me word again that I may come and worship Him also."* To this day there are enemies of Christ that pose as His friends. Christ distinctly says, "He that is not with me, is against me; and he that gathereth not with me, scattereth abroad." According to these words of our divine Lord all those that mean to hold a neutral position, and all those that do not gather with Him, or work for Him and for His kingdom, must be looked upon as His opponents. They are against Him; they are His enemies. You are either a friend of Christ, and then you will act the part of a friend, you will confess His name and work for His kingdom; or you are an enemy of Christ, and then you will act the part of an enemy, though you may do so under the disguise of a friend.

There are many in our days who do not believe in Christ and yet they do not openly speak against Him, or persecute Him. Sometimes there are children who are scoffers and infidels at the bottom of their hearts, and yet they come to church and make an outward profession of the Christian religion on account of their pious parents whom they would not like to offend by an open renunciation of the faith. And then again there are parents who are outspoken unbelievers, and yet they send their children to church and to Sunday-school, because they can not deny the wholesome influence of religion. Then there are such as do not openly join the ranks of blasphemers, because if they did this, it might injure their trade and business, or because by such a step they would hurt the feelings of their Christian friends. And so they do not wish to sever their connection with the church altogether. They pose as Christians whilst their entire mien and demeanor plainly shows they do not care for the church; the word of God has no charms for them; they are unbelievers, enemies of Christ.

But aside from these secret enemies there is another class of bold, out-spoken enemies of Christ and His religion, enemies raging and raving against Christ like Herod in our Gospel, enemies who plot, and seek to destroy Christ, and to wipe Christianity from the earth. Let us consider with the aid of God's Holy Spirit,

HOW THE ENEMIES PLOT AGAINST CHRIST AND HIS KINGDOM; and let us consider

 I. *The craftiness of their plotting.*
 II. *The uselessness of their plotting.*

I.

How ingeniously did Herod plot against the newborn Savior! When the wise men came to Jerusalem from the East, seeking the newborn King of the Jews, he discovered that such a King was expected and that He was to be born in Bethlehem. So he sent those wise men to Bethlehem and instructed them to be sure and come back to tell him whether they had found that King, so that he also might worship Him. The hypocrite! He never thought of worshiping the Child. He meant to kill Him. God, therefore, told the wise men in a dream not to return to Herod, and they departed into their own country another way. "*And when they were departed, behold, the angel of the Lord appeareth to Joseph in a dream, saying, Arise, and take the young Child and His mother, and flee into Egypt, and be thou there until I bring thee word; for Herod will seek the young Child to destroy Him.*" Behold the ingenuity and shrewdness with which this enemy plots and schemes against the Lord's Anointed! So cleverly does he arrange his plans, so secretly does he work, it seems he must succeed. Must not the wise men return to their homes by the way of Jerusalem? Must not gratitude prompt them to bring Herod all the information desired? It was, indeed, a finely laid plot, a scheme which could not but work successfully to the mind of the bloody tyrant, whose soul was as black as night, who brooded death and destruction merely to keep his throne and not to be pushed aside by an intruder.

But Herod not only plotted against Christ's person, but also against His kingdom. We read of Joseph, "*When he arose, he took the young Child and His mother by night, and departed into Egypt, and was there until the death of Herod; that it might be fulfilled which was spoken of the Lord by the prophet, saying, Out of Egypt have I called my Son.''* So the persecution directed against the person of Christ did strike those also that were with Christ   The whole family had to flee for the life of Jesus, and dwell for a time in a strange country, in the land of Egypt.   And not only the near relatives of Jesus had to suffer inconvenience, but also those that were in the same locality were afflicted for Jesus' sake.   For we are told, *"Then Herod, when he saw, that he was mocked of the wise men, was exceeding wroth, and sent forth, and slew all the children that were in Bethlehem, and in all the coasts thereof, from two years old and under, according to the time which he had diligently enquired of the wise men."* Here again we perceive the ingenuity and shrewdness of the bloody tyrant.   The Child that was heir to the throne had to die at all hazards.   And since the wise men had not brought him the information he desired, since he only knew where, but not who the Child was, he determined to slay all the children in and around Bethlehem, of two years and under   How could the mysterious Child escape then?   When those infants were butchered and the blood of the first martyrs was shed, the king was sure of it that he could not have missed the Christ-child.

This cruel king has had his followers at all times from the beginning of the Christian era to this day.   There always have been enemies of Christ who plotted and schemed against the Lord's Anointed and His kingdom.   How did the Jews, notably the Pharisees and chief rulers, persecute Jesus and plan to kill Him !   How did they breathe out threatenings and slaughter against the disciples of the Lord !   And the heathen—how mercilessly did they deal with Christ's followers !   In the first three centuries alone there were seven persecutions waged against the Christians by seven different Roman emperors, and the Christians were put to death by the thousands   Like sheep they were led to the slaughter, tortured, and killed   Later on Mohammed came   He promised heaven to those of his followers who died on the battle-field fighting for the cause of Islam   And now the Christians were again butchered by the thousands   Entire Christian provinces were laid waste and depopulated.   Then the papacy came.   The Roman pontiff sat in the temple of God, in the church "shewing himself that he is God."   And how cruelly did he persecute the true followers of

Christ! Countless is the number of those who under the rule of
the papacy were tortured and slaughtered, because they would not
acknowledge any other authority in matters of faith than the word
of God, and no other ruler and king than the Lord Jesus Christ.
The books of history are full of horrors committed under the
papal rule

And have the enemies ceased at last to plot against Christ
and His kingdom? Have not the most shocking atrocities occurred
within recent years? Have not thousands of Christians been massacred in cold blood by the Turks? Are not anarchists and their
allies continually at work planning how they might overthrow the
established order of things and destroy Christ and His religion?
Do they not openly say that the time will come when by brutal
force they will accomplish their designs, and bring about the desired change with blood-stained hands?—There is no question, to
this day the enemies are plotting against Christ and His kingdom.

II.

And now, in the second place, let us see how useless all their
plotting is.

What did Herod accomplish against the person of Christ?
Did he dethrone Christ? Did he make to naught the prophecy
of God concerning the Messiah? No, contrary to his own will he
had to be instrumental in fulfilling God's prophecy By Christ's
flight to Egypt the prophecy had to be fulfilled which says, "*Out
of Egypt have I called my Son*" And by the massacre of those
innocent infants in the borders of Bethlehem another divine
prophecy had to come true, the prophecy of Jeremy, saying,
"*In Rama was there a voice heard, lamentation, and weeping,
and great mourning, Rachel weeping for her children, and would
not be comforted, because they are not.*"

And what did Herod accomplish against Christ's kingdom?
Did his power extend into the realms of the invisible world?
Could he debar God's holy angels from warning the wise men
and Joseph in a dream? Did he not again, contrary to his own
will, have to aid and serve the kingdom of Christ which he meant
to destroy? For did he really harm those innocent infants, those
first martyrs, who bled for Jesus' sake? Many, or perhaps all
of them, would have grown up enemies of Christ, had they lived,

for most of the Jews rejected their Messiah. But now they entered into eternal glory and were among those of whom it is said in the Psalm, "Out of the mouth of babes and sucklings Thou hast perfected praise." As our children, dying in their baptismal grace, invariably go to heaven, so did these infants, who were Rachel's children, children of the covenant, having received the sacrament of Circumcision which in the Old Testament held the place of Baptism, by their premature death, get to eternal happiness and bliss

So we have seen that Herod's plotting against Christ and His kingdom was altogether unsuccessful. Though he succeeded for a while in hiding his diabolical plot before the wise men, he could not hide it from God. Though he formed his plans with the utmost ingenuity and shrewdness and executed them with merciless cruelty, his fight against the Lord and His Anointed was in vain. And so it has always been. The enemies of Christ never did succeed and never will succeed. In the early times of the Christian church both, Jews and Gentiles, combined and arrayed their forces against the Christian religion. Entire libraries have been written against the divine truth of the Gospel, and heathen officials tried to stamp out the pest of Christianity, as they called it, by seizing and burning every copy of the New Testament they could find. Entire Christian provinces were ravaged and depopulated, and the smoldering ruins of Christian homes showed how completely the work of devastation was done. But it was in vain. Christ always survived His enemies. At times it seemed as if the church of God was no more. But the Lord has always made true His promise that even the gates of hell shall not prevail against His church.

And there is one more point to which I would call your attention. Those enemies of Christ who waste their efforts in plotting against Him and His kingdom oftentimes meet their due punishment already in this life. There is but a short notice in our Gospel concerning Herod, "*But when Herod was dead, behold, an angel of the Lord appeareth in a dream to Joseph in Egypt, saying, Arise, and take the young Child and His mother, and go into the land of Israel for they are dead which sought the young Child's life*" Two secular historians, a Jew by the name of Josephus and a Christian by the name of Eusebius, describe the death of this cruel king Herod. They tell us that his body was covered with ulcers emitting such a stench, that it was almost impossible to stay with him. When he saw that he must die, he had the most distinguished Jews incarcerated and ordered that they should be put to death as soon as he would breathe his last, so that, as he himself said, all Judaea would have to mourn, in place of rejoicing, at his death. Then the miserable wretch committed suicide by plunging a knife into his heart. And there is another historian by the name of Lactantius who wrote a book entitled, "Death of Persecutors," showing that nearly every one of those Roman emperors and officials who stained their hands with Christian blood met with a most horrible death.

Indeed, God is not mocked. Even when God does not avenge the blood of His saints on earth, even when those who have been devoting their lives to plotting against Christ and His kingdom and have been persecuting the children of God pass away from this life apparently in peace and without suffering, they shall not escape the punishment which they deserve. They shall perceive whom they have pierced and come to eternal woe.

Let us, then, confidently trust in the Lord. Let the enemies of Christ and His church plot all they wish with the utmost cunning and craftiness, they shall succeed as little now as they did in former times. "The Lord of hosts is with us, the God of Jacob is our refuge." Amen.

EPIPHANY.

Matt. 2, 1—12.

Now when Jesus was born in Bethlehem of Judaea in the days of Herod the king, behold, there came wise men from the east to Jerusalem, saying, Where is he that is born King of the Jews? for we have seen his star in the east, and are come to worship him. When Herod the king had heard these things, he was troubled, and all Jerusalem with him. And when he had gathered all the chief priests and scribes of the people together, he demanded of them where Christ should be born. And they said unto him, In Bethlehem of Judaea: for thus it is written by the prophet, And thou Bethlehem, in the land of Juda, art not the least among the princes of Juda: for out of thee shall come a Governor, that shall rule my people Israel. Then Herod, when he had privily called the wise men, enquired of them diligently what time the star appeared. And he sent them to Bethlehem, and said, Go and search diligently for the young child, and when ye have found him, bring me word again, that I may come and worship him also When they had heard the king, they departed, and, lo, the star, which they saw in the east, went before them, till it came and stood over where the young child was When they saw the star, they rejoiced with exceeding great joy And when they were come into the house, they saw the young child with Mary his mother, and fell down, and worshiped him: and when they had opened their treasures, they presented unto him gifts, gold, and frankincense, and myrrh And being warned of God in a dream that they should not return to Herod, they departed into their own country another way

BELOVED FRIENDS IN CHRIST:

The purport of this Gospel is to inculcate the fact that also the Gentiles have a part in Christ. That the Son of God was to be the Savior of the Jews, there could be no question He had been promised to the chosen people of God for a period of two thousand years And when the time was fulfilled and He was made manifest in the flesh, the Jews were the first to be notified that the Savior was come. On the plains of Bethlehem the angel of the Lord appeared to the shepherds, who were Jews, and brought them the good tidings of great joy that unto them was born, in the city of David, a Savior, which is Christ the Lord. Scarcely, however, had the Jews been made acquainted with this joyful intelligence, when the Lord God informed the Gentiles also that a Savior had come for them. And while the good tidings were brought to the Jews on the very spot, in the immediate neighborhood of Bethlehem, where Jesus was born, the communication of the Savior's birth was conveyed to the Gentiles in the far East, far away from the scene While the Jews received their information by an angel from heaven announcing the Savior's birth, and by the multitudes of the heavenly host singing songs of praises upon earth, the Gentiles beheld in the heavens a wonderful star While the Jewish representatives, to whom God communicated the great event, were plain shepherds, the Gentile representatives were men of wealth and learning

Now, since we are descendants of Gentile nations and our heathen ancestors were converted from heathenism and brought to the faith of the Son of God, O how should we thank God for His great mercy shown unto us ! A special festival, the festival of Epiphany, which we are celebrating to-day, was arranged in the church to commemorate this blessed fact and to give us an occasion to offer up praise and thanksgiving for the inestimable

5

blessing that we have been rescued from heathenism by the wonderful Child in the manger, that we also have a share in the Christ-child, that He is our Savior as well as the Savior of the Jews,' and that we have found Him, recognized in Him our Savior, and have been made members of the Christian church.

Our Gospel, however, also imparts valuable instruction. "Whatsoever things were written aforetime were written for our learning," and there is something to be learned of the wise men in our Gospel. The subject of our discourse shall be with the aid of God's Holy Spirit,

TRUE WISDOM TO BE LEARNED OF THE WISE MEN.

I   *They followed the guide from heaven*
II   *They were not influenced by the infidelity of others.*
III. *When they found Christ, they worshiped and honored Him*

I.

"*Now when Jesus was born in Bethlehem of Judaea in the days of Herod the king, behold, there came wise men from the East to Jerusalem, saying, Where is He that is born King of the Jews? for we have seen His star in the East, and are come to worship Him.*" So these wise men had a guide from heaven, and they followed that guide, making no delay and undertaking a long and expensive journey to find Christ. But we must not think that that wonderful star in itself was their guide The science of astronomy does not teach the way to heaven Men have been endeavoring to show that the Gospel is written in the stars, but that is a mere play of fancy. "The heavens declare the glory of God, and the firmament showeth His handiwork." But where does the word of God say that man should lift up his eyes to heaven and read the Gospel in the stars? No; the Gospel is a mystery which was kept secret since the world began, and is not revealed by the works of nature, but by the great God Himself in His divine word. Those wise men, therefore, must have had some divine revelation concerning that star, or they never would have comprehended its meaning

Another false notion current in our days concerning the star of Bethlehem is, that it was something in the ordinary course of nature. Astronomers have found that about the time when those wise men journeyed to Jerusalem, there was a conjunction of three very bright stars, Mars, Jupiter, and Saturnus; a conjunction which occurs only once in eight centuries. And now it is claimed that the star which those wise men beheld was this conjunction of stars. How absurd! Could that conjunction guide them from Jerusalem to Bethlehem, and then remain in a fixed position over where the young Child was? Is not Bethlehem south of Jerusalem and do not the ordinary stars move from east to west and stand so high above us that they always seem to go with us, and never stop over and above a certain place, while we are walking on? No, we must not seek to explain away miracles. There may have been conjunctions of stars at the same time, but they certainly had nothing to do with this star. This star was a special light placed by the Lord God for this special purpose in the lower regions of the atmosphere.

As intimated, the guide which the wise men really followed was the divine revelation concerning that star. And now, when they came to Jerusalem, we are told that Herod "*gathered all the chief priests and scribes of the people together, and demanded of them where Christ should be born. And they said unto him, In Bethlehem of Judaea: for thus it is written by the prophet, And thou Bethlehem, in the land of Juda, art not the least among the princes of Juda: for out of thee shall come a Governor, that shall rule my people Israel*" And when Herod had told them this and had sent them to Bethlehem, we are informed, "*When they had heard the king, they departed; and, lo, the star, which they saw in the East, went before them, till it came and stood over where the young Child was When they saw the star, they rejoiced with exceeding great joy.*" What was it, then, that really guided and led these wise men to Christ? Which was their true guide to heaven? It was the word of God, the word of divine revelation spoken by the prophet. That was the guide from heaven whom they followed. And how wise were they to follow that guide! Had they remained in the East and paid no attention to the wonderful star, and had they not followed the directions given by the word of God in the writings of the prophet, they never would have come to Christ; they would have remained in darkness, in superstition, and condemnation

Behold, then, here is true wisdom. Follow the guide from heaven. That guide is the divine word. But you must not wait for a special divine revelation in a dream or vision. You have no promise for that. God may send you a star in the shape of great joy or great sorrow, or in some other way give you an indication that He longs and yearns to save you in particular. But then you must place your confidence in the written word of God, and heed the word of God. Let the word of God perform upon you its mission on this earth. Let the word of God convince you that you are a lost and condemned sinner, and persuade you that you have been redeemed from sin and death by the Lord Jesus, by His painful suffering and bitter death on the cross. Let the word of God guide you through this vale of tears to the heavenly mansions. That is true wisdom, that is making a profitable use of your time upon earth, so that you may get to a blessed hereafter.

II.

The wise men showed true wisdom in another way. They were not influenced by the infidelity of others. We read, "*When Herod the king had heard these things, he was troubled and all Jerusalem with him.*" Now imagine how these wise men must have felt. They had come to Jerusalem, expecting to find every face beaming with joy, everybody speaking of the newborn King, and the whole city wild with excitement. What do they find? All is quiet. No one seems to care for that King on whose account they had come so far a way. Aye, when the object of their visit is made known, Herod and all the inhabitants of Jerusalem are alarmed. And then again, such is the indifference displayed by the inhabitants, not a single one of them offers to go along to Bethlehem. Could these people more plainly show that they did not believe in that newborn King? But what do we find the wise men doing? Do they say within themselves, Ah, we have been deceived; we have come here in vain; there is no newborn King of the Jews; if there were, would not His own people know about it? would not the distinguished men, the learned and prominent, come with us and go to Bethlehem? No; the wise men were not disturbed in the least. They were not influenced by the infidelity of others. They simply believed what God had told them, and though not a soul seemed to share their faith, they proceeded to Bethlehem at once.

Behold here true wisdom. You must not be disturbed by the infidelity of others. If you allow yourselves to be influenced by the adverse attitude which the majority of men assume toward Christ, then you will reject Christ, reject the word of God, and be an unbeliever. And is not this the greatest folly to think that truth is to be found with the majority? Have not the most absurd theories been advanced by the philosophers of this world, and almost universally accepted, until they were out of date, and had to make room for other theories equally foolish? And why do you expect the majority, and especially the great men of this world, the rich and distinguished, to follow Christ? Did not Jesus say, "Wide is the gate, and broad is the way, that leadeth to destruction, and many there be which go in thereat"? Did not St. Paul say, "Ye see your calling, brethren, how that not many wise men after the flesh, not many mighty, not many noble, are called"? If, therefore, you would be truly wise and prudent, you must not seek your salvation in great Jerusalem, that is, not with the masses, but in Bethlehem, in the lowly manger. You must not seek your salvation with the scribes and chief priests, that is, with the learned, rich, and great, but with Mary and Joseph, with those who humbly profess their faith in Jesus the Savior.

III.

There is one more point showing the true wisdom of the wise men. When they had found Christ, they worshiped Him. We are told, "*And when they were come into the house, they saw the young Child with Mary His mother, and fell down, and worshiped Him: and when they had opened their treasures, they presented unto Him gifts; gold, and frankincense, and myrrh.*" The wise men had believed in Christ all along. They believed in Him as soon as they were persuaded by the divine revelation that the star which they beheld in the East, was the star of the newborn King of the Jews. We must not think that their faith in Christ did not begin until their eyes beheld Him. But now when they did see Him for whose sake they had come all the way from the far East, what did they behold? Did they find what they surely must have expected? Did they find a royal family surrounded with all the luxury and comfort of Oriental splendor and ease? Did they find a magnificent palace, guarded by sentries in gorgeous attire to protect the approach to the great Prince and King? No, there is a low hut, and the occupants are as poor as they can be, and the Child is a babe like any other child. Must not then faith receive a fatal shock at the sight of all this poverty and lowliness? Yet they were wise men, indeed. They knew that the word of God could not deceive them. And did not the wonderful star remain over above the Child? So they boldly overcame all adverse sentiments, fell down upon their knees, worshiped the Child, and honored Him with gifts. They gave Him gold, and we can well conceive how sorely the Child needed the gold for His impending flight to Egypt. But frankincense and myrrh were not considered especially valuable. There must be a special meaning to these two latter gifts. Frankincense was burned at the sacrifices to honor the deity, and myrrh was used in embalming a corpse. It seems, then, that by presenting these two gifts the wise men meant to profess their faith that this Child was both God and man.

Now, if we would be wise and prudent like the wise men, we must see that we keep the faith when trials and afflictions come, when things do not turn out according to our wishes and expectations, when our faith receives a shock. Having found Christ, you must hold on to Him. It will never benefit you to believe in Christ for a while, and then to turn away from Him. Only he that endureth to the end shall be saved. O be not ashamed, then, of Christ and of His Gospel! Confess Him before men, and He will confess you also before His Father in heaven. Do not mind the scorn of the children of this world. Say before all men that you believe that Jesus is both God and man, that He is your Savior and Redeemer, your Sovereign and King, whom you worship, and whom you mean to serve as long as you are living upon this earth. The wise men honored Him and worshiped Him when He was in lowliness and poverty, how much the more should you worship and honor Him now, since He is exalted above the heavens and sitting at the right hand of God the Father Almighty!

May the Lord, then, grant us all His grace to apply our hearts unto true wisdom and to imitate the example of the wise men, to the glory of His holy name and to the salvation of our souls! Amen.

FIRST EPIPHANY.

Luke 2, 41—52

Now his parents went to Jerusalem every year at the feast of the passover. And when he was twelve years old, they went up to Jerusalem after the custom of the feast And when they had fulfilled the days, as they returned, the child Jesus tarried behind in Jerusalem, and Joseph and his mother knew not of it. But they, supposing him to have been in the company, went a day's journey, and they sought him among their kinsfolk and acquaintance And when they found him not, they turned back again to Jerusalem, seeking him And it came to pass, that after three days they found him in the temple, sitting in the midst of the doctors, both hearing them, and asking them questions And all that heard him were astonished at his understanding and answers And when they saw him, they were amazed and his mother said unto him, Son, why hast thou thus dealt with us? behold, thy father and I have sought thee sorrowing And he said unto them, How is it that ye sought me? wist ye not that I must be about my Father's business? And they understood not the saying which he spake unto them And he went down with them, and came to Nazareth, and was subject unto them but his mother kept all these sayings in her heart And Jesus increased in wisdom and stature, and in favor with God and man

Beloved Friends in Christ:

The visit of Jesus to Jerusalem at the age of twelve years is the only incident recorded of the time of His boyhood.   Beside the remark that He was subject to His parents and that He increased in wisdom and stature, and in favor with God and man, nothing more is said of Him until, at the age of thirty years, He comes to John the Baptist and is baptized in the river Jordan.

Had anything remarkable occurred within this long period, had Jesus done anything to show that He is the Son of God and Savior of the world, had He performed a miracle, for instance, St Luke would probably have mentioned it in his Gospel.   Luke is the only Evangelist who tells particulars of Jesus' infancy and boyhood, and he seems to have his information from Jesus' mother, Mary, of whom he distinctly says at different occasions that she kept these things in her heart.   Had Jesus in any way manifested His divinity, Mary, undoubtedly, would have told Luke, so that he might put it down in his book for future generations.   We are expressly told that at the marriage at Cana in Galilee He performed His *first* miracle, turning water into wine   The only time when rays of divine glory shone forth from the Son of man in the days of His youth was when, at the age of twelve years, He was in the temple of Jerusalem. There He sat, the tender youth, in the midst of the doctors, that is, the men who had grown up in the study of the Scriptures, who were the teachers of the people, and were looked upon as authorities in religious matters. He converses with these highly educated men, He asks them and answers them, and behold, such is the understanding and such are the answers of the boy of Galilee, that the doctors do not know what to make of it. They are amazed. They had never seen and heard the like. And the same amazement comes upon Mary and Joseph when He says to them, *"How is it that ye sought me? wist ye not that I must be about my Father's business?"* Here the rays of His divine glory are darting forth from the Son of God, and He gently reminds His parents of the fact that He is the eternal Son of the Father, a fact which they well knew, but did not bear in mind when they addressed Him.

A special feature, however, of our Gospel is, that it contains an important lesson for parents. It tells in what manner parents should care for their children and exercise their authority over them. This, then, shall be the subject of our discourse, with the aid of God's Holy Spirit,

PARENTAL CARE AND AUTHORITY.

We shall consider

I. *Parental care,* and
II. *Parental authority*

I.

Parents need not be told that they must attend to their children in earthly things. They know that. It is implanted by nature. Even the animals instinctively take care of their young, feed them, and protect them, until they can take care of themselves. Parents loving their children will do for them all they can that they might be happy and become useful members of the human family. They will, above all earthly things, give them a good education. For all the inheritance which they may leave to their children can not outweigh a good education. Success and happiness depends to a great extent on education.

There is one thing, however, which stands even above earthly education, and that is the welfare of the child's immortal soul.

If parents are required to look to the mortal bodies of their children, how much more to their immortal souls! In this respect the parents of Jesus may serve as an example. Of them we read: *"Now His parents went to Jerusalem every year at the feast of the passover."* Mary and Joseph were a pious couple, they walked in the fear of God, they observed the commandments of the Lord, and thereby they set a good example to the child that was entrusted to them. Parents, know that your children will learn more by the example you give them in your daily lives than by anything else. Live Christianity before their eyes, and they will learn Christianity. If sincerely you walk in the fear of God, your children will be imbued with the spirit of godliness, and in this wise you will extend to them the proper care for their souls.

Moreover, the parents of Jesus did not neglect the religious training of their child. They did not content themselves with the good example, but led Him to do as they did. We read, *"And when He was twelve years old, they went up to Jerusalem after the custom of the feast. And when they had fulfilled the days, as they returned, the child Jesus tarried behind in Jerusalem; and Joseph and His mother knew not of it."* So they took the child Jesus along with them to Jerusalem and had Him worship with them in the temple. Parents should teach their children to pray and worship the Lord, and should urge them and influence them to walk in the ways of the Lord as long as they live.

Here is where some parents make a grave mistake. They hold to the principle that their children should form their own judgment as to the religion which they mean to embrace. They say, I do not want to make a hypocrite of my child; I have my children baptized and confirmed, and after that they must make use of their own judgment; if they do not care for the church, I can not help it. That is a wrong principle. God demands of you that you should bring up your children in the nurture and admonition of the Lord. That is an express command of God. Not only should we bestow special care upon the immortal souls of our children in the days of their infancy and childhood. Not only should we have them baptized, and teach them to pray at home, and send them to a Christian parochial school, where they may receive a true Christian training, before we send them to the public school, where religion is not and should not be taught. Not only should we attend to their spiritual needs and have them thoroughly instructed in the true faith, until they are confirmed. But after their Confirmation, when they enter the wicked world, when they come in contact with all sorts of people, when they are being tempted by the devil, the world, and their own sinful flesh more than before, then, O parents, is the very time that we must bestow special care on our children that they should remain true to their God, and that our work upon them in the days of infancy and childhood be not in vain. Of course, we can not force our children to believe. Faith is God's work. But we can and should lead, exhort, and admonish them to make diligent use of the means of grace by which faith is produced and sustained. We can and should beseech them, entreat them, admonish them, warn them. And this we should do as long as we live, even when our children have left the shelter of the parental roof.

Parents should be watchful also that their children do not get into bad company and associate with such as will harm their souls. We read, "*But they, supposing Him to have been in the company, went a day's journey, and they sought Him among their kinsfolk and acquaintance. And when they found Him not, they turned back again to Jerusalem, seeking Him.*" When the Israelites went to a feast in Jerusalem from remoter cities and towns, they always went in large caravans. Such a caravan had been made up at Nazareth. Kinsmen and acquaintances usually kept together, and that was the company to which Jesus kept Himself. His parents knew that they could safely entrust Him to that company, and so they were not disturbed when they did not see Him on leaving Jerusalem. But when the caravan halted and preparations were being made to encamp for the night, they missed their boy and hastened back to Jerusalem. Now, as the parents of Jesus watched over their child, how much the more should all parents keep watch over their children and see that they do not get into bad company! Jesus' parents knew that their boy would do no wrong. But how is it with our children? How easily are they misled! How easily do they fall a prey to the temptations with which they are being beset! Indeed, Christian parents can not be careful enough about the company of their children. They should not let their children associate with everybody that comes along. They should make sure of it that the good seed which they have sown in their children's hearts be not trodden down, and not permit them to make friends with such as seduce them into sin and vice. This is the care which parents should bestow on their children.

II.

Our Gospel contains a lesson on *parental authority* also We read, "*And it came to pass, that after three days they found Him in the temple, sitting in the midst of the doctors, both hearing them, and asking them questions And all that heard Him were astonished at His understanding and answers. And when they saw Him, they were amazed and His mother said unto Him, Son, why hast Thou thus dealt with us? behold, Thy father and I have sought Thee sorrowing.*" These words of Mary were evidently meant for a rebuke. They can not be explained in any other way. The poor mother had worried over her lost child, and had suffered a great deal for three days. And now that she finds Him at last, she means to let Him know that she is His mother and censures Him for all the grief and sorrow she had to bear on His account. This censure would have been in the right place, if Jesus had done wrong and had not been the Son of God. As the Son of God He had to be about His Father's business, and His mother's authority did not exceed the authority of His heavenly Father

It is quite a different thing with other parents. God Himself has established the authority of parents over their children. When God says, "Honor thy father and thy mother," this implies that your father and mother are your superiors, that they stand above you, and that you must obey them. Parents, therefore, do perfectly right when they rebuke and censure their children for the wrongs which they do, and when they punish them for their wickedness. They must do that They are commanded to do it Does not God say in the Book of Proverbs, "Withhold not correction from the child for if thou beatest him with the rod, he shall not die. Thou shalt beat him with the rod, and shalt deliver his soul from hell"? In our days there is a growing sentiment among parents to let the children have their own way, not to punish them for their wrongs, and simply to tell them that it is for their own detriment if they do wrong. Children brought up in that way soon trample upon their parents and do what they please, irrespective of anybody   Parents who really love their children will and must exercise their authority and make their children understand that they must obey.   They will mould the characters of their children and train them to be good men and women in future years.   They will bend the tree while it is young, so that it might grow up to the joy and to the delight of others

And as the parents should exercise their authority, so are the children required to submit to this parental authority   We see this in the example of Jesus, of whom the end of our Gospel says, "*And He went down with them, and came to Nazareth, and was subject to them   but His mother kept all these sayings in her heart.   And Jesus increased in wisdom and stature, and in favor with God and man.*"   The heavenly Child, the Son of God, was subject to His earthly parents, that is, He submitted to their authority.   Though He was God, and, therefore, stood above them, He did not make use of His divine authority, He did not exhibit Himself as their superior   No, He obeyed, that in all things He might be like as we.   What a fine example for children !   If the eternal Son of God obeyed His earthly parents, He who was not subject to anybody, how much the more should Christian children walk in obedience, and do all they can to serve their parents!   Children, you can never repay your father and mother for what they did for you.   The sleepless nights, the care and worry, the attention paid to your mortal bodies and to your immortal souls, these are things for which you can never give your parents an adequate compensation.   Obey your parents, then; hold them in love and esteem as long as they live. A Christian child, even when already advanced in years, will not undertake an important step without consulting the parents and seeking their advice.   And if thus you honor your father and mother, you will not only inherit the promise of the fourth commandment that you shall live long upon the earth, but you will increase also, as Jesus did, in favor with God and man.   Both God and men are pleased with a child that shows obedience to the parents

Finally, my friends, can we parents say that we always did our duty to the children whom God entrusted to our care?   And can the children say that they always obeyed their parents?

No; in this respect, also, we must admit that we are sinners. Let us look for forgiveness to Him who became man for us, was a child for us, lived upon this earth for us, and died on the cross for our salvation "The blood of Jesus Christ, the Son of God, cleanseth us from all sin," and as He was raised from the dead by the glory of the Father, so should we also walk in newness of life. Let us look to Him for strength, and He will enable us to walk in His commandments to the glory of His holy name Amen

SECOND EPIPHANY.

JOHN 2, 1—11

And the third day there was a marriage in Cana of Galilee, and the mother of Jesus was there and both Jesus was called, and his disciples, to the marriage And when they wanted wine, the mother of Jesus saith unto him, They have no wine Jesus saith unto her, Woman, what have I to do with thee? mine hour is not yet come His mother saith unto the servants, Whatsoever he saith unto you, do it. And there were set there six waterpots of stone, after the manner of the purifying of the Jews, containing two or three firkins apiece Jesus saith unto them, Fill the waterpots with water And they filled them up to the brim And he saith unto them, Draw out now, and bear unto the governor of the feast And they bare it When the ruler of the feast had tasted the water that was made wine, and knew not whence it was. (but the servants which drew the water knew,) the governor of the feast called the bridegroom, and saith unto him, Every man at the beginning doth set forth good wine, and when men have well drunk, then that which is worse· but thou hast kept the good wine until now This beginning of miracles did Jesus in Cana of Galilee, and manifested forth his glory, and his disciples believed on him

BELOVED FRIENDS IN CHRIST.

In our Gospel we find the Lord Jesus at a wedding. Wedding day is always a day of rejoicing But in the holy state of matrimony two kinds of days are to be expected, days of prosperity and days of adversity And there are two kinds of married couples, such as are never truly happy, even in the days of prosperity, and such as are always happy, even in the days of adversity.

Unhappy are those who have not Jesus with them, who do not believe on the Lord Jesus, and refuse to admit Him to their home. Let such a married couple be apparently ever so happy,

let them love each other ever so fervently; let them possess
health, and wealth, and beauty; let them be free from want and
sickness and sorrow and trouble of any kind, and fare sumptuously every day — they are poor, miserable, unhappy, after
all, even in such days of prosperity. "There is no peace unto
the wicked," says the Word of God, and God's Word must be
true. There is no peace unto them, no peace with God. Their
hearts resemble the troubled sea. The accusations of their own
conscience are never at rest, and the consequence is, they are
miserable, even in the midst of joy and plenty.

But there are also days of adversity for those married couples
that do not admit Jesus to their homes. Be they ever so fortunate in this life, as far as mutual affection, health, and wealth,
and social standing is concerned, they are not exempt from the
cross which God has laid on the matrimonial state. They must
bear their share of it. And oh! how dreadful are the homes of
the wicked when mutual love should cease to exist between man
and wife, when misfortunes come, when poverty sets in, when
want is felt, when they begin to disagree and to quarrel! Then
there may be divorce suits and social scandals; or even murder
and suicide may sever the union from which the Lord Jesus had
been excluded.

Quite a different place is the home of a truly Christian married couple, of a couple that had invited Jesus to their wedding,
and then retains Jesus with them during all the days of its married
life. There the words of the Psalm are being made true. "Blessed
is every one that feareth the Lord; that walketh in His ways.
For thou shalt eat the labor of thine hands: happy shalt thou be,
and it shall be well with thee."

Now in our Gospel we are told of such a couple that invited
Jesus to their wedding, and it is shown how well they fared hav-
ing Jesus with them. Let us, therefore, consider with the aid of
God's Holy Spirit,

THE BLESSEDNESS OF THOSE WHO HAVE JESUS WITH THEM IN THE MATRIMONIAL STATE.

Their blessedness

    I *in the days of prosperity*, and

    II *in the days of adversity.*

I.

We read, "*And the third day there was a marriage in Cana of Galilee; and the mother of Jesus was there. And both Jesus was called, and His disciples, to the marriage.*" Groom and bride, most likely, were Christ's own relations, because, as we are told, "*the mother of Jesus was there.*" But not for this reason did John the Evangelist hand down to posterity this narrative, because Jesus' mother was there, but because Jesus Himself was there and His disciples. As the context shows, Jesus had shortly before been baptized in the river Jordan, had just entered upon His public office, and chosen several disciples. As yet He had not performed a miracle, for we read at the end of our Gospel, "*This beginning of miracles did Jesus in Cana of Galilee, and manifested forth His glory, and His disciples believed on Him.*" Still, though Christ had just entered upon His public office to teach the people, He does not decline the invitation to that marriage. He honors the young couple with His presence and thereby adds to their joy. From the account given in our Gospel we perceive that Jesus was considered the most distinguished guest at this wedding. He is honored above all and by all. He is the center of the group, and He it was that brought happiness into the home of the newly married couple.

Behold, then, the blessedness of those who have Jesus with them in the matrimonial state! Behold their blessedness in the days of prosperity! They love Jesus and Jesus loves them, and, O, what blessedness is there in the love of Jesus! What blessedness for man and wife to know, Jesus is present with us in our home, and if it were ever so lowly a place; He is our Friend, our Guide, our Savior and Redeemer! Be their days ever so fair and their joys ever so great, there is no earthly joy, no earthly pleasure to eclipse the Sun of Life which illuminates their path and directs them where to go—Jesus and His love. All their treasures and worldly possessions they value for naught, if thrown into the scales against Jesus, the Lover of their souls; so much do they love Him. Jesus it is whom they consult when about to enter into the matrimonial state. They take it to the Lord in prayer, and ask Him for wisdom and prudence in the selection of their partner with whom they are to be united for life. They are careful not to be deceived by wealth, beauty, and prominence.

They do not form a betrothal secretly, against their parents' will, and take heed not to transgress the commandment which says, "Honor thy father and thy mother." They enter into the holy state of matrimony with a clean conscience, so that Jesus can enter with them into their homes and dwell with them.

And still more is their blessedness enhanced by praising Jesus. They not only love, they also praise Jesus, and to praise Jesus is not an arduous task for them, but pleasant work. The days of prosperity are the most dangerous for a Christian couple. In such days God is easily forgotten, and we are apt to turn to the world and to its evil lusts. But a Christian couple will practice what the Psalm says, "Bless the Lord, O my soul, and forget not all His benefits!" A Christian couple will adopt for its own and live up to the motto of Joshua, "As for me and my house, we will serve the Lord." They will neglect neither their daily prayers nor the reading of the Scriptures. They will not permit amusements or worldly enjoyments to keep them away from the house of God, while the Word of God is being preached. They will make it a point to come regularly to the Lord's Supper. If their union is blessed with children, they will have their little ones baptized according to Christ's command, "Suffer the little children to come unto Me," and will bring them up in the nurture and admonition of the Lord. When their children are of age and leave the parental roof, they will watch them carefully, so that they do not go astray, but remain with Christ, and walk the path that leads to eternal life. Their most intimate friends and associates they will not seek among infidels and godless people, but among those who confess the Lord Jesus. If the Lord God grants them riches, they will neither squander what they have, and thus abuse the gifts, nor will they drift into the vice of avarice and make mammon their god. They will always be willing to help the poor and distressed, and to aid in spreading God's kingdom.

What blessedness of such couples in the days of prosperity! Jesus is their joy, their treasure, their soul's delight. They always realize that it is Jesus whom they have to thank for all they are enjoying. By faith in the Lord Jesus they have peace with God, and their conscience is at rest. They know that their sins are all forgiven through Jesus' blood and merits, and that for Jesus' sake God looks down upon them as if they had no

sin, looks upon them as a loving father upon his dear children.
O how much more do they enjoy the days of prosperity than unbelievers, who know not what it is to be joyful in the Lord and
to be perfectly contented! How much easier for a true Christian
couple to be pleased with what little they possess than for unbelievers who restlessly crave for more and labor under the delusion that money, riches, wealth is the source of true happiness!
If God grants them more than they need, a Christian couple will
praise him for it and make good use of their possessions: but
content they will be with food and raiment.

One thing in particular adds to their blessedness in the days
of prosperity. They know that God is pleased with them, even
as the Lord Jesus was pleased with the newly married couple at
Cana. They know that their marriage is honorable and pleasing
to God And so are all their works pleasing unto the Lord.
When the husband toils and labors in the sweat of his face, or
when the wife does her humble housework, those are all good
works, better works than the prayers and fasting of all the monks
and nuns in the world, and God will reward them in heaven.
So much about the days of prosperity.

II.

But there are also days of adversity in the matrimony of
God's children, and since they have Jesus with them always, He
is with them in the days of adversity also, and blessedness does
not leave them.

In our Gospel we are told that "*they had no wine.*" Want
was felt on the very first day of the union of this couple Jesus'
mother informs the Lord of their want, and He says to her,
"*Woman, what have I to do with thee? Mine hour is not yet
come.*" This was a rebuke, and from it we see that Mary must
have said something that was out of place. She had no right
to interpose in this matter. But she took the reproof very sub-
missively, and said to the servants, "*Whatsoever He saith unto
you, do it.*" Hereupon Jesus ordered them to fill the six waterpots set there for the purifying, and containing a number of
gallons each, with water, and without any ceremony, simply by
His will, He turned the water into wine, and into wine of the
best quality For we read, "*When the ruler of the feast had*

tasted the water that was made wine, and knew not whence it was (but the servants which drew the water knew), the governor of the feast called the bridegroom, and saith unto him, Every man at the beginning doth set forth good wine, and when men have well drunk, then that which is worse: but thou hast kept the good wine until now."

Now as there was want in the house in Cana, so must all Christian couples meet times of affliction. There are the days of adversity, the days of which we say, We like them not. There are the days of illness, when we must cope with diseases, and all our joy is turned into sadness, or when death comes and we are overwhelmed with grief and sorrow to see those depart from us whom we loved so dearly. Again there are days of actual want, when the husband is out of work, or when the wages are so poor that it is impossible to make both ends meet. At such times a Christian couple may be tempted to fear for the future and to exclaim, "What shall we eat? or, What shall we drink? or, Wherewithal shall we be clothed?" Then again there is, perhaps, a special cross which a Christian couple must bear, ill-will on the part of others, persecution, losses. Sometimes their own children will cause trouble and create days of adversity. Even as Abraham had a godless son, Ishmael, and Adam a godless son, Cain, so unto this day a disobedient and godless child may come forth from a true Christian family, to fill the hearts of Christian parents with the utmost grief. There are many tribulations for Christian families in this world of sorrow. Who could enumerate all the days of adversity?

But how do Christians take such days of adversity? Do they chide with God and murmur against Him because He permits misfortunes to come? Do husband and wife rebuke one another and curse the day when they were married, and wish for a divorce? No, like Mary in our Gospel, they will tell it to the Lord Jesus, in whose name they entered into the holy state of matrimony. If it is illness or want which they suffer, they will in such distress call upon their almighty Savior for help, and will rest assured that He will procure for them, when His hour is come, all that they need, and that He will never leave nor forsake them. If it is some special cross which they must bear, they will apply to Him who said, "Come unto Me, all ye that labor, and are heavy laden, and I will give you rest." If they get into such straits and conditions as to make them feel at loss what to do, they will consult Jesus and do what He tells them in His Word, in the Scriptures.

O the blessedness of Christians even in the days of adversity! Unbelievers find no comfort, no consolation in such days. They must sullenly endure their misery and know of no helper. What glorious privilege of a Christian husband and wife, that in every distress, in every affliction and tribulation they can appeal to their God and Savior and say to Him, Lord, such and such is my trouble, help me, deliver me! And, verily, they shall not ask Him in vain. He is to-day the same that He was in times of old, just as loving, and merciful, and powerful, and mighty to deliver us from all evil. And if at times He does suffer us to shed many tears and to pass through many evil days, it must be for our own good, and we will submit to His will. But when His hour is come, He will rescue us from all misery and turn our sadness into joy and gladness.

Let us always remain with Jesus, and keep Jesus with us, at our fireside, both in the days of prosperity and adversity which fall to our lot in the matrimonial state, and we shall experience the truth of the words in the Psalm, "O Lord of hosts, blessed is the man that trusteth in Thee." Amen.

THIRD EPIPHANY.

Matt 8, 1—13

When he was come down from the mountain, great multitudes followed him And, behold, there came a leper and worshiped him, saying, Lord, if thou wilt, thou canst make me clean. And Jesus put forth his hand, and touched him, saying, I will. be thou clean And immediately his leprosy was cleansed And Jesus saith unto him, See thou tell no man, but go thy way, shew thyself to the priest, and offer the gift that Moses commanded, for a testimony unto them And when Jesus was entered into Capernaum, there came unto him a centurion, beseeching him, and saying, Lord, my servant lieth at home sick of the palsy, grievously tormented And Jesus saith unto him, I will come and heal him The centurion answered and said, Lord, I am not worthy that thou shouldest come under my roof: but speak the word only, and my servant shall be healed For I am a man under authority, having soldiers under me and I say to this man, Go, and he goeth. and to another, Come, and he cometh; and to my servant, Do this, and he doeth it. When Jesus heard it, he marveled, and said to them that followed, Verily I say unto you, I have not found so great faith, no, not in Israel. And I say unto you, That many shall come from the east and west, and shall sit down with Abraham, and Isaac, and Jacob, in the kingdom of heaven. But the children of the kingdom shall be cast out into outer darkness: there shall be weeping and gnashing of teeth. And Jesus said unto the centurion, Go thy way, and as thou hast believed, so be it done unto thee. And his servant was healed in the selfsame hour.

BELOVED FRIENDS IN CHRIST:

The great central theme of our Gospel is faith, faith illustrated both in the leper and in the centurion. The climax is reached when Jesus exclaims, "*Verily I say unto you, I have not found so great faith, no, not in Israel.*"

The unbelieving children of this world have no true notion of faith. Ask them, and what will they say? Some of them will tell you, Faith is but a mask which Christians wear upon their face. They put on a pious outward appearance, pray, go to church, talk religion, and all this they do to some selfish purpose. They are far from truly believing the alleged faith which they profess; and the very sins which they openly condemn in others they commit themselves in secret. This class of unbelievers looks upon all Christians as hypocrites. Others, again, among the unbelieving children of this world will tell you, Faith is a sort of a mental disease, an illusion formed in the mind. Though there be many hypocrites among the Christians, yet they are not all such. There are some who really believe what the Bible says, and imagine it were all true, contrary to the simplest principles of common sense. And this illusion will sometimes get such a strong hold upon them as to cause religious fanaticism and even insanity. This second class of unbelievers looks upon the Christians, as if they were men with an unbalanced mind. And there is a third class of unbelievers who, if you ask them their opinion on faith, will smile and say, Why do you make such a great ado about faith? What good does faith do? Let a man believe ever so much and ever so sincerely, what does that benefit him or others? Faith, rightly looked at, is nothing but an altogether useless act in the mind; and you Christians expect to get to heaven by faith. What foolishness!

Such are the opinions of the children of this world. They have not the least idea of what faith is. They speak of faith as a blind man would speak of colors. And is this to be wondered at? Does not the Word of God say, "The natural man receiveth not the things of the Spirit of God for they are foolishness unto him"? Oh, if such men would only taste of faith themselves and experience for themselves what faith is, they would know whereof they speak, and they would no longer speak as they now speak. But Christians, too, are in need of constant enlightenment on the nature of faith. Our Gospel points out the foundation on which true faith is built, and also tells of the fruits of such faith. The subject of our discourse shall be with the aid of God's Holy Spirit,

TRUE FAITH'S FOUNDATION AND FRUITS.

I. *Its foundation*, and
II. *Its fruits*

I.

On what did the leper in our Gospel rest his faith? We are told, "*When He was come down from the mountain, great multitudes followed Him. And, behold, there came a leper and worshiped Him, saying, Lord, if Thou wilt, Thou canst make me clean.*" Here we must observe that the leper is not praying for a spiritual gift, but for a temporal blessing. He is not asking for forgiveness of sin and the grace of God, but for the removal of his leprosy. Jesus had just delivered His great sermon on the mount, and the leper had probably stood from afar and heard the sermon, because the law did not permit him to approach others on account of his loathsome contagious disease. But when Jesus came down from the mount, the poor man was bold enough to walk right up to the Lord, to fall down before Him, burying his face in the dust, and to utter the request: "*Lord, if Thou wilt, Thou canst make me clean.*" Mark well how he submits to the Lord's will, teaching us by his example that, if ever we ask for a temporal gift, we should leave it to the Lord to deal with us according to His good pleasure. Doubtless the leper knew that man is sometimes afflicted with some temporal evil for the sake of his own welfare, and so he did not venture to ask for the cleansing of his leprosy without affixing the condition: "*Lord, if Thou wilt.*" He meant to say, Thou knowest better than I do, O Lord, whether or not it will be profitable for me to be made rid of this loathsome disease, but as for Thy ability to heal me, I do not doubt that for one moment; if Thou wilt only, Thou canst make me clean.   On what, then, did the leper rest his faith?   On Christ, His good and gracious will and His almighty word.   He desired to hear the word of Christ telling him that he should be clean, and he was confident that instantly his leprosy would disappear, if Jesus only spoke the word   And not in vain did he entrust himself to the Lord, not in vain did he rest his faith on Christ's will and word, for we are informed, "*And Jesus put forth His hand, and touched him, saying, I will; be thou clean.   And immediately his leprosy was cleansed.   And Jesus saith unto him, See thou tell no man, but go thy way, shew thyself to the priest, and offer the gift that Moses commanded, for a testimony unto them.*"

And upon what did the centurion in our Gospel rest his faith?   The centurion also asked for a temporal gift   We read, "*And when Jesus was entered into Capernaum, there came unto Him a centurion, beseeching Him, and saying, Lord, my servant lieth at home sick of the palsy, grievously tormented.*"   And when Jesus answered and said, "*I will come and heal him,*" what was the centurion's reply?   "*The centurion answered and said, Lord, I am not worthy that Thou shouldest come under my roof· but speak the word only, and my servant shall be healed.*"   The centurion does not desire a sign, he does not desire to see Jesus lay His hand upon the sick man   He does not even deem it necessary for Christ to come into the house   All he desires is to hear Christ's word.   Christ's word is the foundation upon which his faith rests, Christ's word and nothing else   Aye, such is his confidence in Christ's word that he says, "*For I am a man under authority, having soldiers under me · and I say to this man, Go, and he goeth, and to another, Come, and he cometh, and to my servant, Do this, and he doeth it*"   He evidently means to say, I am a man under authority   I have superiors whom I must obey.   Yet is my word obeyed by those that are subject to me   But Thou art more than mortal man, Thou art the Son of God, subject to no authority, all the powers in heaven are subject to Thee.   How much more, then, must Thy word accomplish what it says!   Thou speakest and it is done   All that is necessary is

Thy word, and my servant's disease must disappear. And to show that this is true faith, faith as it should be, namely the faith which rests on no other foundation than Christ's Word, our Gospel says, *"When Jesus heard it, He marveled, and said to them that followed, Verily I say unto you, I have not found so great faith, no, not in Israel And I say unto you, That many shall come from the east and west, and shall sit down with Abraham, and Isaac, and Jacob, in the kingdom of heaven But the children of the kingdom shall be cast out into outer darkness· there shall be weeping and gnashing of teeth And Jesus said unto the centurion, Go thy way, and as thou hast believed, so be it done unto thee. And his servant was healed in the selfsame hour."* The faith which brings deliverance is the faith that rests on the foundation of Christ's Word.

Is your faith resting on this foundation, my hearer? In our days thousands of Christians claim to be true believers, and there is no sound and solid basis to their faith. They are not positively sure and certain about the things which they believe. They base their faith on their own repentance, on their conversion, on their emotions, on their feelings, on their virtues, and the like. There are those who say, I believe that I am a child of God, for I did repent of my sins, I felt truly sorry for having sinned against God, and so I confidently believe that in Christ my sins are forgiven Others say, I believe that in Christ I am saved, for my own heart tells me so I felt the wrath of God upon me, and then I went down upon my knees and implored God to have mercy on me, and behold, my fears departed, my soul was quickened, a voice seemed to call to me, Thy sins are forgiven thee, and now I believe that I have made my calling and election sure. Still others say, I felt my misery and my wretchedness, I did not know whither to flee for fear of God's anger and wrath But then I began to pray and to wrestle with God, and I continued therein night and day until the Spirit of God came into my soul, and I felt that I was truly converted. Then I could shout and say, Now I have found grace, Jesus is mine, heaven is mine, I am saved, hallelujah! Others, again, triumphantly call attention to the wonderful change which has come upon them, and expect to get to heaven because they had amended their former sinful lives. Formerly, say these, we took part in the vain pleasures of this world and indulged in certain sins, but now we lead an altogether different life, we read the Bible, we pray, we go to church; why, then, should we not get to heaven? Finally, there are such as claim to be in favor with God because in a dream or in a vision they had seen Jesus, or the holy angels, or had otherwise met with some extraordinary experience, assuring them of the grace of God, the forgiveness of their sins, and the salvation of their souls.

All these foundations of faith which men make unto themselves are like the quicksand which gives way under the feet. Woe unto those who rest their faith on their own repentance, for our repentance is always imperfect and never deserving of God's grace! Woe unto those who rely upon their own feeling, for they rely upon their own sinful heart, and God says, "He that trusteth in his own heart is a fool!" Woe unto those who base their faith on certain emotions and on the inward testimony of God's Holy Spirit, for that testimony may not always be there! Woe unto those who believe that they are God's children because they are walking in newness of life, for even the best of lives is damnable, if not covered with the robe of Christ's righteousness.

The only foundation upon which Christians must rest their faith is Christ's Word. Whosoever simply relies upon that which God has spoken in His divine Word, in the Bible, whosoever believes that his sins are forgiven, and that he shall be received into heaven for no other reason than because God declared in His Word that all men, even the greatest of sinners, are reconciled with God for the sake of the painful suffering and bitter death of His beloved Son Jesus Christ, and that through His name whosoever believeth in Him shall receive remission of sins, he has based his faith on the true and everlasting foundation on which alone it can securely rest. For, while everything else, repentance, conversion, feeling, virtue, is unreliable, the Word of God is truthful and can never fail. Let such a believer experience nothing but God's anger and wrath and feel no joy whatever, let him suffer tribulations, and afflictions, and persecutions, let Satan direct against him his darts, in the very face of death, the Word of God will bear him through. Nothing can prevail against faith resting on such foundation.

II.

And now, in the second place, let us briefly consider the fruits which the faith brings forth that is based on Christ's Word.

The fruit of faith is love, as exemplified in the centurion's care for his slave. The centurion, literally, a captain over one hundred soldiers, was not a Jew, but a Roman. As a rule, these Roman officials, and Roman men and women in general, cared very little for the welfare of their slaves. But behold, what a sympathizing master true faith had made of this centurion. He looks after his servant with no less solicitude than he would devote to his own child. He is grieved to see him tormented and writhing with pain. He does all in his power to allay his pains and to have him restored to health. In his anxiety he applies to the Lord for his slave. That, surely, was not merely a trait of his noble character, but the fruit of his faith.

But let us look at Luke's account and we shall hear still more about the fruits of his faith. Luke informs us that the centurion, deeming himself unworthy, did not go to meet the Lord in person, but at first sent the elders of the Jews to beseech Jesus in his behalf. And what did the elders say about the centurion? They said, "He is worthy for whom Thou shouldest do this: for he loveth our nation, and he hath built us a synagogue." The fruit of his faith was, then, that he also loved God's chosen people, though they were despised and held in contempt by the Romans, and to show them his appreciation of their religion, he built them a synagogue, a house of worship, where, doubtless, he himself was a regular attendant.

Love of God and the neighbor is another fruit which invariably grows upon the tree of that faith which is based upon the Word of God. Unbelievers and enthusiasts frequently speak despicably of that faith which rests upon the Word of God alone, and claim that such a faith were a dreary thought of the heart. But they know not of what they speak. For if anything will change man's heart, and make him a new creature, and move and urge him to love God and his neighbor, to feed the hungred and thirsty, clothe the naked, give shelter to the homeless, and to do works of charity without ceasing, it is that faith which is based upon the Word of God alone. Such faith is God's work in man, and how can that which God has quickened into life be a dead and powerless thing? Rather could the sun be without light or the fire without warmth than true faith without deeds of love. But one thing must well be borne in mind here. While the unbelievers and many enthusiasts make a great show and display of what they call charity, arranging charity balls and advertising their donations, so that men should admire their generosity, the children of God, who base their faith on the Word of God alone, prefer not to let the left hand know what the right is doing. In sincere humility they do not make a boast of their sympathy for others and of the great good which they do. Quietly they bring forth the fruits of their faith, incessantly and without murmuring, building the kingdom of God, supporting the holy ministry, aiding those that are in need, and, in general, doing good unto all men, especially unto them which are of the household of faith

Another fruit of faith is apparent both in the leper and in the centurion. It is true humility before God and men. The leper yields up his own will and wisdom to Christ and His will and wisdom and goodness, saying, "*Lord, if Thou wilt*" And the centurion humbles himself, though a Roman officer, before the Man of Nazareth and Son of God. He deems himself unworthy of receiving Jesus in his house and extending to Him his hospitality He does not claim at Jesus' hands any measure according to his own thoughts or desires, but leaves the manner of the fulfillment of his petition entirely to the Lord This was not a fruit of his sinful nature, but of faith engendered in him by the Word of God He, who would otherwise have been a haughty Roman officer, was thus made a meek and humble petitioner before the meek and humble Nazarene And thus to-day faith makes men meek and humble who would by nature be haughty and puffed up with pride. Faith, a firm reliance upon God's grace in Christ Jesus, disposes the believer to mercy, to sympathy with the afflicted, though they be lowly, as was the centurion's slave.

There are still other fruits of faith which might be here enumerated. But let this suffice May the Lord grant us all that faith which is based on the Word of God alone, and we shall not only be sure of our faith, but also bring forth the blessed fruits of faith and never grow weary in welldoing. May He grant us this by His Holy Spirit for the sake of Jesus Christ, His beloved Son, our only Mediator and Redeemer Amen.

FOURTH EPIPHANY.

MATT 8, 23—27

And when he was entered into a ship, his disciples followed him. And, behold, there arose a great tempest in the sea, insomuch that the ship was covered with the waves. but he was asleep. And his disciples came to him, and awoke him, saying, Lord, save us. we perish. And he saith unto them, Why are ye fearful, O ye of little faith? Then he arose, and rebuked the winds and the sea; and there was a great calm. But the men marveled, saying, What manner of man is this, that even the winds and the sea obey him?

BELOVED FRIENDS IN CHRIST:

Jesus had been busily engaged all day preaching and healing the sick. There was such a vast throng and so much to attend to, He had not found time to eat. When night came, the people still remained, and all that Jesus could do to obtain rest was to withdraw from them. So He told His disciples to have a boat ready that He might cross the lake. "*And when He was entered into a ship, His disciples followed Him.*" Straightway Jesus made for the stern of the boat, where He laid down His weary head on an improvised pillow, probably made of a fisherman's coat, and, worn out and fatigued as He was, He was soon fast asleep. Out went the frail craft upon the dangerous deep in the black night. But as they pushed from the shore, there was not the slightest indication of any impending danger. Safely did the boat glide along driven by a gentle breeze. They had probably reached the middle of the lake, when suddenly, without the least warning, a squall was upon them. "*Behold, there arose a great tempest in the sea, insomuch that the ship was covered with the waves: but He was asleep.*" The disciples were fishermen. They knew how to manage a boat. They had braved many a storm on this lake. But such a tempest they, most likely, had never encountered before. They lose control of the ship. It is tossed upon the crest of the waves like a nutshell. The water dashes in afore and aft, much faster than they can bail it out. It dawns upon them that they are lost. In such a tempest there is no escape. The boat must either be capsized or swamped. And there is their Master with them in the boat, resting in sweet repose, so fast asleep as not to be aroused by all the noise around Him, by the roaring of the storm and the splashing of the angry waves and by all the jolting and buffeting caused by the rocking of the boat. They can no longer bear it. They *"came to Him, and awoke Him, saying, Lord, save us we perish."* St. Mark tells us that in their fright and frenzy they even dared to censure the Lord, saying to Him, "Master, carest Thou not that we perish?" And what is Jesus' answer? *"Why are ye fearful, O ye of little faith?"* So the great fault of the disciples in this storm was that they were of little faith, that their faith was not what it should have been, that their faith was weak. And this shall be our subject to-day with the aid of God's Holy Spirit. Having shown you last Sunday an example of strong faith, let me speak to you to-day of

THE WEAK FAITH,

and explain,

I *That the weak faith differs from unbelief*, but

II. *That weakness of faith is a dangerous thing.*

I.

The disciples did not call upon Jesus in vain. *"He arose, and rebuked the winds and the sea; and there was a great calm."* The manner in which He rebuked the winds and the sea is described by St. Mark. "He said unto the sea, Peace, be still, and the wind ceased." In an instant the tempest was hushed. The sea lay before them in its wide expanse as smooth as glass, while a serene sky was overhead. So astonishing was this miracle that *"the men marveled, saying, What manner of man is this, that even the winds and the sea obey Him!"*

But Jesus not only shows that He is the Lord of nature, whom even the winds and the sea must obey. He, at the same time, reproves His disciples, saying to them, "O ye of little faith!" He means to say, If your faith were great and strong, you would not fear even this gale, since I am with you in the ship; you would not doubt for one moment that even while asleep I am keeping watch over you, and that nothing shall harm you while I am near. In the disciples we have an example of weak faith, and by that example we may learn how the weak faith differs from unbelief

This, my friends, is a subject of vital importance. We know that faith saves and that unbelief condemns. Faith, and if there were ever so little of it, if it were ever so weak: faith leads to a blissful eternity, while unbelief in every shape and form will lead to eternal woe. Does not Jesus say, "He that believeth and is baptized, shall be saved; but he that believeth not, shall be damned"? But where is there a Christian, a true child of God, whom the thought did not trouble at times, Ah, perhaps you have no faith, perhaps you are an unbeliever who shall be damned? Weak faith sometimes so strongly resembles unbelief that the one may be mistaken for the other, though there is an essential difference between the two. How vastly important, then, to know exactly in what the weak faith differs from unbelief!

Now, to enable you to ward off Satan's darts tempting you that you should despair of your own salvation because you had not faith, let me bring out a few points of our Gospel, showing the difference between the weak faith and unbelief. As long as a man is void of faith altogether, he will, perhaps, not even think of God, much less approach God in the days of distress. He will either seek help and succor in earthly things alone, or sink into despair. And if he does make an attempt to call upon God, the almighty Ruler of heaven and earth, he will do so with an unbelieving heart, without trust in God, only to try whether prayer will do any good when everything else has failed. But if your faith is weak, as it was with the disciples, though you may get to the point of abandoning all hopes, where you may even have to cope with doubts as to whether God can help you, yet, if there is faith in you, that faith will exert its divine power, and will be strong enough to overcome your doubts and fears, so that you will sincerely trust in God and confidently exclaim, as did the disciples, "Lord, help me!" You will say with the holy psalmist, "God is my refuge and strength, a very present help in trouble." As long as your thoughts are with God, in communication with God, sighing to the Lord, trusting in the Lord, you are a true believer, though your faith may be very weak.—Furthermore, as long as a man is void of faith altogether, he will not sincerely trust in God's grace and mercy. This becomes apparent especially when great misfortunes come upon him. And when such a man must leave this world, when on his deathbed he perceives that now he must cross the dark valley of death, the voice of his conscience perhaps once more will make itself heard. His sins will come to his memory, and though he tries ever so hard to find rest and comfort against his sins, he cannot. God's grace and mercy is proclaimed to him in vain. He does not desire Christ. He attempts to clothe himself before God in the filthy rags of his own righteousness. In such a state of mind he passes into eternity. But if your faith is weak, you will, at all events, hold on to God's grace and mercy. You may get into such deep distress as to say with the disciples, "Lord, carest Thou not that I perish?" Hast Thou forgotten to be merciful? But though your faith be ever so weak, it will enable you to hold on to God's grace and mercy. You will be confident that God cannot mean you any harm, in spite of all the trials and temptations and misfortunes that you must endure. You will say, God hath given me His beloved Son, His one and all; how, then, can I doubt His grace and mercy? Confidently you will appeal to God and implore Him, saying, Lord, help me, or I must perish! I know Thou wilt hear my prayer, for Thou hast said, "Call upon Me in the day of trouble; I will deliver thee, and thou shalt glorify Me," and, "My mercy is from everlasting to everlasting upon them that fear Me." How can I doubt Thy promise? Though I am a sinner, not worthy of Thy grace, Thou canst not forsake me. As long, then, as thus you humble yourself before God and desire His grace, though that desire be ever so faint, you are a believer, and your faith, though weak, is true faith, and has the promise of eternal life.

The difference, then, between weak believers and unbelievers is simply this: While unbelievers either ignore God altogether or sink into utter despair, weak believers will finally triumph over their temptations and sincerely call upon the Lord in prayer. While unbelievers fail to lay hold on God's grace and mercy, shown to the whole sinful world in the sacrifice of His beloved Son, weak believers, though frightened and greatly disturbed, will cling to God's grace after all and expect of Him alone their help. And their trust is not in vain. For "a bruised reed shall He not break, and a smoking flax shall He not quench."

II.

Now since also a weak faith is true faith and has the promise of eternal life, a person might think that a weak faith is all that needs be desired That is a grave mistake. Let me endeavor to show you that weakness of faith is a dangerous thing

Weakness of faith is surely not a state and condition in which a Christian should wish to remain. Did Jesus mean to praise His disciples when He said, "*Why are ye fearful? O ye of little faith*"? Was not this an outright reproof? According to Mark and Luke it was even more than a reproof It was a rebuff. Jesus said, "Where is your faith?" and, "How is it that ye have no faith?" Weakness of faith is nothing pleasing to God, nothing praiseworthy. As a Christian must follow holiness and strive to become always more and more perfect in righteousness of life, so must he strive to grow strong in the faith, and to rid himself of those infirmities that cling to his faith. St. Paul, indeed, says, "I will glory in mine infirmities," but he does not mean infirmities of faith; he means the tribulations he had to endure for Christ's sake.

It is a dangerous thing to be contented with a weak faith. To this day Christians must experience the same things which the disciples had to experience. To this day Christians must follow Christ into the ship and upon the sea of this world And while other ships may have smooth sailing, the ship with Christ in it often seems to be doomed to destruction. It gets into a storm center. The waves dash over into it. The sails are rent. The masts and the rudder are broken It drifts along helplessly, tossed up and down upon the billows of an angry sea, and all seems to be lost and gone. Meanwhile Jesus seems not to care for the fate of the ship. He sleeps What I mean to say is this· Whosoever casts his lot with Christ, whosoever embarks with Him in the ship of life, and confesses Him before men, and sets sail for the beautiful shore of a blissful hereafter under His guidance, must be prepared to meet with disastrous storms in this life, to encounter trials and temptations, persecutions, griefs, sorrows, affliction, and all manner of tribulations. If you love Christ, the world will hate you If you join those that rally around the standard of the Gospel, you will be laughed at, sneered at, scoffed at. If you make it a point not only to hear

Christ's Word, but also to do Christ's will, if you sternly refuse to take part in the world's evil lusts, in drunken revelries, in public dances, and similar works of the flesh, you can depend on it that you will have to suffer for such refusal in some way. If you have entrusted yourself to Christ, to His guidance and governing in life, the common ills of mankind are not kept away from you. You may even have to bear more than those who have not cast their lot with Christ. You may have to suffer illness, reverses in business, trouble in the family, and divers misfortunes. And then the greatest trouble will come. Satan will shoot his darts against you. He will whisper into your ear and say, You are certainly not a child of God. Can a merciful God let His children suffer as you must suffer? Go to, there either must be no God, and all your faith in God and a Savior be a delusion, or, if there is a God, He does not care for you.

Now tell me, my friends, is a weak faith likely to hold out in such fierce tempests and storms? Is not the smoking flax very apt to be extinguished and the bruised reed very apt to break, when the wind blows a gale? Does not Christ tell us in the parable of the sower that those who have no root believe for a while only and in time of temptation fall away? Have not thousands upon thousands fallen away from Christ because they were contented with a weak faith? Does not every weak believer easily fall a prey to error, to temptation, to sins and lusts? Is not this a most dangerous thing to be contented with a weak faith?

O let us all seek, then, to be strengthened in the faith! Let us pray, as did the disciples, and say with them, "Lord, increase our faith." And to increase our faith we must diligently make use of the means of grace. Come to the house of God, my friend, and with devout attention hear the preaching of the divine Word. Come to the holy sacrament and receive the true body and blood of Christ, given and shed for the remission of sins. And thus, by the grace of God, you shall be made "strong in the Lord and in the power of His might, and put on the whole armor of God, that you may be able to stand against the wiles of the devil."

Let us fight the good fight of faith, then, and lay hold on eternal life. And God grant that we all hold out to the end, and finally receive the crown of victory for Jesus' sake. Amen.

FIFTH EPIPHANY.

MATT 13, 24—30

Another parable put he forth unto them, saying, The kingdom of heaven is likened unto a man which sowed good seed in his field but while men slept, his enemy came and sowed tares among the wheat, and went his way But when the blade was sprung up, and brought forth fruit, then appeared the tares also So the servants of the householder came and said unto him, Sir, didst not thou sow good seed in thy field? from whence then hath it tares? He said unto them, An enemy hath done this The servants said unto him, Wilt thou then that we go and gather them up? But he said, Nay, lest while ye gather up the tares, ye root up also the wheat with them Let both grow together until the harvest and in the time of harvest I will say to the reapers, Gather ye together first the tares, and bind them in bundles to burn them but gather the wheat into my barn

BELOVED FRIENDS IN CHRIST·

In the parable of our Gospel the Lord Jesus illustrates the kingdom of heaven. When Jesus speaks of the kingdom of heaven in His parables, He does not mean merely the kingdom of glory, which we generally call heaven. He means His church, which, upon this earth, is the kingdom of His grace, and in heaven will be the kingdom of glory. And that Christ means to illustrate the state and condition of His church here upon earth in this parable of the tares among the wheat is plainly to be seen from His own interpretation of the parable. The parable of our Gospel is one of the few parables of our Lord which He Himself has explained. For this is what we read in the same chapter from which our text is taken: "And His disciples came unto Him, saying, Declare unto us the parable of the tares of the field. He answered and said unto them, He that soweth the good seed is the Son of man: the field is the world; the good seed are the children of the kingdom, but the tares are the children of the wicked one: the enemy that sowed them is the devil; the harvest is the end of the world; and the reapers are the angels. As therefore the tares are gathered and burned in the fire, so shall it be in the end of this world. The Son of man shall send forth His angels, and they shall gather out of His kingdom all things that offend, and them which do iniquity, and shall cast them into a furnace of fire there shall be wailing and gnashing of teeth. Then shall the righteous shine forth as the sun in the kingdom of

7

their Father. Who hath ears to hear, let him hear." So, in the light of Christ's own interpretation, the world appears as a vast field. Upon this field Jesus sows the good seed of His divine Word. That seed is not cast out in vain. Children of God are produced, true Christians, who constitute the church of Christ. Meanwhile, the devil also sows his pernicious seed in between, which produces ungodliness and children of wickedness. These are intermingled with the true Christians, like the tares among the wheat. And in this mixed state and condition the church shall remain unto the end of the world.

The subject of our discourse shall be with the aid of God's Holy Spirit,

TARES AMONG THE WHEAT, OR, THE CONDITION OF THE CHURCH ON EARTH.

And we shall consider,

I. *That upon earth the church appears in a condition resembling tares among wheat*, and

II. *How we are to conduct ourselves in view thereof*.

I.

The church upon this earth appears in a condition resembling tares among the wheat. I deliberately say, it appears in such condition. The godless people that are found in the visible church are not a component part of the church. For what does Christ call the church? He says, "*The kingdom of heaven is likened unto a man which sowed good seed in his field.*" The church is the kingdom of heaven upon earth, and only that which is produced by the good seed of the divine Word pertains to the church. Wherever there are those who believe in Jesus Christ, there is the church. Jesus says, "Where two or three are gathered together in my name, there am I in the midst of them." In the time of the New Testament the church is not confined to a certain locality, to a certain nation or people, as it was in the time of the Old Testament. The whole wide world is its domain, and wherever Christ Himself is the Sower, that is, where the Word of God is taught in its purity and the holy sacraments are administered in conformity with Christ's institution, there is the church of Christ. The church in itself is a pure thing, a glorious church, as St. Paul says, not having spot or wrinkle, or any such thing, holy and without blemish.

But what is the outward appearance of the church upon this earth? Christ says, *"But while men slept, his enemy came and sowed tares among the wheat, and went his way. But when the blade was sprung up, and brought forth fruit, then appeared the tares also."* Behold, then, such is the outward appearance of the church upon earth. It resembles in its outward appearance a field where the tares are mixed among the wheat. Note well, the tares are not a desirable plant. The farmer does not sow them. He does not cultivate them. So the wicked, the hypocrites, false prophets, gross and impenitent sinners, are not of God. They belong to the church only as the tares belong to the wheat-field, or the withered and dead branches to the living tree. They are not members of the church proper, of that mystic body of which Christ is the Head. But such is merely the outward appearance of Christ's church. Where the Word of God is taught in its purity and the holy sacraments are rightly administered, where the true church is established, there you will also find the sad effects of Satan's pernicious work. You will find wicked people among the good, godlessness developing alongside of piety, vice cropping forth on the very side of virtue, and children of the Evil One standing next to the children of God.

This has always been the case, and thus it shall remain unto the end of the world. Was not Cain, who killed his brother Abel, in the first church, the church of Adam? Was there not such corruption in the church of Seth that God determined to make an end of it by the deluge? In the small church saved in the ark, the church of Noah, was there not a black sheep, Ham? Did not such wickedness develop in the church of Shem that God found it necessary to single out Abraham and to make him the father of His chosen people? And what sins, crimes of almost every description, do we find recorded in the Old Testament, crimes committed by members of God's people, the people of Israel! And when in the New Testament the Eternal Son of God came into the flesh and gathered around Him a church of His disciples, were there not tares among the wheat? Did not Judas betray his Master? And when the holy apostles founded the Christian church and organized Christian congregations, beginning at Jeru-

salem and thence extending their missionary labors to the different
parts of the world, were these churches and congregations pure
and faultless, and did the apostles never find cause for complaint?
Did not one of those first seven deacons elected for the congregation in Jerusalem, a man by the name of Nicolas, cause divisions
in the church and become the founder of a most disgraceful sect?
Do we not find divisions in the congregation of Corinth, alterca-
tion among the members, injustice, abuse of the Lord's Supper,
men who denied the doctrine of the resurrection, and even a man
who had committed incest? Did not false prophets succeed in
seducing nearly all the members of the congregations in Galatia
to believe that they were not saved through faith alone, but also
by their own good deeds? Read the epistles in the New Testament, and you will find that under the very eyes of the apostles
Satan sowed his tares among the wheat, and that the church, in
its outward appearance, before men, was never pure, but always
in such a mixed state and condition.

And where should I begin and end, would I enter upon the
history of post-apostolic times and show you how the papacy developed in the church? Show me a church which presents the
appearance of pure wheat with not a blade of any sort of obnox-
ious weed in it. Show me a congregation which has arrived at the
stage of perfection, and where everything is exactly as it should be
among the members. There is no such church upon earth. And
there can never be such a church upon earth, for the simple
reason that Satan will always sow the seed of wickedness upon
the same field where God casts the seed of His divine Word, and
that our own hearts, corrupted with sin, are always susceptible of
all that is evil.

II.

And now, in the second place, let us consider how we should
conduct ourselves in view of this mixed state.

In our Gospel we read, *"So the servants of the householder
came and said unto him, Sir, didst not thou sow good seed in thy
field? From whence then hath it tares? He said unto them, An
enemy hath done this. The servants said unto him, Wilt thou
then that we go and gather them up? But he said, Nay; lest
while ye gather up the tares, ye root up also the wheat with them*

Let both grow together until the harvest: and in the time of harvest I will say to the reapers, Gather ye together first the tares, and bind them in bundles to burn them; but gather the wheat into my barn."

The first thing we learn here is that we must not be offended when we behold tares among the wheat, thinking that a church must be false in which sins occur, and eventually severing our connection with it, though we must admit that it has the marks of the true church, the pure Word of God and the holy sacraments. The children of this world generally make a great ado when a church member is exposed as a hypocrite, or falls into some gross sin even in the eyes of the world. They charge such things to the inability of the church to exercise a wholesome influence upon its members. And ill-advised Christians will sometimes permit their thoughts to run into the same channel. The true church of Christ upon this earth, according to their thoughts, is a net comprising only good fishes, a table spread with holy vessels only. As soon as some public offense is given, they begin to doubt whether this can be the true church of Christ when such horrible things can come to pass.

This is a grave mistake. Must you rest your souls' salvation upon the righteousness and piety of men? Must you not rest your souls' salvation upon the infallible Word of God alone? If, therefore, you are seeking the true church of Christ upon earth, you must seek for a church where the holy Word of God is proclaimed in its truth and purity, without taking anything therefrom or adding anything thereto, where Scripture is explained by Scripture, and where the holy sacraments are administered in conformity with Christ's institution. These are the infallible marks by which you should know the true church. Where these are, there the good seed is sown which must, and invariably will, produce fruit for eternal life; there is the true church of God.

And another thing to be observed in view of this mixed condition of the church is, we must not think that we had to cleanse the church by rooting out the hypocrites, and heretics, and evil-doers from the field of this world. By the church of Rome thousands were put to death not only for evil-doing, but also for supposed witchcraft and for proclaiming doctrines which were termed heresies, because they opposed the papacy. The hands

of that church are stained with the blood of many thousands of
martyrs, true Christians, who confessed Jesus to the end of their
lives, as did John Huss, who was burned at the stake. Woe
unto us if that church ever came to ruling power in our beloved
country! Religious freedom would be at an end. And the so-
called Reformed churches are little better By Calvin the principle was ratified that heretics, or false teachers, should be
destroyed by the sword. To this day the churches based on
Calvinistic doctrine do not comprehend the distinction between
church and state. Time and again they make efforts to govern
the church by secular power and to have the state mix into
church affairs. All of this is on the line of rooting up the tares
with the wheat, of ruling the church with the sword, with temporal power, and not by the Word of God alone.

Still, are we not to mind the sins and evils which occur in the
church? Are we to be indifferent about them? Are we to keep
such within the pale of the church as are open and manifest
sinners? Verily not. Note well that Christ says, " *While men
slept, his enemy came and sowed tares.*' The members of a
Christian congregation should be watchful and wakeful to pre-
vent, as much as possible, the enemy from sowing his tares
among the wheat They should admonish one another to be
steadfast in the faith of the Son of God who died on the cross
for the sins of all men, and to lead a truly Christian life. And
when a church member does fall into sin, the duty devolves upon
the congregation to convince him by the use of the divine Word
of the wickedness of his ways, and to lead him to repent of his
sin, and to seek refuge with Jesus, who is the propitiation for
our sins, and not for ours only, but for the sins of the whole
world. If he repents, his sin is forgiven, and he remains in the
church. But if he does not repent, and persists in the way of
the transgressor, the rule is laid down by the Lord Jesus in the
eighteenth chapter of Matthew that such person shall, after re-
peated fruitless admonitions, be looked upon as a heathen man
and a publican, or excommunicated, excluded from the Christian
congregation

May the Lord, then, grant unto us all His grace to examine
our own hearts, and to see that we are true members of the invisible church, which is built upon the foundation of the apostles

and prophets, Jesus Christ Himself being the chief corner stone. And on the last day, when the mixed state of the church shall cease, we shall not be in those bundles of tares that are cast into the furnace of fire, but in the sheaves that are received into the barn, and be among the righteous who shall shine forth as the sun in the kingdom of our Father Amen.

CHRIST'S PRESENTATION IN THE TEMPLE.

LUKE 2, 22—32

And when the days of her purification according to the law of Moses were accomplished, they brought him to Jerusalem, to present him to the Lord, (as it is written in the law of the Lord, Every male that openeth the womb shall be called holy to the Lord,) and to offer a sacrifice according to that which is said in the law of the Lord, A pair of turtledoves, or two young pigeons And behold, there was a man in Jerusalem, whose name was Simeon; and the same man was just and devout, waiting for the consolation of Israel and the Holy Ghost was upon him And it was revealed unto him by the Holy Ghost, that he should not see death, before he had seen the Lord's Christ And he came by the Spirit into the temple and when the parents brought in the child Jesus, to do for him after the custom of the law, then took he him up in his arms, and blessed God, and said, Lord, now lettest thou thy servant depart in peace, according to thy word for mine eyes have seen thy salvation, which thou hast prepared before the face of all people, a light to lighten the Gentiles, and the glory of thy people Israel

BELOVED FRIENDS IN CHRIST:

The Gospel which I have read to you is intended for a certain day, for the second day of February. The second day of February is the fortieth day after Christmas, and on that day the Child Jesus was taken to Jerusalem by His mother Mary and His foster father Joseph, and presented to the Lord in His holy temple. At the same time, Mary brought the sacrifices of purification, as prescribed by the Law of God.

Now while they were in the temple with the Child Jesus, an old man came into the temple, and when he beheld the Child, his features beamed with joy He took the Child from His mother's arms, pressed Him tenderly to his own bosom, and exclaimed as if in ecstasy, *"Lord, now lettest Thou Thy servant depart in peace, according to Thy word· for mine eyes have seen Thy salvation."* This old man was Simeon , and of Simeon we may

learn a very profitable lesson.   We all know that once we must
die.   There is no balm to save us from the grave.   When our appointed time has come, we must succumb to the inevitable, and
no power can extend our lives beyond the allotted time.   Now
while the children of this world dread and fear death and loathe
even to be reminded of death, a Christian may calmly look into
the face of this grim monster and meet him, as did old Simeon,
without fear and trembling.   We all cling to life, and also a
Christian will use all rightful means to keep death away from his
door; but he has no higher wish than to depart from this life in
peace, when his time is ended.   Let us consider, then, with the
aid of God's Holy Spirit, the question,

WHO CAN DEPART THIS LIFE IN PEACE LIKE SIMEON?

The answer is, *He that*

    I. *beholds Jesus with the eyes of faith,* and
    II. *embraces Jesus with the arms of faith.*

I.

Of Simeon we read, "*And he came by the Spirit into the
temple: and when the parents brought in the Child Jesus, to do
for Him after the custom of the Law, then took he Him up in his
arms, and blessed God, and said, Lord, now lettest Thou Thy
servant depart in peace, according to Thy word: for mine eyes
have seen Thy salvation.*"   And there is an old tradition that
Simeon did not leave the temple alive, but that he expired, closing his eyes in the sleep of death, after he had gazed upon the
heavenly Child and had ended his psalm of praise.

How did Simeon come to depart from this life so peacefully?
He had seen Jesus.   But how many others did also behold Jesus
when He was in the flesh, and did not depart in peace when death
came upon them!   The mere sight of Jesus, seeing Him with
bodily eyes, can, therefore, not be the real cause of Simeon's
peaceful departure from this world.   There must be something
else connected with that seeing.   The fact is, Simeon beheld
Jesus with different eyes than the priests in the temple and the
great majority of the Jews.   He, at the same time, beheld Jesus
with the eyes of faith.   And thus he had been gazing upon Jesus
long before his bodily eyes were permitted to behold Him.

Who, then, can depart this life in peace like Simeon? He that beholds Jesus, he that sees Jesus with the eyes of faith. And how Jesus may be beheld with the eyes of faith is most beautifully shown in our Gospel.

There we are told of Simeon, "*And it was revealed unto him by the Holy Ghost, that he should not see death, before he had seen the Lord's Christ.*" Whom, then, did Simeon recognize in the Child? With the eyes of faith he recognized in Him the Lord's Christ, that is, the Lord's Anointed, the promised Messiah and Deliverer, whom all Israel for many centuries had been expecting to come. He therefore says, "*For mine eyes have seen Thy salvation.*" He obviously has in his mind the words of the dying patriarch Jacob, who, while pronouncing the blessing upon his sons, made a solemn pause, and exclaimed, "I have waited for Thy salvation, O Lord," meaning by the salvation the Savior from sin, in whom all the nations of the earth should be blessed. If, therefore, like Simeon, you would behold Jesus with the eyes of faith, so as to die in peace, you must not look upon Him as did those priests in the temple who took Him for a common child. No; you must recognize in Him the Savior and Deliverer from sin. You must not look upon Him as though He were nothing more than mortal man, only a perfect man and the model for all men. No; you must believe that He is the Lord's Christ, that He is both God and man in one person.

And not only His person, but His office also you must view with the eyes of faith. You must know by faith that He has accomplished the great work of the redemption of the whole fallen human race, when for our sakes and in our stead He put Himself under the Law.

Reference is made to this great work of the Son of God in the beginning of our Gospel, where we are told how Jesus was presented to the Lord in the temple and how the sacrifice of purification was brought for Him. According to the Law of God for the children of Israel, every mother, having given birth to a child, was to be considered unclean; and she had to remain at home for forty days if the child was a boy, and for eighty days if the child was a girl. These were the days of purification. When they were accomplished, the first place a mother in Israel had to visit with her child was the Lord's temple, where the parents had to offer a sacrifice for the birth of the child. Now this Law was evidently to remind the children of Israel that man is conceived and born in sins. But Jesus was not conceived and born in sins. He was conceived by the Holy Ghost and born of the Virgin Mary. Yet of His own will and accord He put Himself under the Law, as though He were a sinner, like all the rest of the children of men. And this He did for us, as our substitute, that He might redeem us. Behold, then, if with the eyes of faith you would see Jesus, you must also look upon Him as the substitute of the sinful human race, who put Himself under the Law for our sakes, and fulfilled for us the Law's demands, that we might not be eternally condemned by the Law which we have not fulfilled, but live before God forever.

II.

Still, my friends, if, like Simeon, we would depart from this life in peace, we must not only behold Jesus with the eyes of faith, but also embrace Him with the arms of faith. This is our second point.

Old Simeon was not satisfied with the mere look which he cast upon the Child. We are informed that he took the Child up in his arms. So great was his joy, he could not constrain himself. He had to press the dear Child to his own bosom.

My friend, do you wish to depart from this life in peace, like Simeon, when your time comes? If so, you must also embrace Jesus. I do not mean that you must embrace Him with bodily arms. You could not do that. For though invisibly and even bodily present with us alway, the Lord Jesus is no longer visible with us. And was it the bodily contact which made Simeon so happy in death? Did not many of the Jews touch Jesus when He was in the flesh, and not see salvation? Did not Judas kiss Him? There must be something else connected with the embrace also of old Simeon. The fact is, Simeon embraced Jesus, at the same time, with the arms of faith. When he tenderly pressed the Child to his bosom, he meant to say thereby, This Child is *my* Savior, *my* consolation, *my* hope in life and in death. And in this manner old Simeon had been embracing Jesus long before he was permitted to hold Him in his arms.

Thus, then, my friends, true faith is not contented with merely beholding Jesus, that is, with knowledge and assent, knowing that He is the promised Messiah, the Son of God, born of the Father in eternity, the Mediator between God and men, the Savior of the fallen human race. The main thing is to embrace Jesus, that is, to make Jesus your own, to receive and accept Him as *your* Savior, to appropriate to yourselves the merits and sufferings of Jesus, in short, to place your confidence in Jesus alone.

And how is that done? How is Jesus embraced with the arms of faith? How is Jesus made our own? Behold Simeon's example. He says, *"Mine eyes have seen Thy salvation, which Thou hast prepared before the face of all people; a light to lighten the Gentiles, and the glory of Thy people Israel."* Do you hear how Simeon places himself in line with the Gentiles and says that Jesus is the Savior of both Jews and Gentiles? Simeon knows that he is a sinner, though he is a member of God's chosen people, and that in the sight of the just and holy God he is not any better than a heathen. Yet he is not frightened by the glory and majesty of the heavenly Child. He firmly believes that in this Child all his sins are forgiven, and that now the gates of heaven are opened before him.

So if you would embrace Jesus with the arms of faith, you must, indeed, humble yourselves before God and admit that you are sinners, not worthy of His grace, but then you must not despair on account of your sins, and if they were ever so great, but come to Jesus and say, Receive me, O Lord, make me Thine own. You must boldly apply to yourselves that which Jesus did for all sinners and confidently believe that in Him you have perfect forgiveness, life, and salvation.

And if you do this with a sincere heart, you will not only lead a godly and holy life, as did Simeon, of whom we are expressly told that he *"was just and devout, waiting for the consolation of Israel, and the Holy Ghost was upon him,"* but you will also be duly prepared at any time to depart this life in peace, to fall asleep in Jesus' name, and to awake in the heavenly mansions, where there is joy for evermore. Amen.

SEPTUAGESIMA SUNDAY.

MATT. 20, 1—16.

For the kingdom of heaven is like unto a man that is an householder, which went out early in the morning to hire laborers into his vineyard. And when he had agreed with the laborers for a penny a day, he sent them into his vineyard. And he went out about the third hour, and saw others standing idle in the market place, and said unto them, Go ye also into the vineyard, and whatsoever is right I will give you. And they went their way. Again he went out about the sixth and ninth hour, and did likewise. And about the eleventh hour he went out, and found others standing idle, and saith unto them, Why stand ye here all the day idle? They say unto him, Because no man hath hired us. He saith unto them, Go ye also into the vineyard; and whatsoever is right, that shall ye receive. So when even was come, the lord of the vineyard saith unto his steward, Call the laborers, and give them their hire, beginning from the last unto the first. And when they came that were hired about the eleventh hour, they received every man a penny. But when the first came, they supposed that they should have received more; and they likewise received every man a penny. And when they had received it, they murmured against the goodman of the house, saying, These last have wrought but one hour, and thou hast made them equal unto us, which have borne the burden and heat of the day. But he answered one of them, and said, Friend, I do thee no wrong: didst not thou agree with me for a penny? Take that thine is, and go thy way: I will give unto this last, even as unto thee. Is it not lawful for me to do what I will with mine own? Is thine eye evil, because I am good? So the last shall be first, and the first last: for many be called, but few chosen.

BELOVED FRIENDS IN CHRIST:

This Gospel has always been considered one of the most difficult texts in the Bible. The difficulty arises when we attempt an explanation of all the points of comparison in the parable. Luther calls such an attempt a great mistake. A parable generally has some points in it which admit of no interpretation, because they stand in no relation whatever to the truth which the parable is to impress on the mind. When Christ says, for instance, that He shall come to judge the world as a thief in the night, does He mean to say that He will do the work of a thief, which is to rob and to steal? No; He simply means to say that He will come unexpected, and nothing more. In another parable, the unjust steward who cunningly deceived his master is praised because he had done wisely providing for the future. But does this mean that fraud and deception is something praiseworthy and commendable? No; it simply means that, as the children of this world are prudent in their own sinful way, so should the Christians be prudent in a rightful way and provide for a blessed hereafter.

So in our Gospel we must not attempt an interpretation of every single point, but see which is the general doctrine, or divine truth, which Jesus means to inculcate by this parable. And this is plainly shown by the context. Jesus had told a young man, who was very rich, that he should give all his goods to the poor and follow Him as a disciple. The young man could not make up his mind to do that. He went away sorrowful. Hereupon Peter said to the Lord, "Behold, we have forsaken all, and followed Thee; what shall we have therefore?" Peter thought that he and his fellow-disciples were entitled to an ample reward for the sacrifice of their earthly possessions for Christ's sake; and now he wanted to know what their reward would be. And what was Jesus' reply? He said, "Every one that hath forsaken houses, or brethren, or sisters, or father, or mother, or wife, or children, or lands, for my name's sake, shall receive an hundredfold, and shall inherit eternal life. But"—adds He significantly—"many that are first shall be last; and the last shall be first." Christ means to say, It is truly not in vain that you follow me and labor in my kingdom as my servants, but take heed; that is a dangerous question, "What shall we have therefore?" For in my kingdom all must labor, some more, some less, every one according to the grace bestowed upon him, but the reward is by grace, not by merit. No one can say that by his labor he merits anything, or that he works for compensation. And this is the general truth which the Lord means to teach by the parable of our Gospel, namely, that all must labor in the vineyard of His kingdom and that their reward is by grace. Accordingly, the subject of our discourse shall be with the aid of God's Holy Spirit,

OUR LABOR IN THE LORD'S VINEYARD, AND OUR REWARD

    I. *Our labor.*
    II. *Our reward.*

I.

The most important and most precious doctrine of the Holy Scriptures is the doctrine of justification by grace, the doctrine that we are justified and saved not by our own good works and righteousness, but by God's free grace and mercy, through faith

in the Lord Jesus Christ. This doctrine is the great central truth
of the Bible and the foundation of our hope. If we had not this
doctrine, we could never be made sure of our soul's salvation.
The doctrine of justification by grace should, therefore, occupy
the foremost part in our hearts and permeate all our thoughts.
Most beautifully does St. Paul set forth this doctrine when he
says in his epistle to the Ephesians, "By grace are ye saved
through faith; and that not of yourselves: it is the gift of God:
not of works, lest any man should boast." Where this doctrine
is received into the heart, and not merely comprehended by the
understanding, there is true happiness, there is God's kingdom,
and a truly holy people.

But oh, how grossly do some men abuse this precious doctrine! Why, say they, if all things are by grace, then we need
not do good works and abound in them. If all things are by
grace, what is the use of watching, praying, searching the Scriptures, and the like? If by grace alone we are saved and our good
works are not taken into account, what is the use of crucifying
the flesh, and toiling and laboring for God's kingdom?

All such blasphemous thoughts are most vigorously de-
nounced by the parable of our Gospel. Here the whole world
is pictured as a market place, where the people are standing
about idle and know not what to do; while the kingdom of heaven
is pictured as a vineyard, where all are kept busy. Some enter
the vineyard early in the day, others come later. All day long
they come into the vineyard, some even in the very last hour.
But from the moment they enter the vineyard they work. They
are engaged for the very purpose to labor in the vineyard. Now
what does this teach us? It teaches us that in the Lord's vineyard there is no idleness, but restless activity. He that is still
standing idle and doing nothing in a spiritual way; he that does
not seek God's kingdom and His righteousness; he that does not
set his affection on things above; he that does not run for the
prize and fight for the incorruptible crown, as we are told in the
epistle of the day — he is not in the Lord's vineyard, not in God's
kingdom, not a true Christian; no, he is still standing idle in the
market place of this world.

As soon as you enter the Lord's vineyard, my friend, you
will toil and labor for your Lord and Master, and faithfully do

your share of the work which He assigns to you. And what will you work for? Not to gain heaven by the labor of your hands.

> Not the labor of your hands
> Can fulfill the Law's demands
> Could your zeal no respite know,
> Could your tears forever flow,
> All for sin could not atone,
> Christ has saved, and He alone

Christ has already gained heaven for all men by His merits, by His innocent suffering and death; and as soon as you enter His vineyard, the forgiveness of sins, life, and salvation is freely presented to you and made yours by faith. You will labor for the Lord prompted by gratitude. You will feel as though you could not do enough for Him, since He has done so much for you, forgiving you all your sins, healing all your diseases, delivering your life from destruction, and crowning you with loving kindness and tender mercies. It will be a pleasure for you to toil and labor in God's kingdom. Your faith, if true and sincere, cannot but produce good works. Is it not impossible for the sun to be without light and for the fire to be without warmth? Behold, just as impossible is it for a true Christian, whose heart is filled with God's love, not to do the works of love in the Lord's vineyard, but to stand idle, and to say, I am saved by grace through faith alone, therefore I need not toil and labor in the vineyard, I need not perform good works.

Examine your own life, my friend. You toil and labor, you diligently perform the works of your earthly calling, that you might get along in the world. That is right. But what labor do you perform in the Lord's vineyard into which God has called you from the market place of this world? Where are the fruits of your faith? In what manner are you making yourself useful in the Lord's vineyard? Are you doing your part and share of the work to be accomplished for the extension of God's kingdom and for the glorification of His holy name? Are you doing all you can for the Lord? Do you not mind going to some trouble and inconvenience? Do you give freely and willingly to support the Lord's cause? Do you deny yourself certain things for the Lord's sake? Or do you think, If others are fools enough to sacrifice themselves for the Lord and to labor in the sweat of their brow, in the Lord's vineyard, let them do so, so much the better for me. I shall labor as little as possible, pay as little as possible, exert myself as little as possible, and the more others do the less shall be required of me? If such is your principle, you are sadly deceiving yourself. The others are not the fools, but you are the fool, and may the Lord grant that you perceive your folly in good time.

Do not say to me, Those who were called and did their work in the eleventh hour also received the reward, and so will I wait until the eleventh hour, until I am old and death is nigh, and then I will quickly repent and get to heaven. True, Christ is ever ready to receive penitent sinners. He pardoned the dying thief. But how do you know whether you will attain to old age, or whether you will find time to fix your account with God? May not death come very suddenly? And can you bring forth the same excuse which those had who were called in the eleventh hour? When the householder asked them, "*Why stand ye here all the day idle?*" did they not make answer and say, "*Because no man hath hired us*"? Can you offer such an excuse? Did not the Lord call upon you in His divine Word and entreat you many a time to go into His vineyard? O, then harden not your own heart. Engage in the Lord's service. He is ever ready to receive you. Go, that is, repent of your sins with a sincere heart and seek refuge with the Savior Jesus, who bled and died for you. And thus you shall be in the vineyard, and your heart shall be filled with a fervent desire to serve God and to labor for Him and for His cause.

II.

And your labor shall not be without a reward.

Speaking of the reward we must bear two things in mind. First, that we merit absolutely nothing by our labor in the Lord's vineyard, and second, that nevertheless every laborer shall receive his reward.

The main purpose of our Gospel, as stated before, is to show that the work in God's kingdom is not done for compensation, that we merit nothing by all the labor we perform for Christ's sake. This is plainly shown by the fact that all laborers are paid alike, every one receives the stipulated price, which is a penny. And when those who had been engaged early in the morning, "*murmured against the goodman of the house, saying, These last have wrought but one hour, and thou hast made them equal unto us, which have borne the burden and heat of the day,*" what answer did they receive? "*He answered one of them, and said, Friend, I do thee no wrong: didst not thou agree with me for a penny? Take that thine is, and go thy way: I will give unto this last, even as unto thee. Is it not lawful for me to do what I will with mine own? Is thine eye evil, because I am good?*"

We must know that God is our Lord and Master. In this respect our relation to God is the same as that of a slave to his master. The slave does not earn anything by his labor, and is in duty bound to do all the work he can. So we are in duty bound to our God and Creator. It is not optional with us to work in His vineyard, or to stand idle in the market place of this world, just as it may suit our own fancy. No; the labor in His vineyard is something we owe Him, something we must do, and we have no compensation to claim. Jesus therefore says in the Gospel according to St. Luke, "Which of you, having a servant plowing, or feeding cattle, will say unto him by and by, when he is come from the field, Go and sit down to meat? And will not rather say to him, Make ready wherewith I may sup, and gird thyself, and serve me, till I have eaten and drunken; and afterward thou shalt eat and drink? Doth he thank that servant because he did the things that were commanded him? I trow not. So likewise ye, when ye shall have done all those things which are commanded you, say, We are unprofitable servants: we have done that which was our duty to do." So it is not more than a plain duty of ours to labor in the vineyard of the Lord, who created us, and gave us life and existence, and preserves us from day to day. A compensation for our labors in His vineyard is altogether out of question.

Nevertheless, my friends, God has promised us that we should be abundantly rewarded for all the labor we perform in His vineyard. His grace and mercy is so bountiful that He not only gives us eternal life for the sake of His beloved Son, but also an additional glory in heaven according to the pleasure of His grace. Did not Jesus say, "Whosoever shall give you a cup of water to drink in my name, because ye belong to Christ, verily I say unto you, he shall not lose his reward"? Whatever you may

8

do in the faith of the Son of God, every stroke in the Lord's
vineyard, even the least and most imperfect work, every mite
given to the Lord, every prayer ascending into heaven, every
good deed proceeding from a truly believing heart, shall be rewarded in heaven. Mark well, heaven itself is not the reward.
Heaven has already been gained for us all by Jesus' blessed work
of the redemption. But in heaven, after we have entered the blissful mansions, we shall be rewarded by our good God and Lord.

O my friends, how ready and willing should we be to work
while it is day, ere the night cometh when no man can work, to
take part in the Lord's work wherever we can, wherever there
is an opportunity for us to pray diligently in our homes and in
the house of the Lord, to give for the support of God's kingdom,
not as little, but as much as possible, to bear our crosses with
patience, to aid the poor and to help those who are in distress;
in short, to labor in the Lord's vineyard!

Let us never tire, then, of our blessed work. Let us remember the words of St. Paul, "He which soweth sparingly shall
reap also sparingly; and he which soweth bountifully shall reap
also bountifully." Let us run that we may obtain the prize,
and never be weary in welldoing, until of us it may be said,
"Blessed are the dead which die in the Lord from henceforth:
Yea, saith the Spirit, that they may rest from their labors; and
their works do follow them." May God grant us this for Jesus'
sake. Amen.

SEXAGESIMA SUNDAY.

LUKE 8, 4—15.

And when much people were gathered together, and were come to him out
of every city, he spake by a parable: A sower went out to sow his seed: and as
he sowed, some fell by the way side, and it was trodden down, and the fowls of
the air devoured it. And some fell upon a rock; and as soon as it was sprung
up, it withered away, because it lacked moisture. And some fell among thorns;
and the thorns sprang up with it, and choked it. And other fell on good ground
and sprang up, and bare fruit an hundredfold. And when he had said these
things, he cried, He that hath ears to hear, let him hear. And his disciples
asked him, saying, What might this parable be? And he said, Unto you it is
given to know the mysteries of the kingdom of God: but to others in parables;
that seeing they might not see, and hearing they might not understand. Now

the parable is this: The seed is the word of God. Those by the way side are they that hear; then cometh the devil, and taketh away the word out of their hearts, lest they should believe and be saved. They on the rock are they, which, when they hear, receive the word with joy, and these have no root, which for a while believe, and in time of temptation fall away. And that which fell among thorns are they, which, when they have heard, go forth, and are choked with cares and riches and pleasures of this life, and bring no fruit to perfection. But that on the good ground are they, which in an honest and good heart, having heard the word, keep it, and bring forth fruit with patience.

BELOVED FRIENDS IN CHRIST:

"*Unto you it is given to know the mysteries of the kingdom of God: but to others in parables; that seeing they might not see, and hearing they might not understand.*" These words of our Gospel almost sound as if it were God's will that some people should not understand and, therefore, should not derive any benefit from the Word of God, though they hear it.

The doctrine of Calvin actually maintains that the reason why so many derive no benefit from the divine Word is, because God, according to the unsearchable counsel of His own will, "whereby He extendeth and withholdeth mercy as He pleaseth," passes by and does not effectually call them through the Gospel. The Word sounds in their ears, but it is ineffectual with them, besause God has not predestinated them unto everlasting life, but foreordained them to everlasting death: such is the Calvinistic theory.

And does not this explanation seem very plausible? Whence that great difference between the hearers of the divine Word? Why is it that some are so quickly moved by the preaching of the Word, and others are not moved at all? Some there be who are deeply impressed when they hear the sermon. They are aroused from their sinful slumber. They are made to rejoice over their salvation. They are comforted in their distresses. Others there be who seem to experience nothing of the kind, though they hear the same divine Word. The preaching leaves them cold and indifferent. Neither are they frightened by the preaching of the Law, nor are their hearts gladdened by the preaching of the Gospel. They draw no comfort from the divine Word. And if their hearts should be moved to some extent during a sermon, it is only a transient emotion and does not last. Why is it, then, that these derive no benefit from the Word?

Why is it that unto them the Word of God is preached in vain, while others experience all the blessings that are connected with God's Word? Calvin's doctrine, which says, God passes by and does not effectually call them, seems to explain the situation at once.

But this explanation is utterly wrong. It contradicts the Scriptures throughout. If there is any truth explicitly stated in the Bible, it is this, that God wills not the sinner's death, that He desires that all men should be saved, that with Him there is no respect of persons, that His Word is intended for the salvation of all that hear it preached unto them.

The words of Christ, "*That seeing they might not see, and hearing they might not understand*," do not mean to say, it were God's will that some people should not understand His Word. They merely explain why the Lord began to speak in parables. Before this He had preached the Gospel in plain words, without the use of figures and illustrations. This the people despised. Now He spoke in parables, in illustrations taken from earthly things, and "*when He had said these things, He cried, He that hath ears to hear, let him hear.*" His intention was not that the people should not understand His words, but that they should search, as did the disciples, for the hidden meaning of His parables.

The true reason, then, why so many derive no benefit from the hearing of the divine Word is not to be sought in God's will, as if God did not want them to understand, but in their own sinful hearts. This is shown in the parable of our Gospel. Accordingly, let us consider with the aid of God's Holy Spirit,

THE TRUE REASON WHY SO MANY DERIVE NO BENEFIT FROM THE HEARING OF THE WORD OF GOD.

It is because their own hearts resemble,

I. *Either the wayside,*
II. *Or the rocky soil,*
III. *Or the thorny soil.*

I.

"*A sower went out to sow his seed: and as he sowed, some fell by the way side; and it was trodden down, and the fowls of the air devoured it.*" This is the beginning of the parable. And here is the explanation, "*The seed is the Word of God. Those by the way side are they that hear, then cometh the devil, and taketh away the Word out of their hearts, lest they should believe and be saved."*

So there is a class of men whose hearts resemble the wayside. When the sower walks along the edge of the field, casting out his seed by the handful, some of the seed will, perhaps, get beyond the tilled soil and fall on the road, where it is crushed under the feet of those who walk by, and the birds come and devour it. What a striking illustration of some of the hearers of the divine Word! There are some such people as get an occasional seed of God's Word, a stray seed, so to say, which falls on the wayside. They are not regular attendants at church. They drop in occasionally, or when there is something going on, or they attend the divine service merely to please some one else. Still, they hear, as Christ says. But what fate does the holy Word of God meet with when they hear it proclaimed to them, and feel how it strikes them and wants to take root in the depth of their souls? It is trodden down and crushed. Perhaps their souls were prejudiced before they entered the house of God, and they only came with the avowed purpose to be confirmed in such prejudice, to gather evidences against the Christian faith and doctrine, to find fault somewhere, and afterwards to put to ridicule what they heard the preacher say. Or, perhaps, they are so indifferent as to pay no attention to the sermon, and sit there with staring eyes, but their thoughts far away, and with open ears taking in the sounds, but not the words, so that seeing they do not see, and hearing they do not understand. And what is the outcome? *"Then cometh the devil, and taketh away the Word out of their hearts, lest they should believe and be saved."* Like as the fowl of the air pick up the seed on the wayside, so does the devil take away from their hearts the divine Word, so that there is not a trace of it left to do them any good, to save them from his power, from sin and from death, and to fill their souls with true consolation and with the hope of eternal life.

What, then, is the true reason why these people derive no benefit from the hearing of the divine Word? Is it because God does not want them to believe and to be saved? No; it is because the devil does not want them to believe and to be saved. And the devil could not have any power over them if they did not yield to him, if their hearts did not resemble the trodden wayside paved with prejudice and indifference, which God, even while they hear the Word, endeavors to remove from them, and would actually remove, if only they would not resist Him willfully, and harden their own hearts against the divine truth

II.

The second class of those who derive no benefit from the hearing of the divine Word are they who resemble the rocky soil. The Lord says in the parable, *"And some fell upon a rock; and as soon as it was sprung up, it withered away, because it lacked moisture"* And this is the explanation, *"They on the rock are they, which, when they hear, receive the Word with joy; and these have no root, which for a while believe, and in time of temptation fall away"* When the seed drops on the rock which is covered with a thin layer of ground, the moisture in the soil and the heat from above will cause it to sprout in a short time; and the blades will come forth very promising. Alas! there is no room in such a thin layer for the roots to grow. The sun scorches, the moisture evaporates, the ground becomes parched, and everything withers away   This is a portraiture of not a few hearers of the divine Word.   There are people who are easily moved. They do not harden their hearts with prejudice and in difference, as does the first class.   Their prejudices, if they entertain such, are quickly removed, and their indifference is completely overcome, while they hear the precious Gospel telling them that God loved them so dearly, in spite of their sinfulness, and has given His only begotten Son to die for them, that they might live.   They are truly converted.   They believe on the Lord Jesus Christ with a true heart.   They begin a new life that is pleasing in the sight of God.   They are God's dear children, and walk in the narrow way that leads to eternal life.

But no Christian can walk that way unencumbered and undisturbed.   Temptations will and must come.   These enthusiastic Christians are assailed by the devil, the world, and their own sinful flesh   They are prevailed upon to leave the narrow way and to enter upon the broad way which is so agreeable to the flesh. And behold, just as easily as they were converted, they are again perverted; just as easily as they were moved to believe in the

Lord Jesus, just as easily are they induced to cast away that precious faith and to join the world with its evil lusts.

And let me tell you right here, such time-Christians, such unreliable Christians are frequently those who are converted in revival meetings, if a conversion takes place at all. You know about these revival meetings. A so-called evangelist is engaged to stir up the people, because there is a sort of spiritual stagnation and the pastor's sermons are ineffective. Big crowds assemble. A great show is made about the good work that is being done and about the large number of those who are being converted. Alas! when the noted evangelist has departed, or even before that, the enthusiasm dies away, and, perhaps, within a few weeks the majority of those newly converted Christians are again outside of the pale of the Christian church; and though a great ado had been made in the press about the number of conversions, the great number of backsliders is never made public.

But what is the true reason why these backsliders derive no benefit from the hearing of the divine Word? Why is it that they lose the faith and join the world, like Demas? Is it because the Lord God neglected them and did not endow them with sufficient grace and power to withstand those temptations and to remain in the faith? No; it is because their own hearts resemble the rocky soil which produces no fruit. The Word of God which they hear is mighty to change their hearts, and the grace which they receive is powerful and sufficient to keep them in the narrow way. But they refuse to obey the Word when temptations come upon them. They resist the Holy Ghost, who warns them and prevails upon them to stand firm. And so the fault lies with them. They themselves are to blame for not deriving any benefit from the hearing of the divine Word.

III.

The third class of hearers deriving no enduring benefit from the hearing of the divine Word, are those who resemble the thorny soil. The Lord says in the parable, "*And some fell among thorns; and the thorns sprang up with it, and choked it.*" And this is the explanation, "*And that which fell among thorns are they, which, when they have heard, go forth, and are choked with cares and riches and pleasures of this life, and bring no fruit to perfection.*"

The seed which falls on the thorny soil will certainly grow. But the thorns also will grow; and thorns are weeds that will thrive and get ahead of good plants. In a short while the thorns will be masters of the field, and the good seed will be choked and retarded in its growth, so that it will not yield fruit to perfection. And thus it is with many hearers of the divine Word. They appear to be true Christians, as far as the outward profession goes. They neither show and manifest their dislike of the Christian faith, as does the first class; nor do they profess Christianity only for a while and then fall away, as does the second class. They are outward members of the church and remain such. They make use of the means of grace. They hear the preaching of the Word of God and come to the holy sacrament of the Lord's Supper. They seem to manifest a desire to provide for the eternal welfare of their immortal souls. They seem really to seek the kingdom of God and His righteousness. But there are other things which they crave for, and which so completely occupy their hearts as to crowd out and subdue their Christianity. They have earthly cares and earthly troubles which draw away their minds from heaven. They chase after riches and have set their mind on wealth. They seek worldly enjoyments and do not shrink back from partaking of those sinful pleasures in which the children of this world find their joy. In short, they want to serve two masters, God and this world. And that is a thing which no one can do. The world will make slaves of such double-faced Christians, slaves that are Christians merely by name, but not in truth. Though they hear the Word of God and apparently receive a blessing therefrom, they will not live up to the Word and will deny by their lives what they profess with their mouths.

What, then, is the true reason why these derive no benefit from the hearing of the divine Word, why they do not bring fruit to perfection? The true reason is to be sought in their own hearts, which resemble the thorny soil. There is always in the Word which they hear the power to change their hearts and to overcome the cares and riches and pleasures of this life. But they refuse to yield to the power of the Word and prefer to follow their own inclinations.

My dear friends, let us always be careful not to resist within ourselves when we hear what God has to say to us. Let us always submit to the divine influence of God's Word. Our hearts shall then resemble neither the wayside, nor the rocky soil, nor the thorny soil, but the good ground. We shall continually enjoy the benefits which the Lord has promised unto them that hear His Word devoutly, and our true portrait we shall find in the last words of our Gospel, where the Lord says, "*But that on the good ground are they, which in an honest and good heart, having heard the Word, keep it, and bring forth fruit with patience.*" Amen.

QUINQUAGESIMA SUNDAY.

LUKE 18, 31—43

Then he took unto him the twelve, and said unto them, Behold, we go up to Jerusalem, and all things that are written by the prophets concerning the Son of man shall be accomplished. For he shall be delivered unto the Gentiles, and shall be mocked, and spitefully entreated, and spitted on and they shall scourge him, and put him to death and the third day he shall rise again. And they understood none of these things and this saying was hid from them, neither knew they the things which were spoken And it came to pass, that as he was come nigh unto Jericho, a certain blind man sat by the way side begging and hearing the multitude pass by, he asked what it meant And they told him, that Jesus of Nazareth passeth by. And he cried, saying, Jesus, thou son of David, have mercy on me And they which went before rebuked him, that he should hold his peace· but he cried so much the more, Thou son of David, have mercy on me And Jesus stood, and commanded him to be brought unto him and when he was come near, he asked him, saying, What wilt thou that I shall do unto thee? And he said, Lord, that I may receive my sight. And Jesus said unto him, Receive thy sight thy faith hath saved thee. And immediately he received his sight, and followed him, glorifying God· and all the people, when they saw it, gave praise unto God

BELOVED FRIENDS IN CHRIST.

"*They understood none of these things: and this saying was hid from them, neither knew they the things which were spoken.*" This is what St Luke has to say of the disciples, after the Lord had told them in plain words that now they were going to Jerusalem, and that there He must suffer and die. None of these things did they understand. How is this to be accounted for? Could the Lord speak any plainer than He did? Were not His words as clear and simple as they could be to communicate unto them the information that He was to suffer and to die? "*Behold, we go up to Jerusalem, and all things that are written by the prophets concerning the Son of man shall be accomplished. For He shall be delivered unto the Gentiles, and shall be mocked, and spitefully entreated, and spitted on; and they shall scourge Him, and put Him to death.''* How can it be possible for anyone not to understand such plain and simple language? The Lord certainly spoke to them in their own native tongue. And this they did not understand? What are we to make of that?

The solution of this problem is obvious. St. Luke does not say, They understood not the words. These they understood perfectly well. They comprehended as well as we do that the Lord spoke of His suffering and death. St. Luke says, *''They understood not these* THINGS.''* How their Lord and Master should be delivered into the hands of the Gentiles to suffer and to die—this is what they could not comprehend. It was incompatible with their opinion of the Messiah and His glorious kingdom. They expected to go to Jerusalem and see Jesus enthroned as the great King of Israel to inaugurate a new era for the Jewish nation. Their own human reason revolted at the idea that He, who more than once had miraculously escaped the murderous grasp of His enemies, should now be delivered into their hands, and that He, who had in thousands of cases soothed the pains and healed the diseases of others and had even restored to life the dead, should now undergo torments and sufferings and Himself be slain. And unto this day human reason is prone to doubt and to be offended in the sufferings and death of our beloved Savior. Let us, therefore, with the aid of God's Holy Spirit, consider,

THE DOUBTS AND OFFENSES OF HUMAN REASON CONCERNING THE SUFFERING AND DEATH OF THE SON OF GOD.

We shall see,

    I. *Wherein these doubts and offenses consist,* and
    II. *How they are removed.*

I.

Though the disciples could not help understanding the literal meaning of Christ's words when He said, *''Behold, we go up to Jerusalem, and all things that are written by the prophets con-*

*cerning the Son of man shall be accomplished   For He shall be
delivered unto the Gentiles, and shall be mocked, and spitefully
entreated, and spitted on, and they shall scourge Him, and put
Him to death   and the third day He shall rise again,"* still this
saying was hid unto them.   Doubts entered their minds as to
the true meaning of these words.   They took it for granted that
these words could not be taken in a literal sense.

And what were their doubts?   They evidently considered it
both impossible and unnecessary that their Lord and Master
should suffer and die.

Impossible they deemed it.   Had they not heard Him say
time and again that He was the true Son of the living God?
Had they not beheld with their own eyes that nothing in this
world could withstand His divine power?   Had they not recognized in Him the divine Master who conquered all diseases, all
the demons of hell, and even death?   And how often had His
enemies attempted both with force and with subtlety to apprehend and to kill Him!   At Nazareth they had led Him to the
brow of the hill whereon the city was built, that they might
cast Him down headlong.   And how did He escape?   Passing
through the midst of them He went His way.   At Jerusalem they
had sent officers to take Him prisoner.   The officers went and
found Him preaching in the market place.   His divine words
so affected them they could not lay hands upon Him   Upon
their return, being asked, "Why have ye not brought Him?"
they made answer, "Never man spake like this Man."   In the
temple the Jews had gone sheer mad when the Lord declared
unto them, "Verily, verily, I say unto you, Before Abraham was,
I am."   They took up stones, stood around Him in a circle, and
made preparations to stone Him to death.   He seemed doomed
right then and there.   And how did He escape?   Majestically
going through the midst of them, He passed out of the temple
No arm was able to move, no stone was hurled at Him.   Of such
things had the disciples been eyewitnesses.   Hence their doubts
as to the possibility of Christ's falling into the hands of His
enemies to suffer and to die

Moreover, they also doubted the necessity of Christ's suffering and death.   From the days of their youth they had been
taught that the Messiah would establish a glorious worldly king-

dom and rule over all the nations. All along the Lord had been instructing them and telling them that His kingdom were not of this world. But they held on to their ideas of Christ's worldly kingdom. What necessity was there for Him to undergo such things as to suffer, and to die, and to rise again from the dead? Could He not ascend the throne of David without doing Himself such harm? These, evidently, were their doubts as to the necessity of Christ's suffering and death. And so deeply were these doubts rooted in their minds as to make it impossible for them to understand the spiritual nature of Christ's kingdom, until the day of Pentecost, when the Holy Ghost came upon them and guided them into all truth.

From the disciples we learn that human reason can comprehend neither the possibility nor the necessity of Christ's suffering and death. The deep humiliation of the Son of God is a mystery which human reason can neither fathom nor reveal. It is and it ever has been a stumbling-block to human reason that Jesus should suffer and die on the cross and, at the same time, be the eternal Son of God. History proves and experience confirms it. Nothing did the Jews and the Gentiles in the days of the apostles consider more foolish and ridiculous than to hear the Christians call Him their God and Savior who had been betrayed by one of His own disciples, mocked, spitefully entreated, spitted on, scourged, and finally nailed to the cross, and killed like a common criminal.

The same objections to the Bible's statements concerning the suffering and death of God's eternal Son are made in the name of human reason and common sense to this day. How can that be possible? says the voice of human reason. Jesus of Nazareth, the homeless man, who had not where to lay His head; who fled before His persecutors; who lay upon His knees in Gethsemane sorrowful and sore amazed; who was altogether helpless in the hands of His enemies; who was taken captive and bound by the officers, and elders, and chief priests; who was condemned to death, ill-treated, scourged, crucified; who Himself complained that God had forsaken Him, and died such an ignominious death—this unfortunate man should be the Son of God? How can that be possible? And even if it were possible—says the voice of human reason—, where is the necessity for such proceedings? The great God, that Supreme Being, who created heaven and earth, who is exalted above all things, who lives in a state of glory and majesty which no mortal tongue can describe, that great God should descend from the throne of His divine glory and become man for the purpose of permitting Himself to be spitefully entreated by a lawless mob, to be buffeted by the vile hands of ruffians, chastised, mocked, murdered? Should God, the God of love, be so cruel as to lay upon His beloved Son the burden of the whole sinful world, all the sins and transgressions of the human race, and have Him suffer the most excruciating pains, and shed His blood in streams, and die a miserable death? Could not the Almighty have devised some other plan to redeem and save the lost human race than with the blood of His own Son? These, my friends, are the doubts and objections and offenses of human reason concerning the suffering and death of the Son of God.

II.

And now, in the second place, let us see how these doubts and offenses may be removed

Concerning the first doubt and offense of human reason, the possibility of Jesus' suffering and death, we must admit that Jesus could not be the Son of God, if accidentally He had fallen into the hands of His enemies and had suffered as a powerless victim to their relentless enmity. How could an accident, how could any unforeseen event, or fate, disturb the plans of the omniscient God? How could human craftiness outwit divine wisdom? How could any power upon earth conquer the Almighty and reverse His decrees? But the foundation of this doubt and offense has been removed long ago by the Scriptures. For the Scriptures tell us that Jesus did not fall into the hands of His enemies unawares, because fate had suddenly turned against Him The Scriptures tell us that He did not suffer and die unwillingly, but willingly, according to God's eternal counsel, and to fulfill the Scriptures. Read the Old Testament, and you will find that for a period of four thousand years God had been proclaiming to the world that His Son should become man to suffer and die for the sins of the world. Even the minutest occurrences connected with His suffering and death are foretold in the Old Testament. And did not Christ Himself show before all men that He could have escaped and that He was able to resist? Not only did He stay the hands of those who wanted to precipitate Him from the rock at Nazareth, and of those who wanted to stone Him in the temple, but even in the hour of His deepest humiliation He exhibited His divine power. Scarcely had He risen to His feet from that terrible struggle in Gethsemane, when His majestic words, "I am He," made the motley crowd, which came to take Him captive, go backward and fall to the ground. He healed the ear of Malchus which Peter had cut off with his sword, and by the simple words, "If ye seek me, let these go," He gained liberty for His disciples. Had He only been willing to do so, He could easily have laid all His enemies prostrate at His feet, and could even have descended from the cross, and transformed that scene of His humiliation into a scene of glory and triumph. But it was of His own will that He consented to reconcile unto God the sinful world by His suffering and death. Willingly He came into this world. Willingly He took upon Himself the form of a servant. Willingly, and well knowing everything that was in store for Him, He undertook His last journey to Jerusalem to fulfill all things said by the prophets concerning the Son of man. Where is there any room now for human reason to come in with its doubts and offenses concerning the possibility of Jesus' suffering and death? They are all removed by the fact that Jesus suffered willingly.

But, says human reason, was all this necessary? Could the merciful God not devise some other plan, a plan not so cruel and bloody, to save the human race? The Scriptures remove also this second offense. The Scriptures tell us that God is not only merciful, but also just and holy, that His justice demands full punishment of the transgressors; and that He cannot be merciful at the expense of His justice and holiness; that He cannot forgive sin in such a way as to act as if sin were nothing serious; that God Himself did not take any pleasure in the cruelty that was connected with the noble sacrifice of His beloved Son for the fallen human race; but that this had to be in order to fully atone for the sins of all men and to satisfy the demands of divine justice. It is true, by nature we have correct ideas neither of the damnableness of sin nor of the strictness of God's justice.

By nature we are disposed to look upon sin, as if it were merely a sort of weakness for which we were not so much to blame; and we are disposed to look upon the great God in heaven, as if He were an over-good and lenient Father who overlooks the wrongs of His children and lets their misdoings go unpunished. Hence, to become perfectly convinced of the necessity of Jesus' bloody atonement for our sins we must, first of all, be enlightened by the holy Word of God. All the doubts and offenses concerning the necessity of Jesus' suffering and death will be hushed in him who yields to the influence of the divine Word. This we may learn from the latter part of our Gospel. There we read, *"And it came to pass, that as He was come nigh unto Jericho, a certain blind man sat by the wayside begging; and hearing the multitude pass by, he asked what it meant. And they told him, that Jesus of Nazareth passeth by. And he cried, saying, Jesus, Thou Son of David, have mercy on me. And they which went before rebuked him, that he should hold his peace: but he cried so much the more, Thou Son of David, have mercy on me. And Jesus stood and commanded him to be brought unto Him; and when he was come near, He asked him, saying, What wilt thou that I shall do unto thee? And he said, Lord, that I may receive my sight. And Jesus said unto him, Receive thy sight: thy faith hath saved thee. And immediately he received his sight, and followed Him, glorifying God: and all the people, when they saw it, gave praise unto God."*

This wonderful event, which occurred immediately after the disciples had been made aware of their own spiritual blindness in the matter concerning the Lord's suffering and death, goes to show how the natural man may be cured of his spiritual blindness, so as to become perfectly convinced of the necessity of Jesus' suffering and death. Like the blind man he must, first of all, know that he is blind spiritually, and then call upon Jesus the Savior to help him, and to enlighten him with His Word and Spirit, so that he may see, that he may behold the wonders of His grace and mercy exhibited in the pains and suffering of the dying Savior.

O blessed is he who calls upon Jesus, as did that blind man! Jesus will hear his prayer and remove from him all those doubts which his own human reason may produce concerning the Lord's

holy passion   The history of the Lord's passion will be unto
him a source of life and salvation, a crystal fountain whence the
healing streams do flow that will comfort him in life and death.

May the Lord grant unto us all His divine blessing during
the coming season of Lent, and strengthen our faith in us, while
we prayerfully contemplate the sacred story of our suffering and
dying Lord and Savior Jesus Christ.   Amen.

FIRST SUNDAY IN LENT.

MATT 4, 1—11

Then was Jesus led up of the spirit into the wilderness to be tempted of the
devil   And when he had fasted forty days and forty nights, he was afterward
an hungred   And when the tempter came to him, he said, If thou be the Son of
God   command that these stones be made bread   But he answered and said, It
is written Man shall not live by bread alone, but by every word that proceedeth
out of the mouth of God   Then the devil taketh him up into the holy city, and
setteth him on a pinnacle of the temple, and saith unto him, If thou be the Son
of God, cast thyself down   for it is written, He shall give his angels charge concerning thee   and in their hands they shall bear thee up, lest at any time thou
dash thy foot against a stone   Jesus said unto him, It is written again, Thou
shalt not tempt the Lord thy God   Again, the devil taketh him up into an exceeding high mountain, and sheweth him all the kingdoms of the world, and the
glory of them; and saith unto him, All these things will I give thee, if thou wilt
fall down and worship me   Then saith Jesus unto him, Get thee hence, Satan
for it is written, Thou shalt worship the Lord thy God, and him only shalt thou
serve   Then the devil leaveth him, and, behold, angels came and ministered
unto him

BELOVED FRIENDS IN CHRIST:

This is a remarkable story — Christ tempted by the devil in
the wilderness.   At first sight we are at a loss what to make of it,
and we fail to see why Christ should be tempted of the devil   But
there is a cause and reason for everything Christ did.   And the
reason why Jesus underwent this temptation in the wilderness
was, because He wanted to make amends for and set aright the
failure of our first parents, of Adam and Eve, in Paradise.   Are
we not told that "for this purpose the Son of God was manifested
that He might destroy the works of the devil"?   And what was
the devil's first work?   It was this.   In the form of a serpent he
approached man in Paradise and tempted him to transgress God's

commandment, to perform an act of disobedience against the divine Maker. And behold, he was successful. Though our first parents possessed the power to resist Satan and to retain their original integrity, yet they did not stand firm in the hour of temptation, but hearkened to the seducing voice of the tempter. Thus sin was brought into the world with all its evil consequences, misery, death, and eternal damnation. And it was not merely the individual that fell, it was the race that fell in Adam and Eve. For their children were flesh of their flesh and blood of their blood, polluted and corrupted with the same sin with which they were infected. The fountain having been contaminated, the entire stream issuing therefrom is stocked with germs of disease and death. This was the devil's work. But our divine Lord came to destroy the works of the devil. Scarcely had He been baptized by John the Baptist and entered upon His public ministry, when He encountered the "old serpent" in the wilderness and subjected Himself to the deceiver's temptations. And lo! Jesus came out victorious. He conquered Satan for us, as our Substitute, and thereby won back the battle which had been lost in Paradise.

Jesus, however, does not only figure as our Substitute in those temptations in the wilderness. He is our Guide at the same time. By His example we may learn how to stand firm in all the temptations with which we are being beset. With the aid of God's Holy Spirit let us consider the question,

HOW MAY A CHRISTIAN STAND FIRM IN TEMPTATIONS?

I. *In temptations to use unlawful means for his sustenance, by an implicit trust in God.*

II. *In temptations to believe false doctrines, by a strict adherence to the divine Word.*

III. *In temptations to seek the world's sinful pleasures, by a stern refusal.*

I.

"Then was Jesus led up of the Spirit into the wilderness to be tempted of the devil. And when He had fasted forty days and forty nights, He was afterward an hungred. And when the tempter came to Him, he said, If Thou be the Son of God, command that

9

these stones be made bread.''   We shall not enter upon the question here, in what disguise or form the devil approached Jesus and tempted Him. The Scriptures say nothing about this, and all we know is, that it was the evil spirit, who had assumed the form of an intellectual, rational, visible being, so that he could converse with Jesus. Neither shall we enter into discussion with those who claim that the things recorded in our Gospel were not an actual occurrence, but merely took place in the mind of Jesus and were a sort of a vision which came to His weakened mind in consequence of a forty days' fast. There is not the least trace of an indication pointing to such an explanation. Our text, on the face of it, is a plain, simple narrative describing what actually took place; and every unprejudiced reader will and must accept it as such.

The question with us is, What did the first temptation imply, when the devil approached Jesus and said, *"If Thou be the Son of God, command that these stones be made bread"* ? The answer is, It implied that Jesus should use unlawful means to provide for His own sustenance. Jesus was hungry, having fasted forty days and forty nights. He was starved and longed for something to eat. Now the devil's object was that Jesus should not trust in His heavenly Father, and expect of Him to provide for His bodily wants, but that He should exert His own power, if He really were the Son of God, and turn stones into bread, against the will of the Father, who had sent Him upon this earth to suffer and to subject His will to the will of His Father in heaven, to be obedient to Him to death, even the death of the cross.

Does not the devil tempt Christians in the same manner to this day? When you are in want and an opportunity presents itself to obtain money or goods in an unlawful way, by practicing upon your neighbor a clever fraud, or by lottery, or gambling, or in some other crooked way, does not the devil whisper into your ear and say,'Here is your chance ! Why should you be such a fool as to let it slip? Go, do it ! Others do it, the most respectable people do it.   There is no wrong in it, especially since you are in such straits and difficulties.   When you are ill at ease about stolen or lost goods, or about things that are concealed before your eyes and that you would like to know, are you not tempted at times to apply to clairvoyants, mediums, fortune-tellers, and to find out with their aid what God does not want you to know? When a disease has fastened upon you which baffles medical skill and no relief may be expected from the physicians, are you not tempted at times to use witchcraft, or to join the so-called Christian Scientists who deny the very existence of sin and its evil consequences, and tell you to simply believe that you are well and your sickness must depart?

How may a Christian stand firm in these temptations to use unlawful means for his sustenance or deliverance? Christ shows us plainly. He answered the devil and said, "*It is written, Man shall not live by bread alone, but by every word that proceedeth out of the mouth of God.*" The Lord quotes this passage from the book of Deuteronomy, where the reason is stated why God fed the Israelites with manna, namely, because He would teach them that man shall not live by bread alone. Jesus here manifests His trust in the heavenly Father, that the Father is able and willing to provide for Him; and that He can do so without bread, even as He did in the wilderness when He fed Israel forty years with manna. Learn from Christ, then, my dear Christian, how to stand firm in the temptation to use unlawful means for your sustenance and deliverance. Trust in God that He will provide for you in some way. Trust in Him so implicitly as not to doubt that the affliction in which you must remain is for your own good, and that He will deliver you when the right time is come. Trust in Him, that without His good and gracious will not a hair shall drop from your head, and that with Him you are always in safe keeping. And if thus you trust in the Almighty God you will stand firm in the hour of temptation and not think of doing anything which is incompatible with conscience and His divine Word.

II.

The second temptation is described in the following words, "*Then the devil taketh Him up into the holy city, and setteth Him on a pinnacle of the temple, and saith unto Him, If Thou be the Son of God, cast Thyself down for it is written, He shall give His angels charge concerning thee: and in their hands they shall bear thee up, lest at any time thou dash thy foot against a stone.*" Now what did this second temptation imply? It implied false doctrine   The false doctrine produced by the devil is, that God will protect those who trust in Him and let no harm come to them, even if wantonly they expose themselves to danger and risk their lives by some foolhardy act   Jesus had declared His trust in the heavenly Father in point of nourishment; now He should show His trust in point of safety.   He should leap from the high roof of the temple, and believe that He would land safely on the ground below, because God's holy angels would bear Him upon their hands   In support of this false doctrine the devil quotes Scripture.   But how does he quote Scripture?   He omits the very point at issue   For the passage quoted from Psalm 91 reads, "In all thy ways the Lord shall keep thee "   What does that mean, "In all thy ways"?   It means, If you go out of your way, out of the way of your duty and calling, you forfeit the promise and have no claim to God's protection.   Now these few little words overthrow the whole doctrine of God's protection in fool-hardiness, which the devil meant to elicit from the Word of God; and therefore he cunningly omitted them.   It was false doctrine with which he tempted Christ.

Does not the devil oftentimes tempt Christians in the same manner to this day?   Is he not constantly breeding mischief by false doctrine?   Are there not false prophets almost everywhere, perverting and distorting the holy Word of God by either omit-ting therefrom or adding thereto?   Is there not a bewildering number of sects, each of them deviating from God's plain Word in some point and claiming to possess the truth?   Is there a divine truth which Satan had not assailed and to which he had not given some false interpretation?   Does he not continually bring forth something new, some new doctrine, or some new method to rob men of their faith in Jesus, the Savior from sin, aside from whom there is no salvation and none other name under heaven given among men whereby we must be saved?

How may Christians stand firm in these temptations of false doctrine?   Christ shows us plainly.   He simply said to the devil, "*It is written again, Thou shalt not tempt the Lord thy God* "   What was the weapon, then, which Jesus wielded against the tempter, and by which He wiped out his fiery darts?   It was the written Word of God.   The devil had quoted the Word of God to support a false doctrine of his own fabrication, and had mutilated the Word to gain the point. Jesus quoted the Word of God in full bearing in plain language upon the point in question. He stood firm in the temptation and overcame Satan by a strict adherence to the divine Word. Learn from Christ, then, my dear Christians, how to stand firm when you are being tempted by false doctrine. It is a vain excuse for a Christian to say, There are so many churches, every one of them claiming to be right and saying the others were wrong, one does not know whom or what to believe. You have the written Word of God, the Bible. Every question of doctrine is settled in that Book. There is nothing to be settled by churches, or synods, or ecclesiastical bodies. God Himself has settled everything once for all in the Bible. Let neither the traditions of men, nor the dictates of human reason, nor the deceptions of your own sinful heart beguile you. Search the Scriptures. Abide by the letter and spirit of the written Word of God; and if this you do, you shall not be deceived by false doctrine, even though men endeavor to support it by Scripture, falsely quoted, and by wonders and signs. Jesus distinctly says, "There shall arise false Christs and false prophets, and shall show great signs and wonders." But if you strictly adhere to the divine Word, you will not be deceived by them.

III.

The third temptation is thus described: "*Again the devil taketh Him up into an exceeding high mountain, and showeth Him all the kingdoms of the world and the glory of them; and saith unto Him, All these things will I give Thee, if Thou wilt fall down and worship me.*" Now what does this third temptation imply? It was calculated to kindle in Jesus a desire for the pleasures of this world. From an exceeding high mountain the devil showed Him all the kingdoms of this world and their glory. This was done, as Luke informs us, "in a moment of time." It was done in a twinkling of the eye. There was a scene presented to the eyes of Jesus which came and went as a flash of lightning. It was, doubtless, "a fascinating delusion of Satan setting forth the wealth and pleasure and gayety of life as indulged in by the children of the world; the crowns, and robes, and palaces, and pleasure gardens, and all the earthly power and splendor of kings and princes." The devil was sure that this dazzling picture must

create a profound impression and produce in Jesus a desire to
enjoy those pleasures. Unhesitatingly he, therefore, makes the
proposal, "*All these things will I give Thee, if Thou wilt fall
down and worship me.*"

Does not the devil tempt Christians in the same manner to
this day? Is not the temptation to seek the world's sinful pleasures the most frequent and the most dangerous delusion of the
prince of this world? From the days of the holy apostles, when
Demas forsook Paul, having loved this present world, to this day,
have not thousands upon thousands lost the faith and swelled the
number of the damned, because they withstood not the temptation to the lusts of the flesh, and of the eye, and the pride of
life? Is not the world and its evil lusts, the desire for nothing
but amusements, enjoyments, pleasures the great temptation of
the day, the temptation that tends to ruin our Christian congregations, and to kill in them the spiritual life, and to induce
the Christians to worship God with their mouths and the devil in
their hearts and with their works?

O my dear Christian hearers, let us stand firm in this last
and severest temptation. Christ has shown us how. He met the
devil with a stern refusal and said, "*Get thee hence, Satan: for
it is written, Thou shalt worship the Lord thy God, and Him
only shalt thou serve.*" Learn from Christ, then, what to do
when you are tempted to seek the world's sinful pleasures. When
the godless children of this world invite you to go with them to
such places as should be shunned by Christians, or to do such
things as are forbidden in the Lord's commandments, the only
way to overcome such temptations is, sternly and most emphat-
ically to refuse, because God demands your whole heart and not
only a part of it, if you would be His child. Say with Joseph,
"How can I do this great wickedness, and sin against God?"
Remember the apostle's entreaty: "Love not the world, neither
the things that are in the world. If any man love the world, the
love of God is not in him. For all that is in the world, the lust
of the flesh, and the lust of the eyes, and the pride of life, is not
of the Father, but of the world, and the world passeth away and
the lust thereof; but he that doeth the will of God, abideth forever." Know that you are actually worshiping the devil, if you
give your heart to the world. But blessed are they that stand

firm in the hour of temptation! At the end of our Gospel we read of Christ, *"Then the devil leaveth Him, and, behold, angels came and ministered unto Him."* So shall the angels of God also minister unto those who stand firm in temptations, and guard and keep them until they arrive

> Where all the ransomed church of God
> Be saved to sin no more.

Amen.

SECOND SUNDAY IN LENT.

MATT. 15, 21—28.

Then Jesus went thence, and departed into the coasts of Tyre and Sidon. And, behold, a woman of Canaan came out of the same coasts, and cried unto him, saying, Have mercy on me, O Lord, thou son of David; my daughter is grievously vexed with a devil. But he answered her not a word. And his disciples came and besought him, saying, Send her away; for she crieth after us. But he answered and said, I am not sent but unto the lost sheep of the house of Israel. Then came she and worshiped him, saying, Lord, help me. But he answered and said, It is not meet to take the children's bread, and to cast it to dogs. And she said, Truth, Lord: yet the dogs eat of the crumbs which fall from their masters' table. Then Jesus answered and said unto her, O woman, great is thy faith: be it unto thee even as thou wilt. And her daughter was made whole from that very hour.

BELOVED FRIENDS IN CHRIST:

The Syrophoenician woman in our Gospel, though coming from the Gentiles, was a true believer in Jesus Christ. *"O woman, great is thy faith!"* says Jesus. She was in God's grace, her sins were forgiven, she was a child of God; and God loved her.

But did she feel these things? Did she joyously experience in her own heart that she was in such a blessed state? No; while Jesus dealt with her as He did when He rebuked her and refused her request, she surely felt no joy. And yet she was a true Christian, in God's grace, even while her soul was filled with darkness.

One of the greatest mistakes is to think that you must feel joyful and happy continually to be a true Christian, that you must be fully aware that your sins are really forgiven and that you are in God's grace, and, if you did not feel that way, you had no claim on the full forgiveness of your sins and on the grace and

mercy of the Almighty. That is the great error under which
many of our American churches are constantly laboring. In
their revival meetings they endeavor to stir up the feelings of the
people and to get them into a state of high excitement. They
urge the sinners to come forward and be converted to Christ.
When any one comes forward signifying his intention to become
converted, they plead with him, and gather around him, and pray
for him, and the question put to him is not, Dost thou believe?
but, How dost thou feel? Dost thou feel that thou art converted,
that thou art in the grace of God? And he is not declared converted unless he says, I feel. These conversions based on a
momentary feeling of joy brought forth under the strain of religious excitement frequently prove to be mere delusions. For
what guaranty of God's grace can your own heart afford? Is not
man's heart a deceitful and desperately wicked thing? Does not
God say in the book of Proverbs, "He that trusteth in his own
heart is a fool"?

It is foolish, therefore, to trust in your own heart, in your
feelings and inward experience for the certainty of your conversion. And equally as foolish it is to think that you are not
converted unless you feel joyful and happy. This shall be the
subject of our discourse to-day. With the aid of God's Holy
Spirit let us consider,

THE FOLLY OF NOT BELIEVING THAT YOU ARE IN GRACE UNLESS YOU FEEL IT.

   I. *Because you can be in grace, though you do not feel it.*

   II. *Because true faith relies on the Word alone, which promises God's grace.*

I.

You can be in God's grace and favor, though you do not
feel it. This truth is clearly set forth in our Gospel. Let us inquire into the state of the woman's mind who, as shown before,
was in God's grace, and see whether she really felt as if the grace
of God was with her.

We are told, in the first place, that she was in great trouble.
When Jesus came near Tyre and Sidon, "*she came out of the same
coasts, and cried unto Him, saying, Have mercy on me, O Lord,
Thou Son of David; my daughter is grievously vexed with a*

devil." How must this woman have felt when she, a firm believer in Jesus, was thus afflicted and her daughter was bodily possessed with the devil! But to add to her misery, what was Jesus' reply? We are told, *"But He answered her not a word."* Did this look to her as if she were in God's grace? How must she have felt when upon her humble prayer to the Lord she was simply ignored by Him who so kindly heard the prayers of all that applied to Him for help in their distress, and cheerfully granted their requests? Picture to your mind the distressed woman following after Christ, crying after Him, asking and beseeching Him; and Christ leisurely walking on, paying no attention to her, not noticing her. How miserable must she feel!

We are told furthermore, *"And His disciples came and besought Him, saying, Send her away; for she crieth after us."* The woman, undoubtedly, heard the disciples interceding for her, and a flash of hope shot through her soul. But how great must have been her disappointment when Jesus *"answered and said, I am not sent but unto the lost sheep of the house of Israel."* Must she not have felt as though there was no hope for her, as though she must not dare to approach Christ, because she was not an Israelite? Meanwhile, as Mark informs us, Jesus entered a house. He was gone, and there the poor woman stood in the street, abandoned and forsaken. How dreary must have been her thoughts! How depressed must have been the state of her mind! Still, she does not give up to despair. She makes another attempt. She enters the house, and *"then came she and worshiped Him, saying, Lord, help me."* Stern and austere is the Lord's reply, *"It is not meet to take the children's bread and to cast it to dogs."* She is made to believe that she is no better than a dog, being of heathen descent. All the hope she had of obtaining deliverance is cut short. O how great must have been her wretchedness, her grief and sorrow! Why did Jesus deal thus with the poor woman? Was He angry? Not in the least. His grace was with her all the while He refused her prayer. But to prove her faith the Lord, for a time, hid from her His goodness.

Note, my dear Christian, you can be in God's grace, though, like the woman in our Gospel, you do not feel it. To this day God will sometimes deal with His dear children as He did with this woman, and deprive them of all those joyful feelings which at other times make them so happy. To this day God will sometimes hide His lovely face, as it were, and let trials, and afflictions, and temptations come upon those whom He loves. To this day God will sometimes deal with us as though He were deaf to our prayers and did not care to answer, and the more we call upon Him, the less we hear of Him, the less we experience His grace and mercy, and the deeper is our soul plunged into the abyss of grief and sorrow. This truth is taught not only by the example of the woman of Canaan; it is attested and corroborated by numerous examples in the Holy Scriptures. There is Job. Was he not a child of God, and in God's grace? And when tried in the furnace of affliction, how did he feel? He says, "I cry unto Thee, and Thou dost not hear me, I stand up and Thou regardest me not. Thou art become cruel to me: with Thy strong hand Thou opposest Thyself against me." There is the pious King Hezekiah, who was smitten with illness. He wept sore, and after his recovery he made a psalm describing his feelings while he was suffering, wherein he says, "Like a crane or a swallow, so did I chatter I did mourn as a dove: mine eyes fail with looking upward O Lord, I am oppressed, undertake for me." There is David. Even when Nathan the prophet had absolved him from his sin, he still felt the pangs of God's anger and wrath and said in the 38th Psalm, "I am troubled, I am bowed down greatly; I go mourning all the day long." There is the sinful woman, Mary Magdalene. Though Christ had given the assurance and said, "Many sins are forgiven her," still she wept bitterly and did not feel the healing balm of grace, until Christ turned to her and said, "Thy sins be forgiven thee: thy faith hath saved thee, depart in peace."

You see, my dear Christians, you can be in God's grace, though you do not feel it. You can be in such a condition as to experience nothing but death and condemnation and, at the same time, be a child of God. You can be weeping and lamenting over your sins, while the angels in heaven are praising the Lord for your repentance. You can have peace with God and, at the same time, your own heart may be filled with fear and uneasiness. When you are in such a depressed and despondent state, do not let false prophets deceive and tell you, you were no Christian, because you did not feel any joy and did not experience

God's grace. Know that God means to prove your faith when He withholds those joyful feelings, that Jesus merely hides His grace, which is yours nevertheless and shall not be taken away from you. Hold on to His grace, as the woman of Canaan did, and say,

When darkness veils His lovely face,
I rest on His unchanging grace.
In every high and stormy gale
My anchor holds within the veil.
On Christ, the solid Rock, I stand,
All other ground is sinking sand.

II.

It is folly not to believe that you are in God's grace unless you feel it, also for this reason, because true faith relies on the Word alone, which promises God's grace.

Jesus praises the woman, because, in spite of His rebukes and the feeling of her own unworthiness and all contrary experiences, her faith in His grace and mercy remained unshaken.

Though Christ seemed to be opposing her, this woman obviously said within herself, It is impossible that Christ, the Son of David, should put you off and not grant your request; He cannot be angry; He must be merciful; you must persevere; He surely is your Savior, His harsh words notwithstanding. When therefore Christ said to her, "*It is not meet to take the children's bread and to cast it to dogs,*" she clings to these words and responds, "*Truth, Lord: yet the dogs eat of the crumbs which fall from their masters' table.*" How adroitly does she turn to her favor what seems to be against her! And does the Lord censure her for such obtrusiveness? No; He is highly pleased and says, "*O woman, great is thy faith: be it unto thee even as thou wilt. And her daughter was made whole from that very hour.*"

Behold, my friends, here is an example showing wherein true faith consists. Faith does not consist in relying on the feelings of your own heart and believing that you are converted, justified, saved, because your own heart tells you so, or because there is a voice within you saying, Now you have grace, now you are born again, now you have passed through and made your calling and election sure, now your sins are forgiven, now you are a child of

God and an heir of the kingdom of heaven Modern revival conversions are largely brought about in that way, and people thus converted claim that they can fix the very minute of their conversion. They mistake for conversion what is merely an outburst of feeling No, true faith has a better and firmer foundation than the fluctuating feelings of our sinful heart. True faith consists in relying on the Word of God alone, which promises the grace of God That is what the woman did in our Gospel. She held on to Christ's words, in spite of all conflicting experiences.

If any one perceives that he is a lost and condemned sinner, for whom there is no help, and flees to Jesus, seeking refuge in His wounds, if in spite of his sins he applies to himself the righteousness of Jesus, who died on the cross for us all, and trusts in the gracious promises of the Gospel, which says, "God so loved the world that He gave His only begotten Son, that whosoever believeth in Him should not perish, but have everlasting life," then can he rest assured that he is in God's grace He that does not want to believe the gracious promises of the Gospel made to all sinners, unless he can feel the beneficent effects of that Gospel upon his own heart and soul, such person does the very same thing which Thomas did when he said, "Except I shall see in the Lord's hands the print of the nails, and put my finger in the print of the nails, and thrust my hand into His side, I will not believe." The Lord had compassion on this doubting disciple, but He also censured him, saying, "Thomas, because thou hast seen me, thou hast believed: blessed are they that have not seen, and yet have believed." Blessed, therefore, are they who rely on the Word of God alone for their salvation and everything that pertains thereto ! But pity on those who are determined not to believe unless they meet with some peculiar experience within themselves ! Their faith is not based on the right foundation. If they believe, they do not believe for the sake of the divine Word, but for the sake of their own feelings Their own feelings will finally be their Gospel, their Christ, their Savior, the foundation of their salvation. And that is a foundation which will crumble into dust and finally plunge them into the vortex of despair

Remember, my hearers, you are saved not by what you feel, but by what you believe It is not written, He that is joyful shall be saved, but, "He that believeth shall be saved." It is not feeling, but believing. We walk by faith, not by sight. When I feel my soul as cold as an iceberg, as hard as a rock, as sinful as Satan, even then does faith not cease to justify. Faith prevails as truly in the midst of sad feelings as of happy feelings. For just then, standing alone, it shows the greatness of its power.

May the Lord grant unto us all such unflinching faith in the words of His promises and enable each one of us to say,

> I cling to what my Savior taught,
> And trust it, whether felt or not.
> Amen.

THIRD SUNDAY IN LENT.

LUKE 11, 14—28.

And he was casting out a devil, and it was dumb. And it came to pass, when the devil was gone out, the dumb spake; and the people wondered. But some of them said, He casteth out devils through Beelzebub the chief of the devils. And others, tempting him, sought of him a sign from heaven. But he, knowing their thoughts, said unto them, Every kingdom divided against itself is brought to desolation; and a house divided against a house falleth. If Satan also be divided against himself, how shall his kingdom stand? because ye say that I cast out devils through Beelzebub. And if I by Beelzebub cast out devils, by whom do your sons cast them out? therefore shall they be your judges. But if I with the finger of God cast out devils, no doubt the kingdom of God is come upon you. When a strong man armed keepeth his palace, his goods are in peace: but when a stronger than he shall come upon him, and overcome him, he taketh from him all his armor wherein he trusted, and divideth his spoils. He that is not with me is against me: and he that gathereth not with me scattereth. When the unclean spirit is gone out of a man, he walketh through dry places, seeking rest; and finding none, he saith, I will return unto my house whence I came out. And when he cometh, he findeth it swept and garnished. Then goeth he, and taketh to him seven other spirits more wicked than himself; and they enter in, and dwell there: and the last state of that man is worse than the first. And it came to pass, as he spake these things, a certain woman of the company lifted up her voice, and said unto him, Blessed is the womb that bare thee, and the paps which thou hast sucked. But he said, Yea rather, blessed are they that hear the word of God, and keep it.

BELOVED FRIENDS IN CHRIST:

In our last Sunday's Gospel we were informed that Jesus cast a devil out of the Syrophoenician woman's daughter, and to-day again we are told, *"And He cast out a devil, and it was dumb. And it came to pass, when the devil was gone out, the dumb spake."*

To believe in the actual existence of devils or evil spirits is now looked upon as a remnant of old superstitions of bygone days by those who claim to be progressing with the times. They themselves use such phrases as, In the devil's name, and the like, and these phrases seem to indicate that they must be believing in the actual existence of the devil after all, their declaration to the contrary notwithstanding. But let any one say to them that he believes in the existence of a personal devil, and he is very apt to be laughed at and called a fool.

Now we must admit that in olden times, and especially during the reign of the papacy in the Old World, and in the days of the Pilgrim Fathers in the New World, in our own country, the most absurd stories were circulated designed to frighten people, telling how the devil appeared with hoof and horns, and what he had done. The most cruel punishments were inflicted upon those who were suspected of having some secret intercourse with the devil. Such persons were horribly tortured to extort from them a confession of their guilt. They were required to undergo tests to prove their innocence. Many an innocent person was put to death.

All of this was an abuse of the doctrine of the Scriptures concerning the devil. It was contrary to the Scriptures. But are we to cast away this doctrine, because it was and is still being abused? Are we to deny the very existence of Satan because so much superstition clusters around his name? Verily not. The Scripture is the divine truth. The Scripture is just as true in what it says of the devil as it is in what it says of God. And does not the Scripture contain a complete history of the devil, of his origin, his works, his intentions, and his final doom?

This Sunday's Gospel also treats of the works of Satan. After the Lord Jesus had cast out a devil of the man who was dumb, we are told, *"The people wondered. But some of them said, He casteth out devils through Beelzebub, the chief of the devils. And others, tempting Him, sought of Him a sign from heaven."* From this Christ takes occasion to discourse copiously on the kingdom of Satan. Let us therefore consider with the aid of God's Holy Spirit,

CHRIST'S DISCOURSE ON SATAN'S KINGDOM,

showing,

I *Wherein Satan's kingdom consists*, and

II. *How his kingdom is overcome.*

I.

Christ says, "*Every kingdom divided against itself is brought to desolation; and a house divided against a house falleth If Satan also be divided against himself, how shall his kingdom stand? because ye say that I cast out devils through Beelzebub And if I by Beelzebub cast out devils, by whom do your sons cast them out? therefore shall they be your judges. But if I with the finger of God cast out devils, no doubt the kingdom of God is come upon you. When a strong man armed keepeth his palace, his goods are in peace: but when a stronger than he shall come upon him, and overcome him, he taketh from him all his armor wherein he trusted, and divideth his spoils.*" From these words of our Savior we see clearly that there is such a thing as the kingdom of Satan, that there are palaces which he inhabits, and that there is an armor wherein he trusts.

And what is Satan's kingdom? His kingdom is this world: his palace is the human heart; his armor are all those things which Satan makes use of to establish or keep his sovereignty in the human heart.

The whole world is Satan's kingdom. He is, therefore, called the prince of this world, the god of this world He did not create the world, neither does he preserve and govern the world; but Satan it was who brought about the present deplorable state of the world. He corrupted the world He seduced man to sin and thereby introduced sin, and woe, and misery, and death: and he established a kingdom of his own in God's beautiful creation. All men are born sinners and, therefore, born subjects of Satan in his kingdom. Had not God had compassion on the fallen human race, not a soul would be saved, but all men would have to remain in Satan's kingdom and share with him his terrible doom of eternal damnation But God did have mercy on us. He had His only begotten Son, Jesus Christ, live and suffer and die for us, and thereby destroy the works of the devil. Whosoever is baptized in Jesus' name is no more a subject in Satan's

kingdom, though he is still in the world, which is Satan's kingdom.
God is his Father, Jesus is his King, and Satan has no claim upon
him. Alas! many that were baptized do not remain in their baptismal grace. They lose the faith, lead a godless life, and let
Satan rule over them. Hence it is that Satan's throne is established even in Christian lands. The heathen and Mohammedan
lands with their people and the remnants of Jewry that are scattered over the whole world, are the strongholds of Satan, which
he holds by ignorance and superstition, so that rarely a soul
escapes. But even in the midst of Christendom there are millions of palaces, millions of human hearts that are occupied by
the prince of this world. Not only does Satan hold in his clutches
those who are outspoken infidels and enemies of the divine truth,
but even many of those who claim to be Christians are his loyal
subjects.

For what does Christ say in our Gospel? He says, *"He that
is not with me is against me: and he that gathereth not with me
scattereth."* What does that mean? In the connection in which
it is said it means this. Not only such as claim to be neutral and
neither to hold to me nor to Satan are against me and, therefore,
Satan's servants; but even such as do not gather with me, such as
do not work with me, and are not in a true union with me, though
they claim to be Christians, are Satan's subjects. Oh, Satan is a
cunning spirit. He does not demand of his subjects to worship
him openly, he permits them to go by the name of God's servants,
and is perfectly satisfied, if they will only do his works. Whosoever indulges in some sin and nourishes and cherishes that sin and
cannot make up his mind to rid himself of that sin with the power
of God, his heart is Satan's residence and palace, and if he were
ever so good a Christian outwardly before the world. A heart
given to licentiousness is Satan's domain. The drunkard's heart
is Satan's possession. Hearts that are continually possessed with
pride, arrogance, conceitedness, hatred, enmity, or any such sinful
emotions, are the devil's palaces. For these are the weapons, the
armor, by which he keepeth his own. In short, where sin is not
being resisted, where sin is permitted to prevail and to hold its
sway in the heart, there Satan's kingdom is established. Drunkards
will sometimes make an effort to keep sober and even swear never
to touch another drop of strong drink, but their appetite is so

strong that they cannot keep themselves under control Sensualists will sometimes make a desperate effort to lead a chaste and decent life, but the next temptation gets the best of them. Persons given to lies and falsehoods will sometimes make up their minds to be truthful and sincere, but before they are aware another falsehood crosses their lips. Whence this irresistible power of sin? It is because the power which holds them in bonds and fetters is more than human. It is diabolic. Satan has possession of such hearts.

And not only such has Satan bound with his chains and fetters as live in open sin and shame, but also many of those who lead an honest and upright life before men. Sometimes his fetters are so hidden and concealed as to make it impossible for man to detect them. When we see a drunkard staggering in the street, or when we hear some person cursing, and swearing, and using filthy language; or when we see some one performing an extremely wicked deed, we may justly form an opinion that the hearts of such persons must be palaces of Satan. But the evil spirit does not dwell exclusively in the hearts of the grossly immoral and profane and in the slums of sin and vice. Sometimes he has even a stronger hold upon the self-righteous and upon those who are highly educated and appear to be beyond reproach. Satan has his dominion not only in the hearts of the illiterate and ignorant, sometimes his kingdom is even more firmly established in the hearts of the educated who disseminate errors and do this, perhaps, even in the name of divine truth

II.

And now, in the second place, having heard wherein Satan's kingdom consists, let us consider how his kingdom is overcome. Christ says, "*When a strong man armed keepeth his palace, his goods are in peace: but when a stronger than he shall come upon him, and overcome him, he taketh from him all his armor wherein he trusted, and divideth his spoil.*" Here Christ tells us that, when Satan dwells in man's heart, he is there as a strong man armed, and he will remain and keep his own, except one stronger than he come upon him and overcome the evil spirit. But who is stronger than Satan? No mortal man. No mortal man can by his own natural power break Satan's fetters and rid himself of

10

Satan's dominion. Satan is too strong for him. Sometimes it seems as if by his own will power a man could overcome Satan and his destructive work. Drunkards, and licentious persons will sometimes abandon those evil practices in which previously they had indulged. But, at the same time, they are fettered by other sins, as, by self-righteousness or covetousness, and their hearts remain virtually unchanged. Is Satan really overcome if one sin is dispensed with and another remains, or is substituted in its place, if, for instance, the drunkard drinks no more, but prides himself in self-righteousness before God and man? No; in such cases Satan is not overcome at all. He only puts on a different garb. His power remains undisturbed.

The only possible way for man to be saved from Satan's power is through Jesus Christ, the eternal Son of God. He is the stronger who comes upon and overcomes the strong man armed, who taketh from him all his armor and divideth the spoils. The only possible way to overcome Satan's kingdom, to rend asunder his fetters, to rid yourself from the bondage of sin, to become a truly free man, who is not the slave of some pet sin, to become truly converted from the power of Satan to God, is through Jesus Christ. You must not attempt to overcome Satan's kingdom by your own power, or you will fail invariably. Christ alone can free the sinner from Satan's power.

And how will Jesus do this? He will, first of all, lead the sinner to perceive the damnableness of his sin, to feel true remorse, not so much because of the evil consequences of sin, a name tainted before the world, or health impaired or ruined, but most of all because by sin he transgressed God's divine Law, and stood in league with God's enemy, the devil, permitting him to occupy his heart as a palace, while it should have been the temple of God.

But Jesus will do more for the sinner than that. He will not only let his heart be filled with remorse by the Law. He will also take possession of his heart by the Gospel; and Satan will have to depart. Christ will replenish that heart with true faith, with the assurance that all sins have been blotted out by His suffering and death on the cross. Thus will He rid the heart from the love of sin and evil ways and lead the soul to hate and despise all works of darkness and with strength from on high to resist all temptations.

Behold, thus is Satan's kingdom overcome in man's heart through Jesus Christ

But so strong and so cunning, at the same time, is Satan, even when driven out of man's heart and completely put to flight, he will watch his chances to return and to recapture the palace which he was forced to abandon. And if not properly guarded against, he may regain his dominion and reestablish his kingdom. Christ says, "*When the unclean spirit is gone out of a man, he walketh through dry places, seeking rest: and finding none, he saith, I will return unto my house whence I came out. And when he cometh, he findeth it swept and garnished. Then goeth he, and taketh to him seven other spirits more wicked than himself; and they enter in, and dwell there: and the last state of that man is worse than the first.*" Christ means to say, If a Christian is not on his guard, Satan will again get him under control and triumph over him. If a Christian ceases to watch and to pray, to use diligently the means of grace, to battle against sin in his own heart; if he begins to grow indifferent as to his soul's salvation and to desire after the world's evil lusts, then is his heart swept and garnished and duly prepared for the reception of the evil spirit. And woe unto him if he yields to the desires of his own flesh! Not only will his own pet sin return, but other sins will follow in its wake, and the last state will be worse than the first. It is always a more difficult thing for a backslider to be reconverted than for a sinner who had not yet tasted the good Word of God and the powers of the world to come, to come to repentance

O let us all be mindful of the apostle's warning, "Let him that standeth take heed lest he fall." Let us diligently make use of God's holy Word and wield that Sword of the Spirit freely against him who goeth about as a roaring lion, seeking whom he may devour. And ours shall be the promise of our Savior, "*Blessed are they that hear the Word of God and keep it.*" Amen.

FOURTH SUNDAY IN LENT.

JOHN 6, 1—15.

After these things Jesus went over the sea of Galilee, which is the sea of Tiberias. And a great multitude followed him, because they saw his miracles which he did on them that were diseased. And Jesus went up into a mountain, and there he sat with his disciples. And the passover, a feast of the Jews, was nigh. When Jesus then lifted up his eyes, and saw a great company come unto him, he saith unto Philip, Whence shall we buy bread, that these may eat? And this he said to prove him: for he himself knew what he would do. Philip answered him, Two hundred pennyworth of bread is not sufficient for them, that every one of them may take a little. One of his disciples, Andrew, Simon Peter's brother, saith unto him, There is a lad here, which hath five barley loaves, and two small fishes: but what are they among so many? And Jesus said, Make the men sit down. Now there was much grass in the place. So the men sat down, in number about five thousand. And Jesus took the loaves; and when he had given thanks, he distributed to the disciples, and the disciples to them that were set down; and likewise of the fishes as much as they would. When they were filled, he said unto his disciples, Gather up the fragments that remain, that nothing be lost. Therefore they gathered them together, and filled twelve baskets with the fragments of the five barley loaves, which remained over and above unto them that had eaten. Then those men, when they had seen the miracle that Jesus did, said, This is of a truth that prophet that should come into the world. When Jesus therefore perceived that they would come and take him by force, to make him a king, he departed again into a mountain himself alone.

BELOVED FRIENDS IN CHRIST:

In this day's Gospel we are told that the people intended to take Jesus by force and make Him a king. The time seemed to be favorable. The Passover was nigh. From all parts of Judea and from other parts of the world the Jews were flocking to Jerusalem to celebrate the great annual feast which, according to their Law, they were required to celebrate in their magnificent temple at the capital city. Thousands among the common people took Jesus for the great Prophet of whom Moses had spoken, saying, "The Lord, thy God, will raise up a Prophet unto thee, like unto me; unto Him ye shall hearken." They looked upon Jesus as the promised Messiah, as the long-expected Deliverer, who should restore the glory of the house of Israel. Like a gloom rested upon the whole nation the shame of having been conquered by the Gentiles and being held in bondage by the mighty Romans. And since the whole nation was inspired with a fervent desire to cast off the Roman yoke and to be an independent people again, would not the Passover have been the most opportune time to proclaim a king? Is it not very likely that the multitudes coming to Jerusalem to worship would have made an attempt to expel the Roman intruders and hailed with delight the man who should restore the throne of David and Solomon?

But what are we told of Christ? When He perceived what the people were about, "*He departed again into a mountain Himself alone*" He secreted Himself. He did not mean to be the kind of savior they expected and desired. He did not mean to be a worldly king. And Christ is the same to-day, though most men expect of Him something different The subject of our discourse shall be with the aid of God's Holy Spirit,

CHRIST QUITE A DIFFERENT SAVIOR THAN MOST MEN DESIRE.
We shall see,

I *What kind of savior most men desire*, and,
II. *What kind of Savior Jesus is.*

I.

At the time of Christ there were two classes of men who desired a different kind of savior than Jesus was. The one class were those who persecuted Christ. This class was composed of the Sadducees and Pharisees, two different sects at variance with each other, but one in their opposition to Christ. The Sadducees were the agnostics and scoffers of those days. They believed in no resurrection, nor angel, nor spirit. Their sole aim was to enjoy this life, to eat, drink, and be merry, and not to worry about the hereafter. They looked upon those as fools who said that there was a heaven and a hell. Still, they also desired a savior. But the savior whom they had in their minds was to be a man who should teach them how to enjoy this life still more and who should procure for them more of the pleasures of this world

There was quite a contrast between these and the Pharisees. The Pharisees believed in the resurrection of the dead, in heaven and hell, in a retribution after this life, and showed great piety. But they meant to get to heaven by their own righteousness. The savior whom they desired was to be a man who should preach morality, admire their outward holiness, keep aloof from publicans and sinners, and make the Jews the leading nation of the world in external magnificence and splendor. Since Jesus in no way came near their standard of the Messiah they opposed Him, And the same thing was done by the Sadducees, who looked upon Jesus as a man who was far behind the times.

Aside from these outspoken enemies of Christ there was another class of men who did not oppose Christ and yet desired a different kind of savior than Jesus proved to be. These are described in the following words of our Gospel, "*After these things Jesus went over the Sea of Galilee, which is the Sea of Tiberias And a great multitude followed Him, because they saw His miracles which He did on them that were diseased.*" The miracles which Jesus performed convinced them that He must be, at least, a great prophet, and all the threats and blasphemies of Pharisees and Sadducees could not keep them from following after Christ and hearing His preaching.

Still, Jesus was not the kind of savior they were wishing for. This is plainly shown in our Gospel All those miracles which Jesus performed before their eyes, all the divine sayings which they had heard from His lips did not move them to proclaim Him their King and Savior But no sooner had He fed them in the wilderness with a little bread and fish and supplied their wants in a miraculous way, so that even more was left over than the original supply — no sooner had Jesus performed the great miracle of feeding five thousand men with only five barley loaves and two small fishes, than the people shouted in an ecstasy, "*This is of a truth that Prophet that should come into the world.*" Now they owned that He was the Prophet promised by Moses, the true Messiah. Even such was their excitement over what Jesus had done for them, that they made ready to take Him by force and make Him their king at once. Why did not the previous miracles of Christ produce upon the people the effect which this miracle of feeding them produced? The reason is obvious. The people desired a savior who should give them plenty to eat, a savior not of the soul, but of the body; not for heaven, but for the earth. When, therefore, on the following day Jesus met some of them at Capernaum they said to Him, "Lord, evermore give us this bread." That shows plainly what kind of savior they desired. They were bread-Christians and wanted a bread-savior

But the same state of things exists to this day. To this day the same two classes of men are to be found who at the time of

Christ desired a different kind of savior than Jesus was. We have Sadducees in our days. These are the infidels who mock and scoff at every form of religion, who say that there is no God, who deny heaven and hell, and claim that man has no more soul than the brute. Jesus is not a savior to their taste. Then saviors, the men whom they admire, are those who assail and denounce the Bible, and the Christian religion, and everything in connection therewith. We also have the Pharisees. These sometimes lay claim to the Christian name. They are the self-righteous who protest most vigorously if you tell them that they are lost and condemned sinners, and that they cannot get to heaven in any other way than by faith in Jesus Christ, the Lamb of God that taketh away the sins of the world. Jesus is not a savior to their taste either. Their saviors are those who proclaim shallow morality, praise the achievements of man, and urge people to show sympathy to their fellow men, presupposing that, if there is a yonder life, man must get there by his own exertions.

And then there are such in our days as are very much like the people whom Jesus fed in our Gospel. Like the multitude they follow Jesus into the wilderness. In a certain sense they separate themselves from the children of this world. They go to church and hear the preaching of the divine Word. But what is it they seek with Christ? Redemption from sin? Life everlasting? Far from it. To say it in plain words, they seek with Christ nothing but bread and fish. They expect Him to give them the riches and pleasures of this world, to permit them to enjoy this life to their heart's content, to do the same things which the children of this world call their greatest delight, to go to dances, balls, and theaters, and thus to participate in the world's evil lusts. And when they are told that Jesus is not such a savior, that Christians must crucify their flesh and the lusts thereof: then they feel disappointed and offended. Their conduct shows that Jesus is not the savior whom they desire.

II.

And now, in the second place, let us see what kind of Savior Jesus really is.

St. Mark also has an account of this great miracle. He says that, when the multitude came to Jesus, *"He was moved with compassion toward them, because they were as sheep having no shepherd; and He began to teach them many things."* So from St. Mark's account we see that the first thing which Jesus did was that He administered to the spiritual wants of the people. He fed their immortal souls with the bread of life. His heart was filled with compassion toward them, not so much because they were in bodily needs, but, above all, because they were as sheep having no shepherd for their souls to lead and guide them. From this we see what kind of Savior Jesus is. He is a Savior, first of all, for the souls of men. Those who come to Him and receive Him as their Savior are required, first of all, to seek the kingdom of God and His righteousness; first of all, to look upon Him as the Savior from sin "who has redeemed us lost and condemned creatures, purchased and won us from all sins, from death and from the power of the devil, not with gold or silver, but with His holy, precious blood and with His innocent suffering and death, that we may be His own, and live under Him in His kingdom, and serve Him in everlasting righteousness, innocence, and blessedness."

All this is well known. It is being preached and proclaimed continually. But where are they who desire such a Savior and wish to be His disciples in the manner indicated? Ah, these are comparatively few. There are many, indeed, who follow Christ into the wilderness, as did the multitude in our Gospel, many who hear the preaching of His divine Word, many who perform the outward works of Christians, say their daily prayers, give to the poor, show benevolence, support the church, and help to extend the kingdom of God. But if the inmost thoughts of their hearts were exposed, how many would we find doing all these things from pure, untainted love of the Savior, because He loved them first and did so much for them? How many would we find doing these things with cheerfulness of heart and with rejoicing that they can, in some way, show their gratitude for the great work of the redemption wrought upon their immortal souls? They do, indeed, in their way, believe in the Bible and call Jesus their Savior. But when they are informed that Jesus is a Savior of the soul, and that they must give Him their hearts, serve Him alone, shun the world and its evil lusts, and set their affection on things above, where Christ sitteth on the right hand of God, then it becomes

apparent that Jesus Christ, the eternal Son of God and Mary's
Son, is not the Savior whom they really desire.

Still, we must not think that Jesus showed no care for our
bodily needs Though providing, first of all, for our immortal
souls, He does not neglect our mortal bodies. Having taught the
multitude and shown them the way to eternal life, He also administered to their bodily needs. He gives them bread to eat and
by a miracle of His divine power not only supplies their present
wants, but also furnishes enough food for them on their way
home. Our Gospel tells us, " *When Jesus then lifted up His eyes,
and saw a great company come unto Him, He saith unto Philip,
Whence shall we buy bread, that these may eat? And this He
said to prove Him · for He Himself knew what He would do
Philip answered Him, Two hundred pennyworth of bread is not
sufficient for them, that every one of them may take a little. One
of His disciples, Andrew, Simon Peter's brother, saith unto Him,
There is a lad here, which hath five barley loaves, and two small
fishes · but what are they among so many? And Jesus said, Make
the men sit down. Now there was much grass in the place So
the men sat down, in number about five thousand. And Jesus
took the loaves, and when He had given thanks, He distributed
to the disciples, and the disciples to them that were set down; and
likewise of the fishes, as much as they would When they were
filled, He said unto His disciples, Gather up the fragments that
remain, that nothing be lost. Therefore they gathered them together, and filled twelve baskets with the fragments of the five barley
loaves, which remained over and above unto them that had eaten.*"
From this we see what kind of Savior Jesus is. He is such a
Savior as will never forsake those who trust in Him. He will in
some way furnish for them all they need for the support of this
body and life, and if He should have to do so by miracle He
does not promise them riches, not an abundance of goods and
earthly possessions. But He will from His vast stores supply
them with the necessaries of life. He therefore says to all His followers, "Take no thought for your life, what ye shall eat, or what
ye shall drink; nor yet for your body, what ye shall put on Is not
the life more than meat, and the body than raiment? Behold the
fowls of the air: for they sow not, neither do they reap, nor gather
into barns; yet your heavenly Father feedeth them. Are ye not

much better than they?" But above and beyond this He provides for our immortal souls. To the multitude by the seaside He had preached words of eternal life before He fed them to sustain this temporal life. And for all mankind He came into the world to seek and to save those who without His saving grace must have been lost forever. And to this day He rules in His kingdom of grace by His Word, calls and enlightens and sanctifies and preserves in saving faith, through His Spirit, those who shall be gathered about His throne in the kingdom of glory.

Tell me, then, my friends, could we wish for a better Savior than Jesus? a Savior who takes charge of our immortal souls, and providing for us richly and daily, does not neglect the mortal body? Is it not the height of folly to desire a different kind of savior than Jesus is? What should we be benefited, if we had a savior who would give us all the riches and pleasures of this world, and who would desert us in the hour of death, and leave us to our fate, which is eternal woe and misery for all the children of men who die in their sins and have not obtained forgiveness of their transgressions? "What is a man profited, if he shall gain the whole world, and lose his own soul?"

May this, then, be our prayer,

> Jesus, Lover of my soul,
> Let me to Thy bosom fly,
> While the nearer waters roll,
> While the tempest still is high!
> Hide me, O my Savior, hide,
> Till the storm of life is past;
> Safe into the haven guide,
> O receive my soul at last.

Amen.

FIFTH SUNDAY IN LENT.

JOHN 8, 46—59

Which of you convinceth me of sin? And if I say the truth, why do ye not believe me? He that is of God heareth God's words: ye therefore hear them not, because ye are not of God. Then answered the Jews, and said unto him, Say we not well that thou art a Samaritan, and hast a devil? Jesus answered, I have not a devil, but I honor my Father, and ye do dishonor me. And I seek not mine own glory: there is one that seeketh and judgeth. Verily, verily, I say unto you, If a man keep my saying, he shall never see death. Then said the Jews unto him, Now we know that thou hast a devil. Abraham is dead, and the prophets; and thou sayest, If a man keep my saying, he shall never taste of death. Art thou greater than our father Abraham, which is dead? and the prophets are dead: whom makest thou thyself? Jesus answered, If I honor myself, my honor is nothing: it is my Father that honoreth me, of whom ye say, that he is your God: yet ye have not known him, but I know him: and if I should say, I know him not, I shall be a liar like unto you: but I know him, and keep his saying. Your father Abraham rejoiced to see my day: and he saw it, and was glad. Then said the Jews unto him, Thou art not yet fifty years old, and hast thou seen Abraham? Jesus said unto them, Verily, verily, I say unto you, Before Abraham was, I am. Then took they up stones to cast at him: but Jesus hid himself, and went out of the temple, going through the midst of them, and so passed by

BELOVED FRIENDS IN CHRIST:

"*Why do ye not believe me?*" This question is asked by the Lord Jesus in our Gospel. The Jews to whom the question was put answered with scorn and malediction. In our days men generally couch their answer to this question in polite words. If you ask an infidel, Why do you not believe on the Lord Jesus? he will say now-a-days, I cannot, I would like to, but I am sorry to say, I cannot. Some years ago a pastor had a conversation with a Congressman on a train coming from Washington. The Congressman told him that nearly all the highly educated men that make the laws of the land were infidels, and that he, too, was an infidel, but that he was not happy in that state; his mother was a devout Christian, and he knew that she was a happy woman. But as for himself, he could not believe the Christian doctrine, though he desired very much that he could do so and be a happy man. But in the course of the conversation it developed what the man's trouble was. It was that he had contrived for himself an obstacle to keep him from the faith. He had fixed in his mind the idea that to be a faithful believer you must be ignorant to a certain extent and prone to superstition. So he preferred to be an infidel and to claim for himself the name of a highly educated man who was no more bound with the ties of old traditions and superstitions of bygone days.

Let us not be deceived by these pretensions of infidels when they say that they would like to believe on the Lord Jesus, but that they could not, because they were too highly educated, they knew too much, they had made a thorough study of the laws of nature, had traveled and seen so much of the world, and the like. Infidelity has not monopolized education, and never will. Among the greatest men, the most profound thinkers, the wisest statesmen, the highest men in literature, there always have been and there are to this day professed Christians. Washington professed the Christian faith, and so did Newton and Noah Webster. Bismarck and Gladstone, the greatest statesmen of modern times, were believers on the Lord Jesus; and many learned men of our days are, at the same time, prominent men in the Christian church. Learning and education are not barriers against the Christian faith. The true cause of infidelity is always to be sought in man's will. A person may think that he does not believe because he cannot on account of his own convictions to the contrary, but if he will examine his own heart honestly and sincerely, he will always find that he does not like to part with some pet sin, or that he is loath to put up with some things that true believers must endure. This is shown in our Gospel by the example of the Jews with whom Jesus disputed in the temple. Let us, therefore, consider, with the aid of God's Holy Spirit, the question,

WHY IS IT THAT SO MANY CANNOT BELIEVE ON THE LORD JESUS CHRIST?

The answer is threefold,

    I. *Because they do not want to hear the truth.*
    II. *Because they despise the Lord's grace.*
    III. *Because Christ's divinity is foolishness unto them.*

I.

In the third article of the Creed we confess according to our Catechism, "I believe that I cannot by my own reason and strength believe in Jesus Christ, my Lord, or come to Him."

This means that natural man cannot by his own natural power decide for Christ and himself make up his mind to believe. But it does not mean that such natural inability may be tendered as an excuse and that it could not be overcome. The root and source of this inability lies in man's perverted will. He cannot believe because he does not want to believe.

This is clearly shown in our Gospel. Christ says to the Jews, "*Which of you convinceth me of sin? And if I say the truth, why do ye not believe me?*" The Jews did not want to hear the truth, as Jesus testifies here. He asks, "*Which of you convinceth me of sin?*" He had lived among them. They had closely watched His deeds and sayings. Now they should bear witness to the truth and own the truth. They should either name and prove a sin which He did, or openly confess His sinlessness and believe Him. Do they convince Him of sin? They know that they cannot. Do they, then, admit His holiness? They do not. By such conduct they prove that they are opposed to the truth and do not want to hear the truth, and for that very reason do not believe on the Lord Jesus.

Christ says, furthermore, "*He that is of God, heareth God's words; ye therefore hear them not, because ye are not of God.*" They had God's words, the Law and the prophets. Both Moses and the prophets wrote of the Messiah and His works, and Jesus did exactly the works which the Messiah was to perform. Why did the Jews not pay any attention to that? Jesus proved His sayings by the Scriptures of the Old Testament; He Himself spoke the Word of God. Why did they not listen to Him? They show by such conduct that they are enemies of the truth, and for that reason do not believe on the Lord Jesus.

Yea, they resort to lies and blasphemy. For we are told, "*Then answered the Jews, and said unto Him, Say we not well that Thou art a Samaritan, and hast a devil?*" They cannot answer the Lord's questions, their conscience smarts, they know that they are doing wrong; still, from pure hatred they will not admit this, and they give vent to their ill feeling by uttering blasphemy. Did these Jews have any excuse for their infidelity? Verily not. They did not want to hear the truth.

And to this day why is it that so many who possess the Bible and live among the Christians cannot believe on the Lord Jesus?

Is it because they are too well educated, too far advanced in wisdom and knowledge, too much enlightened? That claim is persistently made by their champions. But facts are stubborn things, and the fact is that some of the greatest thinkers were Christians. Why, then, do learned men among the infidels not believe? Certainly not because of their high intellectual standing, but because they do not want to hear the truth. Christ's sinlessness, His divine works, His precious Gospel is before them, they cannot gainsay it, it is attested by better evidence than any historical fact which they believe. Why are they so ready to believe almost any theory that opposes religion, and so eager to discredit the Gospel? The fault lies in their own sinful heart which cannot bear the truth.

Furthermore, if these infidels, as they often claim, would like to believe if only they could, why do they not hear the Word of God, through which faith is planted in the heart? Why do they shun the preaching of the Word? Why do they not read the Bible? Must not Christ say to them the same words which He spoke to the Jews, *"He that is of God heareth God's words: ye therefore hear them not, because ye are not of God"*? Do they not show by such indifference that they do not want to hear the truth?

Finally, such infidels as resort to lies and blasphemy, as unscrupulously pervert the Word of God and denounce the Christian religion as fraud and hypocrisy, why can they not believe on the Lord Jesus? Because of their sincerity and conscientiousness? No; like those obdurate Jews, with whom Christ disputed in the temple, they do not want the truth.

II.

The second reason why so many cannot believe on the Lord Jesus is because they despise the Lord's grace. We read, *"Jesus answered, I have not a devil; but I honor my Father, and ye dishonor me. And I seek not mine own glory: there is One that seeketh and judgeth."* These Jews dishonored Jesus. They had made up their minds that this man should not be their Messiah, and they opposed Him so much the more, because all the indications were in His favor. In their council they said, "What do we? for this man doeth many miracles. If we let Him thus alone all men will believe on Him, and the Romans shall come and take away both our place and nation." They would not humble themselves under this man Jesus, who claimed to be the Messiah, and was not such a Messiah as they expected, not a great worldly ruler, who could smite the nations and establish the throne of David. They were too proud and worldly-minded to accept His grace and to receive from Him eternal life. When, therefore, Jesus said to them, "*Verily, verily, I say unto you, If a man keep my saying, he shall never see death,*" then the Jews said unto Him, "*Now we know that Thou hast a devil. Abraham is dead, and the prophets; and Thou sayest, If a man keep my saying, he shall never taste of death. Art Thou greater than our father Abraham, which is dead? and the prophets are dead whom makest Thou Thyself?*" Behold how angry they get when Jesus speaks of eternal life, to be received by the keeping of His saying, that is, by faith in Him! Behold how they pervert the words of His mouth and construe them as if He were speaking of natural death! Behold how they despise His grace and mercy! It is apparent, they are too proud, too self-righteous to humble themselves and to receive eternal life as a gift of His grace, by faith in Him. Hence their infidelity.

And, to this day, why is it that so many cannot believe on the Lord Jesus? Is it not because they are self-righteous and expect to get to heaven by their own good works and righteousness? Is it not because they despise the Lord's grace? They are puffed up with pride, with egotism, with arrogance, and conceitedness. Is it, then, to be wondered at that they despise the Lord's grace and cannot believe? Unto such people the doctrine of justification by grace through faith in the Lord Jesus Christ is foolishness. They are too proud to admit that they are damnable sinners. It is too degrading for them to think so low and little of themselves. They are too proud to humble themselves before their divine Maker. They will even criticise His doings, His works in nature, His dealings with mankind, and prescribe to the Almighty how He must rule the universe. They are too proud to receive eternal life as a gift of God's grace and mercy. If still they believe in a Supreme Being and a future world, they expect to get there by their own efforts, by their

good behavior in this life, by their own virtues, by doing what
they themselves consider to be right and pleasing to the Creator.
But a Savior of sinners they despise and the blood of Jesus
Christ, the Son of God, which flowed also for them, they tread
under foot. They despise the Lord's grace. And that is the
true reason why they cannot believe.

III.

But there is one thing in particular which is especially ob-
jectionable to an infidel, and that is Christ's divinity.

At the end of our Gospel we read, *"Jesus answered, If I
honor myself, my honor is nothing: it is my Father that honoreth
me, of whom ye say, that He is your God. Yet ye have not
known Him; but I know Him: and if I should say, I know
Him not, I shall be a liar like unto you: but I know Him, and
keep His saying. Your father Abraham rejoiced to see my day:
and he saw it, and was glad. Then said the Jews unto Him,
Thou art not yet fifty years old, and hast seen Abraham? Jesus
said unto them, Verily, verily, I say unto you, Before Abraham
was, I am."* Here Christ attests His divinity. He says that
Abraham rejoiced to see His day, believing on Him as the Seed
in whom all the nations of the earth should be blessed. The
Jews well understood the meaning of these words. Scornfully
they retort, *"Thou art not yet fifty years old, and hast seen
Abraham?"* And what is Christ's reply? He says, *"Verily,
verily, I say unto you, Before Abraham was, I am."* Our Eng-
lish Bible reads, "Before Abraham *was*," but the exact trans-
lation is, "Before Abraham *was made*." This implies that Abraham was a creature of God. And in opposition thereto Christ
says, "I am," and this implies that Christ is not a creature, that
He is eternal, that He is God. This is just as plain as when He
says, "Unto me is given all power in heaven and in earth;" just
as plain as when St. Paul says, "Christ is God blessed forever;"
just as plain as when St. John says, "This (Jesus Christ) is the
true God and eternal life." And what response do the Jews
make? *"Then took they up stones to cast at Him: but Jesus hid
Himself, and went out of the temple, going through the midst of
them, and so passed by."* They cannot find words with which
to express their disgust. They mean to stone Jesus as a blas-

phemer The assertion of His divinity it was which enraged them and made them act like madmen

Why is it, to this day, that so many cannot believe on the Lord Jesus? Is it not because Christ's divinity is utter foolishness and such a great stumbling-block unto them? Like the Jews in our Gospel they make Him the greatest liar and impostor that ever lived. There is a class of infidels who claim to be Christ's true disciples and say that they walk in the footsteps of Christ, proclaiming the Gospel of love, while, at the same time, they deny His miracles, His divinity, His redemption, and all the essentials of the Gospel truth. What an absurdity to claim the Christian name, and yet deny Christ! Others, more true to the evil designs of their wicked hearts, say, Jesus was led to proclaim Himself the Son of God and the Lord's Anointed from human weakness, being intoxicated with the homage paid to Him by His disciples. Why, then, can these infidels not believe on the Lord Jesus? Is it because they are so conscientious concerning the Gospel truth? No, it is because the Gospel is foolishness unto them, because they harbor ill feelings in their own bosoms against the divine Lord, and will not concede His divinity, in spite of overwhelming evidences.

Let us not be deceived by the pretensions of infidels, when they say that they feel sorry because they could not believe on the Lord Jesus. Whosoever is sorry for his infidelity, in him God has already begun His work, and his sorrow, if true, will soon turn into joy and saving faith. The Lord grant unto us all His grace that we may not resist His Holy Spirit, but yield to the life-giving power of His Word, and believe with all our soul on Him who has bought us with His own precious blood and with His innocent suffering and death. Amen.

11

PALM SUNDAY.

ADDRESS TO THE CATECHUMENS.

Rom 1, 16

I am not ashamed of the Gospel of Christ for it is the power of God unto
salvation to every one that believeth

My Dearly Beloved Children

As often as you came to this church before this day, you
came to hear God speak to you   His divine Word was proclaimed to you, and where His Word is proclaimed there God
speaks Himself   But what is the purpose of your visit in the
house of God on this day? To-day you came not only to hear
God speak to you, but also to speak before God yourselves And
what is it you intend to say to God? You intend to give Him
a solemn promise, a promise which the entire congregation shall
hear and by which you shall bind yourselves to your God for all
the days of your lives. You shall promise Him faithfulness unto
death   You shall promise Him that you will always serve and
obey Him, never forsake Him, never desert Him, that neither
poverty nor riches, neither honor nor reproach, neither life nor
death, that absolutely nothing in this world shall ever sever your
connection with God and the true Church. Will you keep this
promise? O my dearly beloved children, before the omniscient
God, who searches the depths of the heart, I ask you, Will you
keep this solemn promise? Will you all, every one of you, remain with Christ and His Church? 'Oh, it is a sad experience
that by a great number of children the confirmation vow is soon
set at nought.   Thousands of children stood before the altar on
confirmation day with tears in their eyes and the best resolves in
their hearts and promised to be faithful unto death   And what
became of them later on? For a while they appeared to be
walking the narrow way that leads to eternal life, but gradually
they drifted away from the church and from their God and
swelled the large number of the lost   They did not stand firm
in the hour of temptation.   They began to love the world and
its evil lusts.   They felt loath to bear the cross of Christ and the
reproach which the world heaps upon them that pray, and go to
church, and make an open profession of the Christian faith. And

so they felt ashamed of Christ whose name they solemnly confessed before men on the day of their confirmation; ashamed of their faith, of their God, of their church; ashamed of prayer, ashamed of being seen going to church, ashamed of confessing their Savior before the world, ashamed of being true Christians. With a seared conscience they deserted the Christian ranks and joined the host of Christ's enemies, walking the broad way that leads to eternal perdition. O may the Lord grant that not a single one of you shall ever do such a thing! May the Lord grant that on the last day every one of you shall be found standing at the right hand of Christ and hear His words "Come, ye blessed of my Father, inherit the kingdom prepared for you from the foundation of the world!"

Now to enable you to stand firm in all the temptations of life, let me call your attention to a precious Word of God. This Word of God you must always bear in mind and never forget as long as you live. And if this you do, you will certainly keep the great promise of the day. We find the same recorded Rom 1, 16:

I AM NOT ASHAMED OF THE GOSPEL OF CHRIST. FOR IT IS THE POWER OF GOD UNTO SALVATION TO EVERY ONE THAT BELIEVETH.

I.

"*I am not ashamed of the Gospel of Christ.*" Who said this? The greatest and most learned man among the apostles, St. Paul. Not always could he say, "I am not ashamed of the Gospel of Christ." There was a time when he hated and detested nothing more than the Gospel of Christ. That was before his conversion, when his name was Saul. When Stephen, the first Christian martyr, was stoned to death, Saul watched the clothes of those who did the killing and took great pleasure in the martyr's death. And then he searched the houses in Jerusalem and committed to prison all the Christians whom he could find. Not satisfied therewith, he proceeded to Damascus to persecute the Christians. But on his way to Damascus the most unexpected thing in the world came to pass. Saul, the persecutor of the Church of God, was converted to Christ in a most wonderful way. There was a light from heaven blinding him, and a voice, which called to him, "Saul, Saul, why persecutest thou me? — I am Jesus, whom thou persecutest." He was led

to Damascus now and remained blind for three days. But he
no more thought of persecuting the Christians. When his sight
had been restored by a Christian named Ananias, he was baptized and immediately began to preach in the synagogues that
Jesus is the Son of God. And from this time forth he was not
ashamed of the Gospel of Christ. He traveled from place to
place, and visited nearly all the principal cities of the Old World,
and wherever he appeared he proclaimed the Gospel that Christ
Jesus is come into the world to save sinners. He was beaten,
scourged, cast into prison, stoned for preaching the Gospel. He
was mocked, scoffed, laughed at by the would-be wise men of
this world, because he believed such a silly thing as was to their
minds the Gospel of Christ. But he never faltered, never
wavered, never changed his opinion. Boldly did he confess the
faith before Jews and Gentiles, before the rich and the poor,
before the learned and unlearned, even before princes and kings.
He was a man who was not ashamed of the Gospel of Christ.

My dear children, will you ever be ashamed of this Gospel?
O that I could fasten upon your souls in indelible characters,
never to be forgotten, always to be remembered, these blessed
words: *I am not ashamed of the Gospel of Christ.* In the
wide world which is before you and through which you are to
pass, you will meet with all sorts of people, and many of them
will be wicked people, godless people, people who will do all
they can to make you ashamed of the Gospel of Christ. They
will laugh at you and sneer at you because you pray, and go to
church, and lead a Christian life. They will tell you that you
were the greatest fools to believe what the Bible says, that in
this age of enlightenment and progress no intelligent person could
hold on to what is called the faith of our fathers, that there is
neither a heaven nor a hell, and that it were doubtful at least if
there be a God. And not only by infidels and open blasphemers
will you be approached; there will be others who will do all in
their power to make you ashamed of the Gospel. False prophets
also, men who claim to be Christians and pervert the true Christian doctrine, will endeavor to lead you astray. They will come
to you in sheep's clothing, that is, in Christian disguise, and pre-
tending to mean well with you. They will talk Scripture and
act as though they would only have you know the truth, and be

God's dear children, and be sure of heaven. But inwardly they are ravening wolves. Their real object, though themselves they might not be aware of it, is to make you ashamed of the Gospel of Christ. They will tell you that you must rely on the feelings of your own sinful heart for your conversion and salvation, or that you must gain heaven by your own earnest endeavors. And what is that but setting aside the Gospel of Christ? My dear children, be not deceived. You have been instructed in the pure doctrine of the divine Word, in God's Word and Luther's doctrine pure. Let no man take from you that which has been entrusted to you, whether he be an infidel or a false prophet. Remember Paul's words to the Galatians, "If any man preach any other Gospel unto you than that ye have received, let him be accursed."

But it will not suffice to confess the Gospel with the lips only. For in this case you would be numbered with those of whom Jesus says, "Not every one that saith unto me, Lord, Lord, shall enter into the kingdom of heaven." By your lives you must show that you are not ashamed of the Gospel of Christ. Once more, dear children, I warn you, at this solemn occasion, as I have warned you many a time, Beware of sin! Obey the commandments of the Lord. Never do such things or say such things as you would feel ashamed to say or do in the presence or with the knowledge of your father and mother. Always remember that God knows and sees everything you say or do. Do not neglect your daily prayers. He that prays no more is spiritually dead and is ashamed of the Gospel of Christ. Attend the divine services regularly. He that does not go to church and has no desire to hear the preaching of God's Word is not of God and plainly shows that he is ashamed of the Gospel of Christ. Come frequently to the Lord's Supper. He that will no more comply with Christ's command, "This do ye in remembrance of me," is no less ashamed of the Gospel of Christ than he who despises preaching and God's Word.

II.

And why should you not be ashamed of the Gospel of Christ? The apostle says, "*For it is the power of God unto salvation to every one that believeth.*"

Must you not say from your own experience that the Gospel of Christ is the power of God unto salvation to every one that believeth? Did not the Spirit of God often move your hearts by this precious Gospel? Have you not been led to say with St. Paul, "This is a faithful saying, and worthy of all acceptation, that Christ Jesus came into the world to save sinners"? When the inestimable love of God to us poor lost and condemned sinners in His beloved Son Jesus Christ was pictured to you, when you were shown how kind God is to us and how He longs and yearns to have all men to be saved, were you not sometimes made to feel as though you must leave this world and hasten to God and to your blessed Savior Jesus and be with Him forever?

O dear children, abide with Jesus, then, and with His precious Gospel. Solemnly I declare unto you in the presence of God and this congregation that the Gospel of Jesus Christ is the only thing which will make you happy, truly happy both in this life and in the world which is to come. The Gospel is the glad tidings of the grace of God in Christ Jesus, and as long as you sincerely believe in the Savior Jesus, you will find that the Gospel is truly the power of God unto your salvation. The Gospel will assure you that it was for your sins also that Jesus died on the cross, that, though you be and remain sinners as long as you live, your transgressions have all been blotted out, that God is pleased with you for His dear Son's sake, and that nothing can happen to you against the will of your good God and Lord. And when death comes and you must leave this world, the Gospel will enable you to face the last grim foe without fear and trembling. You will commend your soul into God's hands and depart in peace, falling asleep in Jesus.

Let this be your highest aim, then, and the main object for which you strive upon this earth, to obtain eternal salvation. What good will all the pleasures of life, all the honor among men, and all the riches of this world do you, if in the end you would have to share the rich man's fate in hell and torments? "What is a man profited, if he shall gain the whole world and lose his soul?" Therefore, "Fight the good fight of faith, lay hold on eternal life, whereunto you are also called, and have professed a good profession before many witnesses." Never be ashamed of the Gospel of Christ, which is the power of God unto salvation to every one that believeth. Be faithful, be faithful unto death, and you shall receive the crown of life, which the Lord has promised to them that love Him. Amen.

GOOD FRIDAY.

Dear dying Lamb, Thy precious blood
Shall never lose its power,
Till all the ransomed church of God
Be saved to sin no more.

LUKE 23, 46—48

And when Jesus had cried with a loud voice, he said, Father, into thy hands I commend my spirit and having said thus, he gave up the ghost   Now when the centurion saw what was done, he glorified God, saying, Certainly this was a righteous man   And all the people that came together to that sight, beholding the things which were done, smote their breasts, and returned.

IN THE LAMB THAT WAS SLAIN BELOVED FELLOW CHRISTIANS:

What shall we do? Shall we weep, or shall we rejoice? To-day we must sing,

Alas, and did my Savior bleed,
And did my Sovereign die?

And surely, if ever there was an occasion for shedding tears, it is the memorial day of Jesus' death, who died for us all and gave His life as a sacrifice to atone for our sins. But again we know, had Jesus not died for us, we should all be lost and suffer eternal misery in the world to come; and it was the death of our divine Lord that rescued us from this terrible doom and opened unto us the gates of paradise, that we might live in happiness and bliss which words cannot describe. Must not Good Friday, viewed from such a point, be unto us all a day of great rejoicing, since this day we were rescued from hell, and the gates of heaven were thrown open before us?

If ever a minister of the Gospel, whose sacred duty it is to proclaim the divine truth, must feel his own inability, it is on this day, when he is confronted with the most important event in the history of this world, when he is to dwell upon that which came to pass on Mount Calvary. "That spot is the center of all things. The streams of ancient history converge here, and here the river of modern history takes its rise. The eyes of patriarchs and prophets strained forward to Calvary, and now the eyes of all generations and of all races look back to it   The seeker after truth who has explored the realms of knowledge comes to Calvary, and finds at last that he has reached the center. The weary heart of man that has wandered the world over in search of perfect sympathy and love, at last arrives here and finds rest."

Still, though the theme be too high for human thought, we will venture forward, and occupy our minds with it, and receive into our hearts as much as we can of the truth that has a breadth and length, a height and depth which pass understanding. With the aid of God's Holy Spirit let us consider,

THE DEATH OF JESUS,

and see

    I. *How Jesus died*, and
    II. *What is the effect of His death.*

I.

Jesus died on the cross. His last suffering began the night before in the garden Gethsemane, where He felt the approach of this last terrible struggle and, in consequence thereof, His agony became so intense that drops of sweat intermingled with blood fell from His face upon the ground. During that sleepless night He was abused in various ways. He was taken captive, and led from one place to another; and in the morning He was delivered to the Roman governor Pontius Pilate. Then He was scourged, and crowned with thorns, and illtreated until He was almost exhausted from pain and fatigue. At last He was affixed to the cross, His hands and feet being pierced with nails.

But how did Jesus die on the cross? What was the cause of His death? Did He die from exhaustion? Did He hold on to life as long as He could, and did He grow weaker and weaker while hanging on the cross, until His strength failed Him and life passed away? Did life ebb away and vanish slowly and finally disappear, like a stream that is lost in the sands of the desert? St. Luke says, "*He cried with a loud voice.*" Loud did His voice ring through the darkness that attended His death on Mount Calvary. A man dying from exhaustion can scarcely utter a faint whisper in his last moments, and his attendants must strain their ears to catch his last words. Jesus, therefore, did not die from exhaustion. He was in full possession of His strength to the last minute. This is one of the most remarkable features connected with His death. It was so surprising to all who witnessed the

death of the divine Sufferer, that they did not know what to
make of it We are told, "They feared greatly," and even Pilate
marveled when he was informed that Jesus was already dead.
The crucified generally lingered from twelve to forty-eight and
even to seventy-two hours. And to see a crucified man die shouting with a loud voice, this was something unheard of.

Perhaps some one will say, What is the difference? Is it not
sufficient simply to know that Jesus died for us? What does it
concern us whether He died from exhaustion or in full strength?
My friends, that is not a matter of indifference. Had Jesus died
from exhaustion, had He held on to life until He had to give up
His soul, then it would be apparent that He was not God but a
mere man. Then the old serpent really would have conquered
Him in this great struggle. This crying with a loud voice shows
that Jesus did not die because He had to yield to the inevitable,
that His death was not an irresistible doom, but an act of His will.
Jesus certainly suffered and endured all the pains of a dying man.
But while mortal man dies because he *must*, Jesus, the Son of
God, died because He *would*. He certainly could have more than
outlived the thieves that were crucified with Him. But He died
voluntarily. Did He not say to the Jews, "I lay down my life
that I might take it again No man taketh it from me, but *I lay
it down of myself*"? Voluntarily Jesus surrendered Himself to
His enemies Never would they have been able to apprehend
Him, or to do Him any harm, had He resisted But it was of
His own will that He submitted to their ill treatment, to the
scourging, crucifixion, and all the sufferings It was of His own
will that He brought the great sacrifice of His life and gave up
the ghost.

We are also told which were His last words. The last words
of a dying friend or relative are dear to us, especially if they are
words of Scripture. Christ's last words were a quotation from
that most precious of all the books in the Old Testament, from
the thirty-first Psalm. "*He said, Father, into Thy hands I commend my spirit: and having said thus, He gave up the ghost.*"
Satan, who tempted the divine Sufferer in the wilderness, certainly was close at hand when Jesus was dying, and eager to seize
His departing soul. But Jesus plucked His spirit away from
these hostile hands and securely placed it in the hands of the

Father. His spirit was now in paradise, while His lifeless body
was in the hands of men, and was afterwards borne to the grave.
The terrible struggle was ended and the Man of Sorrows was beyond the reach of all the enemies, visible and invisible, by whom
He had been beset.

II.

And what is the effect of His death? Two most remarkable
incidents are recorded in our text, as a direct result of Jesus'
death, that of the centurion glorifying God, and that of the people
smiting their breasts.

We read, *"Now when the centurion saw what was done, he
glorified God, saying, Certainly this was a righteous man."*
How wonderful! The centurion was a heathen and his soldiers
had abused the divine Sufferer, had mocked Him, spitted on
Him, crowned Him with thorns, and illtreated Him from the
moment He fell into their hands until the very last. The centurion himself may have taken an active part in these proceedings,
at least he did not interfere. But what a change in this man as
soon as the head of the Man upon the cross drops upon His breast
and life departs! The centurion was standing opposite the cross
and watching the dying victim. Perhaps it had been dawning
upon his mind for some time that this Man must be, after all,
what He claimed to be. He had heard each of Christ's remarkable words on the cross. He had witnessed the wonderful conversion of the robber and the inexplicable signs of revolting nature, the darkening of the sun and the earthquake. Now that
Jesus' eyelids close in death he cannot keep his peace. He bursts
forth in praise of the dying Savior and calls Him the Son of God,
as the holy Evangelists report. Tradition says that this centurion's name was Longinus, that afterwards he became bishop of
Cappadocia, and ultimately died a martyr.

The other incident illustrating the effect of Jesus' death is
recorded in the words, *"And all the people that came together
to that sight, beholding the things which were done, smote their
breasts, and returned."* What a wonderful change did Jesus'
death produce in the hearts of the people! Misled by the elders
and chief priests, persuaded and moved by the heads of the
Jewish nation, they had been crowding around Pilate's judgment

seat like a pack of hungry wolves, shouting until they were hoarse, "Crucify Him! Crucify Him!" When Pilate finally consented to grant them their bloodthirsty wish, and washed his hands before the multitude, saying, "I am innocent of the blood of this just person, see ye to it," they all cried of one accord, "His blood be on us and on our children!" And even while Jesus was hanging on the cross the people that passed by railed on Him, wagging their heads and saying, "Ah, Thou that destroyest the temple and buildest it in three days, save Thyself, if Thou be the Son of God, come down from the cross." But what is it we hear of these same people when they behold the lifeless body of their victim? Their lips are sealed. They dare not say any more. But they smite their breasts, thereby indicating their sorrow and remorse for what they had been doing.

And this, my friends, is the effect of Jesus' death unto this day. When you fix your eyes upon the dying Lord, when you behold Him nailed on the cursed tree and pouring out His soul in death amid heartrending agonies and suffering, what will be the effect upon your soul, if you do not willfully resist and harden your own heart, as did the chief priests and elders? The first effect will be extreme sorrow, sorrow for your sins which have caused the innocent suffering and painful death of your divine Savior. You will be moved to smite your breast and to say, Oh, what have I done? I have nailed the Son of God to the cross! My sin it was which made Him suffer and die. And the second effect of Jesus' suffering and death is that you will glorify God, as did the centurion. You will praise God and His wonderful grace and mercy, the great love wherewith He so loved the world that He gave His only begotten Son to die that we might live. You will feel assured now, since Jesus died for you, that your sins are all wiped out, and that the penalty is fully paid for all your transgressions.

May the death of our dear Savior produce in us all this double effect; and thus we shall behold the Lamb of God which taketh away the sin of the world. Amen.

EASTER SUNDAY.

MARK 16, 1—8.

And when the sabbath was past, Mary Magdalene, and Mary the mother of
James, and Salome, had bought sweet spices, that they might come and anoint
him. And very early in the morning, the first day of the week, they came unto
the sepulcher at the rising of the sun. And they said among themselves, Who
shall roll us away the stone from the door of the sepulcher? And when they
looked, they saw that the stone was rolled away: for it was very great. And
entering into the sepulcher, they saw a young man sitting on the right side,
clothed in a long white garment; and they were affrighted. And he saith unto
them, Be not affrighted: Ye seek Jesus of Nazareth, which was crucified: he is
risen; he is not here: behold the place where they laid him. But go your way,
tell his disciples and Peter that he goeth before you into Galilee: there shall ye
see him, as he said unto you. And they went out quickly, and fled from the
sepulcher; for they trembled and were amazed: neither said they any thing to
any man; for they were afraid.

> Hallelujah, lo, He wakes,
> Lives o'er death and hell victorious,
> Earth in awe with trembling quakes,
> As the Hero rises glorious,
> He who died on Golgotha.
> Jesus lives! Hallelujah!
>
> Hallelujah, see the tomb,
> Ye who o'er His death are pining,
> Dry your tears, to joy give room,
> While the radiant sun is shining,
> Hear the angel's gloria,
> Jesus lives! Hallelujah!

Yea, "The stone which the builders refused is become the
head stone of the corner. This is the Lord's doing; it is marvelous in our eyes. This is the day which the Lord hath made;
we will rejoice and be glad in it." Thus did David rejoice in the
Old Testament when in the spirit, by divine inspiration, he saw
the glorious day in which the Lord's Anointed, whom the Lord
would not suffer to see corruption, would leave the tomb.

But we live in the time of the New Testament. What David
saw in the dim future has been fulfilled. Christ is risen from
the dead. He rose almost nineteen hundred years ago. What
thrills of joy should fill our hearts as we meditate on this glorious
event! Is there another day in the history of this world that has

brought greater blessings for all generations, past, present, and to come? another day that has brought greater deliverance for the fallen race? another day that has witnessed a greater miracle than the day of Christ's resurrection? Must we not exclaim with David, "This is the Lord's doing; it is marvelous in our eyes This is the day which the Lord hath made; we will rejoice and be glad in it"?

No greater miracle can be performed than to raise the dead. How astounded should we be if some one would take us to the cemetery and before our eyes would call forth and restore to life the decaying body of a friend who sleeps beneath the sod. This was done. Christ of His own power, and the prophets and the apostles in the power of God, did raise the dead. But what are these resuscitations compared with Christ's own resurrection? Christ was not passive in His resurrection He was not merely *raised* from the dead by the glory of the Father, He was active in His resurrection He Himself of His own power *rose* from the dead. Though Death had claimed Him and bound Him with his fetters and chains, though He was truly and perfectly dead, His heart ceasing to beat and not a spark of life remaining in His chilled and motionless body, He raised Himself, He freed Himself from Death's cold embrace, He restored Himself to life. Can there be a greater miracle?

But is Christ's resurrection beyond doubt? Is our joy on Easter day well founded? May not all these things be a dream? No, my friends, these things are not a dream. If ever we Christians can lift up our heads in triumph, and defy all unbelievers, and rejoice in the faith, it is on the day of Christ's resurrection. Let us consider with the aid of God's Holy Spirit,

THE FACT AND THE MEANING OF CHRIST'S RESURRECTION

I. *The indisputable fact,*
II. *The glorious meaning.*

I.

To be convinced of the fact of Christ's resurrection all doubts as to His actual death must be removed The theory has been advanced by the opponents of Christianity, that Christ could not have been actually dead, that He must have been in a trance, and that the coolness of the sepulcher must have restored Him to consciousness. How absurd and utterly impossible is this theory! What does our Gospel say? *"And when the Sabbath was past, Mary Magdalene, and Mary the mother of James, and Salome, had bought sweet spices, that they might come and anoint Him. And very early in the morning, the first day of the week, they came unto the sepulcher at the rising of the sun. And they said among themselves, Who shall roll us away the stone from the door of the sepulcher?"* Would these women have come to the sepulcher on Easter morn to anoint the body of Christ, to embalm His body, if the least doubt could have been entertained as to His actual death? if the slightest possibility had existed that He might be in a trance? O how anxious would they have been to think that He was merely in a deathlike sleep! But they knew that He was truly dead. Had they not seen Him bow His head on the cross and give up the ghost? Had they not seen with their own eyes how the soldier had thrust a spear into His side and pierced His heart, to make sure of His death? Is it not madness to claim that a man may be merely in a trance when the heart, the center of life, is destroyed?

The fact of Christ's resurrection is evinced by the empty tomb. We read, *"And when they looked, they saw that the stone was rolled away: for it was very great."* On Friday evening, when Jesus was buried by Joseph of Arimathea and Nicodemus, these women were present at the interment. They saw how their beloved Master was wound in a clean linen cloth with spices. They saw how the corpse was deposited in the new rock-hewn grave. They saw how a great stone was rolled to the door of the sepulcher. And what do they behold now on Easter morn? The stone is rolled away. The black, yawning opening of the sepulcher stares upon them. Its occupant is gone. How is this to be accounted for? Was the body stolen? The murderers of Christ had made theft impossible. They came to Pilate and said, "Sir, we remember that that deceiver said, while He was yet alive, After three days I will rise again. Command therefore that the sepulcher be made sure unto the third day, lest His disciples come by night and steal Him away, and say unto the people, He is risen from the dead: so the last error shall be worse than the first." Whereupon Pilate stationed a guard consisting of several soldiers at the sepulcher and had them seal the stone with the imperial Roman signet. How could the body be stolen in the face of such precautions? And yet the body was no longer there on Easter morn. The imperial signet was broken. The stone was rolled away. The watch had fled. The tomb was vacant.

And it was an angel from heaven that announced the fact of His resurrection We read, "*And entering into the sepulcher, they saw a young man sitting on the right side, clothed in a long white garment; and they were affrighted. And he saith unto them, Be not affrighted Ye seek Jesus of Nazareth, which was crucified: He is risen; He is not here· behold the place where they laid Him*" Can we, dare we doubt a fact which God makes known to us by one of His own messengers? Must not Christ's resurrection be an indisputable fact when we hear God informing us that He is risen from the dead? And how was this resurrection accomplished? Matthew tells us, "And, behold, there was a great earthquake: for the angel of the Lord descended from heaven, and came and rolled back the stone from the door and sat upon it. His countenance was like lightning and his raiment white as snow: and for fear of him the keepers did shake and became as dead men." Not did this angel assist Christ in His resurrection. Christ had risen already and had passed with the body of His glorious resurrection through the sealed stone. The angel's mission was merely to reveal the fact of His resurrection and to show by the vacant sepulcher that death no longer holds the Prince of Life.

Who can dispute the fact of Christ's resurrection? Did He not walk upon this earth for forty days after His resurrection, and show Himself to His disciples at different times and in various places, and eat and drink with them, and hold long conversations with them, and instruct them, until He bade them farewell and ascended into heaven before their eyes? A favorite theory with the enemies of Christianity is, that the disciples were deceived, that the Christ of the resurrection was a Christ of their own imagination. Is not this theory as absurd as it can be? Did not the risen Lord have the greatest trouble to convince His disciples of the fact of His resurrection? What trouble did He have with Thomas! How slow of heart were they all to believe! Another theory is, that the entire account of Christ's wonderful accomplishments, including His resurrection, is a piece of fraud, a

made-up story playing upon the credulity of the common people.
Is not this theory as absurd as the rest? Did the disciples of
Christ, and the writers of the New Testament in general, ever
show the slightest signs of willful or involuntary deception? Were
they not the most competent and truthful witnesses, who knew
what they said and meant what they said? And, finally, what
did the disciples get for preaching the crucified and risen Christ?
Were they not persecuted and put to death for their testimony?
Can we conceive how a whole class of men will go into poverty,
disgrace, persecution, death for the sake of a flagrant, willful lie,
rather than to tell the truth and thereby to avoid hardships and
ignominy, and to live? No; Christ's resurrection is a fact which
has been sealed with the heart's blood of the most trustworthy
witnesses, a fact which is even better established than most of the
universally credited events in the annals of history, a fact which
every man in this world, using his own common sense and not
blinded by prejudice, will and must admit, an indisputable fact.

II.

A glorious meaning is connected with this indisputable fact.
This is the second part of our discourse.

The angel said to the women, "*But go your way, tell His
disciples and Peter that He goeth before you into Galilee: there
shall ye see Him, as He said unto you.*" "As He said unto
you." The angel refers to Christ's words and tells the women
that now, after His resurrection, He would make true all that He
had said. And this is the meaning which, above all, is implied in
Christ's resurrection: Christ's Word is true, God's Word is true.
Christ's resurrection is the crowning evidence of our Christian
faith. Christ's resurrection puts the stamp of genuineness on
every word that is contained in the Bible. Even one of the bit-
terest enemies of Christianity that ever lived and who has, perhaps, done more harm than all the rest, calls the resurrection of
Christ "the center of the center—the real heart of Christianity,"
and adds, "It can scarcely be doubted that with it the truth of
Christianity stands or falls." With singular unanimity the enemies of the Christian religion have agreed that, if the resurrection of Jesus Christ from the grave be granted, all else that Christianity claims must be conceded. How triumphantly, then, can

we profess the faith! We can say to the unbeliever, Christ is risen from the dead; you cannot gainsay this fact; you yourself must and do admit it by your inability to disprove it. What, then, do your arguments amount to which you bring forth against the Christian religion? They amount to nothing, however cleverly they are made. They are as shining soap bubbles. And do you not behold the living monument which the risen Christ has erected in the world, that great monument which stands to this day and will stand unto the end of the world? Do you not behold the Christian Church, which is built on the fact of Christ's resurrection and in which He invisibly lives and reigns?

The meaning of Christ's resurrection, however, is not only to furnish us with an invincible proof for the truth of the Christian religion, but also to make us joyful in the faith and in the hope of eternal life. Three things that are contained in the third article of the Creed have been made sure by Christ's resurrection: the forgiveness of sins, the resurrection of the body, and life everlasting.

We must remember that Christ is our Substitute in everything He did, that for us He lived and led a life in strict obedience to the divine Law, that for us He died on the cross and suffered the punishment which we deserve for our transgressions, that for us He was laid in the grave and entered into the dark chambers of death. And as He was our Substitute in life and death so was He our Representative in His glorious resurrection. God raised His beloved Son from the dead and thereby solemnly declared that His great work for us is approved, that the Law is fulfilled for all men, that the penalty is paid for the sins of the world. O glorious meaning of Christ's resurrection! It means that our blessed Mediator and Redeemer has not only finished the redemption, but that His great work for us has also been accepted of the Father. It means that the divine subscription and seal has been affixed to the document which attests to us the remission of all our guilt. It means that God's wrath and anger upon our sins is appeased, that His stern justice is satisfied, that He is perfectly reconciled to the whole fallen world. It means that not only a universal pardon has been extended to all sinners from the beginning to the end of the world, but that even a solemn public absolution has been pronounced upon all the children of men, declaring them free from guilt and exempt from the damnation which for their sins they deserve. Does not Paul distinctly say that Christ "was delivered for our offenses and raised again for our justification," and "that God was in Christ, reconciling the world unto Himself, not imputing their trespasses unto them"? O the glorious meaning of Christ's resurrection! Come, whoever thou art, here is the forgiveness of all thy sins. God has sealed it unto thee in Christ's resurrection. Take it, receive it, accept it, believe it, and you have it.

And as Christ rose from the dead, so we await the resurrection of the body. We must all sink into our graves when our time has come. But if with the forgiveness of our sins we depart from this life, death shall harm us as little as it has harmed Christ. He says, "I am the resurrection, and the life: he that believeth in me, though he were dead, yet shall he live: and whosoever liveth and believeth in me shall never die." Death shall be for us nothing more than a sweet slumber. "This corruptible must put on incorruption, and this mortal must put on immortality." Christ rose from the dead, and we shall follow Him. He became the first fruits of them that sleep. O glorious day when our bodies shall come forth from the earth and be like unto the glorious body of the risen Christ, bodies that shall be freed from all infirmities, bodies that shall be spirit-like, as Christ's body was when after His resurrection He passed through the thickest walls and appeared and again vanished from sight! O glorious day when in our flesh we shall see God!

Finally, Christ's resurrection means for us life everlasting. St. Paul says Romans, chapter sixth, "Now if we be dead with Christ, we believe that we shall also live with Him: knowing that Christ being raised from the dead dieth no more; death hath no more dominion over Him." What a glorious life into which Christ entered by His resurrection! Not an enemy of His was permitted to behold and abuse Him. No sorrow filled His heart. Not a tear did He shed. But He ascended into heaven, He was received into the beautiful realms above amid the hallelujahs of the heavenly host, seated at the right hand of God the Father Almighty, and lives and reigns to all eternity. Thus shall we also enter into heaven, into life everlasting, into joy and bliss which no language can tell; for the Psalm says, "In Thy presence is fullness of joy : at Thy right hand there are pleasures for evermore," and our dear Redeemer Himself has given us the blessed promise, "My sheep hear my voice, and I know them, and they follow me: and I give unto them eternal life."

Praise, then, and glory be to our risen Lord, to our heavenly King, who liveth in us and we in Him, and who is the same yesterday, and to-day, and forever. Amen

EASTER MONDAY.

Luke 24, 13—35

And, behold, two of them went that same day to a village called Emmaus which was from Jerusalem about threescore furlongs. And they talked together of all these things which had happened. And it came to pass, that, while they communed together and reasoned, Jesus himself drew near, and went with them. But their eyes were holden that they should not know him. And he said unto them, What manner of communications are these that ye have one to another, as ye walk, and are sad? And the one of them, whose name was Cleopas, answering, said unto him, Art thou only a stranger in Jerusalem, and hast not known the things which are come to pass there in these days? And he said unto them, What things? And they said unto him Concerning Jesus of Nazareth, which was a prophet mighty in deed and word before God and all the people and how the chief priests and our rulers delivered him to be condemned to death, and have crucified him. But we trusted that it had been he which should have redeemed Israel: and beside all this, to-day is the third day since these things were done. Yea, and certain women also of our company made us astonished, which were early at the sepulcher, and when they found not his body, they came, saying, that they had also seen a vision of angels, which said that he was alive. And certain of them which were with us went to the sepulcher, and found it even so as the women had said: but him they saw not. Then he said unto them, O fools, and slow of heart to believe all that the prophets have spoken: ought not Christ to have suffered these things, and to enter into his glory? And beginning at Moses and all the prophets, he expounded unto them in all the scriptures the things concerning himself. And they drew nigh unto the village, whither they went: and he made as though he would have gone further. But they constrained him, saying, Abide with us: for it is toward evening, and the day is far spent. And he went in to tarry with them. And it came to pass, as he sat at meat with them, he took bread, and blessed it, and brake, and gave to them. And their eyes were opened, and they knew him; and he vanished out of their sight. And they said one to another, Did not our heart burn within us, while he talked with us by the way, and while he opened to us the scriptures? And they rose up the same hour, and returned to Jerusalem, and found the eleven gathered together, and them that were with them, saying, The Lord is risen indeed, and hath appeared to Simon. And they told what things were done in the way, and how he was known of them in breaking of bread.

BELOVED FRIENDS IN CHRIST.

The event of our Gospel occurred on the day of Christ's resurrection. As we are told in the tenth chapter of Luke, Christ, besides the smaller circle of twelve disciples, had another, a larger circle of seventy disciples. The two disciples that walked from Jerusalem to Emmaus in the afternoon of the resurrection day, most likely, belonged to this larger circle of Christ's disciples. The name of the one was Cleopas. The other some take for St Luke himself, who modestly withholds his name, while others take him for James, because St. Paul says in the first epistle to the Corinthians that Jesus after His resurrection appeared unto James also

Now these two disciples, as it seems, did not feel safe in the city. They were in a state of bewilderment. A rumor had been circulated that Christ was risen. This fills them with fright. They haste away from the miserable place where their dear Lord and Master was apprehended, condemned, crucified, and taken down from the cross a corpse; away from the dangerous spot where they themselves were in jeopardy of life and had to hide for fear of the Jews. Who could vouch for them that the chief priests and the elders of the people would not keep on in the course which they had begun? that they would not send out their servants to search for the disciples of Jesus of Nazareth and have them share the fate of their Master? So these two flee from the city. With the city behind them they feel more at ease, and the topic of their conversation, as they walk along, is the tragic end of Him whom they loved and of whom they had expected that He would redeem Israel.

And lo ! while they walk along in sad conversation a stranger overtakes them. They probably took him for one of those pilgrims who came from distant parts to attend the feast of the Passover, and who was now on the way home. It was Jesus, the risen Lord, and their eyes were holden that they should not know Him. So we find the risen Lord with the two disciples of Emmaus, walking with them and then abiding with them at Emmaus

The subject of our discourse shall therefore be with the aid of God's Holy Spirit,

THE RISEN LORD WITH THE DISCIPLES OF EMMAUS,

I. *As their companion,* and

II. *As their guest*

I.

"What manner of communications are these that ye have one to another, as ye walk, and are sad?" By this question the risen Lord interrupts the two disciples in their conversation. He cannot see them sad and depressed. He inquires about their trouble. Now had they recognized Him immediately, how great would have been their amazement and their joy. *"But their eyes were holden that they should not know Him."* So one of them, Cleopas, makes reply and expresses his surprise at this question, saying, *"Art Thou only a stranger in Jerusalem and hast not known the things which are come to pass there in these days?"* What he would say is this, Though a stranger, you ought to know what has been the talk of the town for the last days, and you ought to know something at least about that which is disturbing our minds. But Jesus, as if totally ignorant of those things, asks again and thus leads them to express the doubts and troubles of which He would make them free. *"He said unto them, What things? And they said unto Him, Concerning Jesus of Nazareth, which was a prophet mighty in deed and word before God and all the people: and how the chief priests and our rulers delivered Him to be condemned to death, and have crucified Him. But we trusted that it had been He which should have redeemed Israel: and beside all this, to-day is the third day since these things were done. Yea, and certain women also of our company made us astonished, which were early at the sepulcher; and when they found not His body, they came, saying, that they had also seen a vision of angels, which said that He was alive. And certain of them which were with us went to the sepulcher, and found it even so as the women had said: but Him they saw not."* What ignorance concerning Christ's person and office, what doubts and uncertainties, do their words betray! They admit that Jesus was a prophet mighty in deed and word before God and all the people; but what do they think of Him now? He is nothing more to them now than Jesus of Nazareth, condemned to death and crucified by the chief priests and rulers. Why do they not dare now to call Him the Son of the living God? Oh, they are very much in doubt about that now. They say, *" We trusted that it had been He which should have redeemed Israel."* They speak as if all their hopes and expectations were blasted. For what could they expect of a dead Messiah? Could a dead

Messiah redeem Israel, restore the glorious kingdom of God's chosen people, and reestablish the throne of David and Solomon? As long as He was alive they firmly believed in His future glorious kingdom, and though Christ informed them time and again that His kingdom was of a different nature than they supposed, that it was a kingdom in the hearts of men, still they held fast to their own fancies and pictured Jesus to their minds as a great worldly ruler to be honored by all the nations upon the earth. But now that He was dead, what could they hope for? It seems to them that all was a dream. Still there is something mysterious in this matter, something they cannot account for, something encouraging them not fully to abandon their hopes. This is the third day, and had not Jesus told them that on the third day He would rise again from the dead? And did not the women who had been at the sepulcher early in the morning claim they had seen a vision of angels, saying, He is alive? Had not some of their own number gone to the sepulcher and found it empty? This is what puzzles them and makes them feel uneasy.

Christ, their companion, hears what they have to say and then replies, "*O fools, and slow of heart to believe all that the prophets have spoken: ought not Christ to have suffered these things, and to enter into His glory? And beginning at Moses and all the prophets, He expounded unto them in all the Scriptures the things concerning Himself.*" What a powerful sermon that must have been! Christ removes all their doubts and sets aright all their prejudices. He shows that according to Moses and the prophets the Messiah had to suffer precisely those things which Jesus of Nazareth had suffered, and that He had to die and rise again from the dead. He expounds to them all the prophecies concerning the suffering and death of the Son of God, and thus convinces them by Scripture. O how their hearts burn within them now, how they hang upon the lips of their companion, how convincingly His words penetrate their soul! They are so charmed with their companion's conversation that they loathe to part when they arrive at their journey's end.

And I would have you note, my hearers, that unto this day the risen Lord is a comforting companion unto all His disciples upon life's pathway. Note well, this is the benefit, this is the blessing of Christ's resurrection that He is with us alway. He is invisibly, but really present, present not only according to His divinity, but according to His exalted humanity also, present in the body of His resurrection, present with us where we go and stand ; invisibly present both in the days of prosperity and in the days of adversity. He speaks to us in His holy Word, in the Scriptures, and we again can address Him in our prayers. He is our companion on life's pilgrimage, even as He was the companion of those two disciples on their way to Emmaus.

II.

But let us hear the continuation of our narrative We read, "*And they drew nigh unto the village, whither they went · and He made as though He would have gone further But they constrained Him, saying, Abide with us · for it is toward evening, and the day is far spent. And He went in to tarry with them*" Their companion now became their guest He had won their hearts They felt as if they could not part with Him. So they constrain Him, that is, they entreat and prevail upon Him, to remain and pass the night with them And their dear companion accepts their kind invitation He enters the house with them. Meanwhile the sun has gone down. Supper is served. And what do we hear? "*And it came to pass, as He sat at meat with them, He took bread, and blessed it, and brake, and gave to them.*" How strange ! He is their guest and still He assumes the duties of the landlord He takes the bread, pronounces the blessing, and distributes to the disciples. The defenders of the papacy claim that the risen Lord celebrated the holy communion at this instance, using merely the bread and not the wine They do so to support their erroneous practice of withholding the cup from the laity. But, in the first place, there is not the slightest intimation in the text that this was to be a celebration of the holy communion. And, in the second place, even if it was, the fact that Jesus distributed the bread certainly does not warrant the assertion that He declined to give them wine also. Does not St. Peter say in the epistle of the day that Jesus did both eat *and drink* with His disciples after His resurrection? Christ simply did here as He was wont to do when eating with His disciples. He said the prayer, brake the bread, and gave the pieces to His disciples.

And what was the effect of these proceedings? "*Their eyes were opened, and they knew Him.*" Like a flash of lightning it dawned upon them, it is the Lord. They knew Him at once. It was their dear Lord and Master given to them from the grave. The women had not been mistaken and the angels had told the truth. He was risen from the dead. He was again among the living. But how was it that they did not know Him before this, when they looked into His face and He spoke to them? Had He changed His appearance? Had He put on a different form? No; He was the same, His body was the same. But their eyes were holden that they should not know Him. Now, however, when He raised up His hands and gave them the bread, the veil drops from their eyes. They recognize Him. But before they can find words with which to express their amazement, He vanishes out of their sight. For now He had accomplished His object with them. He had removed their doubts concerning His suffering, death, and resurrection. He had, by eating with them, shown and proved that He was alive. Now they are surprised that they did not recognize Him before, and "*they say one to another, Did not our heart burn within us, while He talked with us by the way, and while He opened to us the Scriptures?*"

And what further effect did this manifestation of the risen Lord produce? Though they evidently had intended to stay in the village over night, and had asked their unknown companion to abide with them and not to proceed on His journey, because night was nigh at hand, "*they rose up the same hour and returned to Jerusalem.*" They were anxious to communicate the good news to their fellow disciples and to tell them how He was their companion on the way to Emmaus and their guest in the village. And when they arrived at Jerusalem, "*they found the eleven gathered together, and them that were with them, saying, The Lord is risen indeed, and hath appeared to Simon. And they told what things were done in the way, and how He was known of them in breaking of bread.*"

My friends, this also is one of the comforts and blessings of Christ's resurrection that He will be our guest as He was the guest of those disciples at Emmaus. Not only does the risen Lord accompany His faithful believers in the pathway of life, He enters their homes also and tarries with them invisibly, but really and truly. He even enters into their hearts by means of His Word and sacrament and makes them His holy temple It is not in vain we pray to Him at meat and say, "Come, Lord Jesus, be our Guest and let Thy gifts to us be blest " It is not in vain we call upon Him and say, Abide, O dearest Jesus, among us with Thy grace. It is not in vain we sing,

> Lord Jesus Christ, with us abide,
> For round us falls the eventide,
> Nor let Thy Word, the heavenly light,
> For us be ever veiled in night.

Even when death comes, we can depend on the invisible presence of our risen Lord and can grasp His divine hand, which will lead us safely through the dark valley of death into the heavenly paradise.

May the Lord, then, keep us steadfast in the faith, that we remain His true disciples : and we shall enjoy the benefits of His presence with us unto the end of our pilgrimage, until in Jerusalem our happy home shall be with Him forevermore. Amen.

FIRST SUNDAY AFTER EASTER.

JOHN 20, 19—31

Then the same day at evening, being the first day of the week, when the doors were shut where the disciples were assembled for fear of the Jews, came Jesus and stood in the midst, and saith unto them, Peace be unto you And when he had so said, he shewed unto them his hands and his side Then were the disciples glad, when they saw the Lord Then said Jesus to them again, Peace be unto you as my Father hath sent me, even so send I you And when he had said this, he breathed on them, and saith unto them, Receive ye the Holy Ghost whosesoever sins ye remit, they are remitted unto them, and whosesoever sins ye retain, they are retained But Thomas, one of the twelve, called Didymus, was not with them when Jesus came. The other disciples therefore said unto him, We have seen the Lord But he said unto them, Except I shall see in his hands the print of the nails, and put my finger into the print of the nails, and thrust my hand into his side, I will not believe. And after eight days again his disciples were within, and Thomas with them then came Jesus, the doors being shut, and stood in the midst, and said, Peace be unto you Then saith he to Thomas, Reach hither thy finger, and behold my hands, and reach hither thy hand, and thrust it into my side and be not faithless, but believing And Thomas answered and said unto him, My Lord and my God Jesus saith unto him, Thomas, because thou hast seen me, thou hast believed· blessed are they that have not seen, and yet have believed. And many other signs truly did Jesus in the presence of his disciples, which are not written in this book: but these are written, that ye might believe that Jesus is the Christ, the Son of God; and that believing ye might have life through his name.

BELOVED FRIENDS IN CHRIST:

Two manifestations of the risen Lord are recorded in our Gospel. The first manifestation took place on the day of Christ's resurrection and the second, eight days after.

Who could describe the feelings of joy felt by the whole assembly of Christ's disciples, when their Lord and Master suddenly appeared in their midst, while they were gathered together behind closed and bolted doors in the evening of the day of His resurrection? Did they expect Him this night and did they meet for this purpose? Hardly. But they knew that He was risen from the dead. The women who had been at the sepulcher early in the morning to anoint His body had found the sepulcher empty and had seen a vision of angels, saying that He was alive. Mary Magdalene had seen Him and spoken to Him. Simon Peter had seen Him. The two disciples of Emmaus had just arrived and reported how the risen Lord had walked with them to Emmaus and how He was known of them in breaking of bread. At divers places the Lord had appeared on this day, but most of His disciples had not seen Him as yet. O how great must have been their joy when suddenly, in the stillness of their assembly, they heard His familiar voice, saying, *"Peace be unto you!"* and when they looked up and saw Him standing in their midst!

This was His first manifestation in their assembly after His resurrection. And it was characterized by something peculiar. We are told, *"Then said Jesus to them again, Peace be unto you: as my Father hath sent me, even so send I you. And when He had said this, He breathed on them and saith unto them, Receive ye the Holy Ghost: whosoever sins ye remit, they are remitted unto them; and whosoever sins ye retain, they are retained."* In the most unambiguous terms Christ gives unto His disciples, that is, unto His Church upon earth, the power to forgive sins. This is the seat of the doctrine of absolution. And though this doctrine, according to which sins are to be forgiven by mortal man in the name of Christ, is looked upon by some as one of the remnants of the papacy in our church, still it is an undeniable doctrine of Christ and affords great consolation

But we shall not enter in detail upon this comforting doctrine to-day. There is another Sunday in the ecclesiastical year to be devoted to the contemplation of this doctrine. We shall apply our attention to the second part of our Gospel which treats of the unbelieving disciple Thomas in particular, and tells how the risen Lord, in His second manifestation, on this very day, the Sunday after Easter, healed this straying sheep of His flock of his unbelief. Accordingly, let us consider with the aid of God's Holy Spirit,

THOMAS' UNBELIEF CONCERNING CHRIST'S RESURRECTION,

and see

I. *How outspoken and, at the same time, how unreasonable was his unbelief,* and

II. *How the Lord rebukes him and, at the same time, convinces him of His resurrection.*

I.

We read, "*But Thomas, one of the twelve, called Didymus, was not with them when Jesus came. The other disciples therefore said unto him, We have seen the Lord.*" When Christ appeared unto His disciples the first time, on the day of His resurrection, all were present excepting Thomas. We are not told what was the reason of his absence. But his conduct may give us a clue. His conduct shows that he must have been on the point of severing his connection with his fellow disciples. Doubts had arisen in his mind concerning Christ, who had died on the cross. And while the other disciples entertained the same doubts, his case was more severe. He had evidently made up his mind that their cause was hopelessly lost, since their Master was dead. Why, then, should he go to their assembly? Perhaps he thought within himself, What foolishness to meet in a body and run the risk of being arrested by the officials! I shall have nothing to do with this thing and will not identify myself with these disciples any longer. Still, Thomas was not so far gone as to betray his fellow disciples, not so far gone as to tread in the footsteps of Judas, to go to the chief priests and elders and to tell them, I also was a disciple of Jesus of Nazareth, but now I renounce Him; and I am at your service, if you can make any use of me. No; he is still on good terms with the other disciples. They meet him and say, "*We have seen the Lord.*" They say to him, Thomas, the Lord is really risen from the dead. The rumors about His resurrection have proven true. He appeared in our midst. We have seen Him with our own eyes, and with our own ears we heard His sweet voice. In short, they related to him in detail all that came to pass in Christ's first manifestation after His resurrection. And what does Thomas say? Does he believe? Is his heart filled with joy at the Lord's resurrection? No; stubbornly he adheres to his doubts and says, "*Except I shall see in His hands the print of the nails, and thrust my hand into His side, I will not believe.*" He would say, "Do you think that I am so credulous as to deem it possible for a man who is dead to be moving among the living? Did I not see from a distance how His hands and feet were pierced with nails and how, after His death on the cross, one of the soldiers ran his spear into His side, producing a wound which necessarily would have killed Him, had He not already been dead, an ugly, gaping wound, large enough to lay a hand into it? Let me tell you, then, I shall not believe that He is alive until I shall place my finger in the print of the nails and thrust my hand in His open side." So outspoken was Thomas' unbelief, he would not believe the report of his fellow disciples, say what they would.

And how unreasonable was his unbelief. His fellow disciples were trustworthy men and not given to falsehood. This he knew. There was no reason whatever to doubt their words. It was wrong to discredit their statements. It was unreasonable to be suspicious in the face of their integrity and their emphatic assurances.

But this unbelieving Thomas has had his followers at all times. O how many that had been Jesus' true disciples for a time at length became offended in Christ because of His deep humiliation, shunned the assembly of their fellow Christians, and drifted away upon the waves and billows of their own unreasonable doubts and unbelief! "*We have seen the Lord,*" these words of Christ's disciples are addressed to all of us. The Lord's chosen apostles bear witness unto all those things that the Savior did and said. Jesus did not Himself write and publish a book containing His doctrine. But the Gospel which He did preach and the work which He did perform has been handed down to us by His chosen disciples, by His order and command, and it is written for all generations unto the end of the world in that divine book, the Holy Scriptures. The apostles were with the Lord Jesus from the beginning of His ministry. They were eyewitnesses of what He did. They accompanied Him whither He went. They heard His sayings. They witnessed His miracles "We have seen the Lord," believe in Him, all generations, this is what His disciples proclaim in the New Testament.

And what say the unbelieving Thomases? To this day they reply, Had our own eyes seen the miracles that are ascribed to Jesus in the New Testament, the healings of the sick, and the halt, and the maimed, and the blind, the stilling of the tempest, the feeding of thousands with a few loaves of bread, the calling forth of the dead, and all those wonderful deeds which, it is alleged, Christ performed; had we ourselves witnessed all those wonderful things presumably connected with His life, suffering, death, and resurrection, then should we not hesitate a moment, but believe in Him forthwith. But these things we did not see. They are incredible. They are inconsistent with the common order of things in this world. And therefore we do not believe.

Have these unbelievers who discredit the statements of the Bible any sound reason, any just cause to justify their unbelief? No: then unbelief is just as unreasonable as was that of Thomas, unto whom the disciples said, "We have seen the Lord." The writers of the New Testament were men who were both able and willing to give a truthful statement, to present things exactly as they were. They were able to do this because they themselves had seen those things and had heard what Christ said. And they were willing to tell the truth, since they were honest and upright men who would rather die than deviate from the truth. Had the disciples been men of dubious character, or had they gained some temporal advantage by the preaching of the Gospel, then perhaps might we suspect that they were impostors and had made up this story to gratify their own ambition, or to fill their pockets. But what earthly benefit did the apostles reap from the preaching of the Gospel? Did they gain any earthly advantage thereby? Did they gain fame, honor before men, riches, worldly possessions? No: they were hated, ridiculed, persecuted, banished, tortured, and put to death for their testimony. Who ever heard that a man with a rational mind would make up a lie and maintain that lie, that he might suffer and be put to death, while he could save his life if he told the truth? The apostles sealed with their own heart's blood the truthfulness of their report.

II.

And now, having heard how outspoken and, at the same time, how unreasonable was Thomas' unbelief, let us consider how the Lord rebuked and, at the same time, convinced him of His resurrection.

We read, "*And after eight days again His disciples were within, and Thomas with them: then came Jesus, the doors being shut, and stood in the midst and said, Peace be unto you.*" "Peace be unto you." This expression is to this day the common form of greeting among the nations in the East. But in the mouth of Jesus it signifies more. He is the Prince of peace, and where He is faithfully received, there strife and discord must depart and peace prevail. O let us remember this, my hearers; where there is not peace, where there is strife and discord among relatives, those of the same kin hating one another, husband and wife chiding another, children and parents opposing another, there Jesus cannot remain, and a peaceless heart cannot retain the true faith in the risen Lord, who is the Prince of peace.

But what do we hear of Christ after He has greeted His disciples? "*Then saith He to Thomas, Reach hither thy finger and behold my hands; and reach hither thy hand and thrust it into my side: and be not faithless, but believing.*" How wonderful! The Lord knows everything and all that came to pass within the last eight days between Thomas and the rest of the disciples. We are not told that He appeared unto any of them. But He knows every word that Thomas spoke. He knows his very thoughts. He knows all about his doubts and faithlessness. Straightway He approaches Thomas and commands him to satisfy his curiosity, to behold the pierced hands and to make sure of it that they were pierced with nails by passing his finger over the print, and to thrust his hand into His side. All of this was intended for a rebuke of Thomas' skepticism. The Lord did not approve of his stubbornness in not accepting the testimony of his fellow disciples. He, therefore, adds, "And be not faithless, but believing."

Unto this day the Lord rebukes those who are straying away into the barren fields of doubt and infidelity, those who are on the point of leaving His flock, because they are offended in this or in that, and things do not suit them. "Be not faithless, but believing." These words are intended for all the unbelieving Thomases in the world. Your faithlessness is not only unreasonable, so that you cannot satisfy your own mind with those poor arguments produced to overthrow the Gospel truth; it is sinful also. By your unbelief you abuse God's chosen messengers whom He has sent forth to proclaim His divine truth, and you stamp them as liars and impostors. By your unbelief you even make God a liar and place yourself above your divine Maker, contradicting His testimonies and refusing to acknowledge His supreme authority.

But what did Thomas do after the Lord had rebuked him for his unbelief? "*Thomas answered and said unto Him, My Lord and my God*" So taken with surprise was Thomas, he did not attempt to satisfy his curiosity and to stretch forth his finger and his hand. Christ had convinced him of His resurrection, so perfectly convinced him that both with amazement and with exultant joy he exclaims, "My Lord and my God!" He is completely cured of his doubts and unbelief Happy for him that he did not miss this assembly! Happy for him that he came once more and joined the gathering of those with whom he previously had been associating! O how miserable must he have felt all along in the state of unbelief, how despondent and comfortless ! And his fellow disciples were so confident, so joyful and happy. But now his soul is filled with delight; and Jesus says to him, "*Thomas, because thou hast seen me, thou hast believed: blessed are they that have not seen, and yet have believed.*"

Even now the risen Lord can and will convince the faithless who are found in the gatherings of His faithful disciples. It is true, no more does He appear visibly since the day of His ascension into heaven. No more does He visibly approach these unbelieving Thomases and show them His wounds. But He approaches them invisibly in His Word And by His life-giving Word He changes their hearts and minds and fills them with faith, with true, persevering, and unwavering faith. Whosoever will hear the Word of God and not willfully resist within himself, while he feels the convincing power of that Word, will soon find all his doubts and uncertainties removed; and the day will dawn and the day star will arise in his heart. He will believe, though he did not see, and will be blessed.

May the Lord, then, help us all sincerely and constantly to believe that Jesus is the Christ, the Son of God; and that believing we may have life through His name. Amen.

SECOND SUNDAY AFTER EASTER.

JOHN 10, 11—16.

I am the good shepherd: the good shepherd giveth his life for the sheep. But he that is an hireling, and not the shepherd, whose own the sheep are not, seeth the wolf coming, and leaveth the sheep, and fleeth: and the wolf catcheth them, and scattereth the sheep. The hireling fleeth, because he is an hireling, and careth not for the sheep. I am the good shepherd, and know my sheep, and am known of mine. As the Father knoweth me, even so know I the Father: and I lay down my life for the sheep. And other sheep I have, which are not of this fold: them also I must bring, and they shall hear my voice; and there shall be one fold, and one shepherd.

BELOVED FRIENDS IN CHRIST:

"*I am the Good Shepherd,*" says Jesus. He claims that He is the great Shepherd spoken of by the prophets. Jesus Christ is the great central figure of God's revelation. "To Him give all the prophets witness, that through His name whosoever believeth in Him shall receive remission of sins." And as Christ is the great central figure in the writings of the prophets, so is He the one great topic of the apostles' speech. St. Paul, therefore, says to the Corinthians, "I am determined not to know anything among you save Jesus Christ, and Him crucified."

Christ is the great central figure of Christianity also. What is it that constitutes a Christian? It is faith in Jesus Christ. Christ must be our one and all. As the heart is the center of bodily life, so is Christ the center of spiritual life. Christ is our sole Comfort, our Light in darkness, our Hope in distress, dearest to us in heaven and upon earth, our Jewel, our Treasure, our

Wealth, our Joy; our thoughts center in Christ Jesus as the one
great object of our desires. A Christian is a branch on the Vine,
which is Christ, and lives in Christ, and Christ in him. To begin
to be a Christian is to find Christ; to be a Christian is to abide
with Christ, to remain a Christian is to hold fast to Christ; to
die a Christian is to fall asleep in Christ

If a person desires to be saved he must come to Christ and
learn to place confidence in Christ alone. There is no other way
to eternal salvation. Christ is the door that leads to heaven, and
the only door Christ alone can save our immortal souls. Christ
alone can reconcile us lost and condemned sinners with the offended God and secure for us a dwelling place in the heavenly
mansions When, therefore, Christ is portrayed before our eyes
in the holy Scriptures, the aim and purpose is always to draw us
to Christ, to invite us tenderly to trust in Christ, to urge us to
place all our confidence in Christ, our beloved Savior. This is
done in our Gospel also, where Christ is portrayed as our Good
Shepherd and His great love toward us is made manifest The
subject of our discourse shall be with the aid of God's Holy Spirit,

CHRIST THE GOOD SHEPHERD,

I. *Giving His life for the sheep,*
II *Lovingly providing for the sheep,*
III *Restoring those who have strayed away*

I.

Jesus says, "*I am the Good Shepherd: the Good Shepherd
giveth His life for the sheep. But he that is an hireling, whose
own the sheep are not, seeth the wolf coming, and leaveth the sheep,
and fleeth, and the wolf catcheth them, and scattereth the sheep.
The hireling fleeth, because he is an hireling, and careth not for
the sheep.*" In this beautiful parable the Lord exhibits Himself
as the Good Shepherd as distinguished from a hireling who shows
no concern for the sheep entrusted to his care. What can you
expect of a careless hireling? Can you expect of him to put
his life at stake when the wolf rushes into the flock to create
havoc among the sheep? No; the hireling's first thought in case
of danger is not how to save the sheep, but how to save himself
and secure his own life. He runs, he flees at the top of his

13

speed, while the wolf has things his own way, tearing to pieces
the defenseless sheep and lambs and scattering the flock in all
directions. I am no such hireling, says Jesus. As a true shepherd will fight a wild beast that attacks the flock, and deliver his
sheep, and slay the brute, even though in the encounter he should
receive wounds that will cause death, so do I, at the price of my
own life, deliver my sheep and save them from the bitter pains
of eternal death. I am the Good Shepherd that giveth His life
for the sheep.

Now, to understand the meaning of this parable more accu-
rately, we must remember that by nature all men are as lost sheep.
Our first parents were sheep of the heavenly fold as long as they
were in the garden of Eden. Alas! they did not remain in this
blessed state. They were seduced into sin and fell a prey to
Satan. Since the fall all men are born in sin, and not a soul is
by nature born into the sheepfold of the Lord. By nature we are
all deaf to the voice of our Good Shepherd. We do not heed His
words. We do not follow Him. We seek our pleasures upon
the barren fields of the world and our nourishment among the
poisonous weeds that are so destructive to our eternal welfare.
By sin the whole human race has been scattered, as Isaiah says,
"All we like sheep have gone astray; we have turned every one
to his own way." And the wolf is lurking behind the bushes.
Satan is only waiting for man's temporal death, that he might
seize his victim and get eternal possession.

But behold! the Good Shepherd came. The eternal Son
of God appeared on the scene to deliver the fallen human race
from the jaws of the ravening wolf, to gather them into the kingdom of His grace, to pasture them, and finally to lead them into
Paradise. But oh, what did our Good Shepherd endure that He
might deliver the lost sheep! He that meant to be our Shepherd
had to fight the devil in our stead and die for us. This is what
the Lord Jesus Christ did for us as our Good Shepherd. As the
Lamb of God which taketh away the sin of the world He came
down from the throne of His divine glory and Himself assumed
the form of the lost sheep. He became man. He abstained from
the full use of His divine power. He became the same as we all,
with the exception of sin. He undertook the combat with the
wolf that was after the sheep, with the prince of darkness, the

enemy of our eternal welfare. In this fierce struggle our Good Shepherd not only put His life at stake, but actually did give His life. He died for us on the cross. O how must Satan have triumphed when our Substitute was slain, when the Good Shepherd was dying, as His blood was ebbing away! The Shepherd conquered, the whole flock seemed to be his. But things turned out contrary to Satan's expectation For behold, Christ rose again from the dead. His death now turned out to be the sheep's life, His blood-shedding their deliverance, His sacrifice their freedom. In giving for us His precious life our Good Shepherd redeemed us all from sin, from death, and from the power of the devil.

II.

But in the portrait of the Good Shepherd, as shown in our Gospel, the Lord is pictured also as lovingly providing for the sheep. Jesus says, "*I am the Good Shepherd, and know my sheep, and am known of mine. As the Father knoweth me, even so know I the Father and I lay down my life for the sheep.*" To understand these words the better we must know that in the East the sheep of different herders are usually taken to a great gathering-place, to a large fold, for the night. The shepherd is out all day, watching his sheep and leading them from pasture to pasture. But when night comes he brings them into the common enclosure, where they mix up with the sheep of other shepherds. Now in the morning, when the shepherds come to take their sheep out for the day, how does each shepherd know which are his sheep? He simply calls them, and they know his voice and follow him. The sheep will always follow their own shepherd and never hearken to the voice of a stranger.

Now Jesus says, "*I know my sheep,*" and when He says, "I know my sheep,' He does not merely mean to say that He knows which are the sheep that belong to His flock, but that He acknowledges them to be His own and lovingly provides for them. He pays attention to the special condition of every sheep in His flock. He knows their needs and helps them. He knows their ailments and heals them. He knows their faults and leads them in the paths of righteousness. He knows their dangers and protects them. He knows their weakness and upholds them.

O blessed is every one that has committed himself to the care of Jesus! Blessed is every one that knows the Good Shepherd, knows Him by faith and trusts in Him! As a good shepherd provides for his sheep, so will Jesus lovingly provide for him. A good shepherd will wash his sheep from uncleanness; and so does Jesus wash off the sins of His sheep in holy Baptism. "Though their sins be as scarlet, they shall be as white as snow; though they be red like crimson, they shall be as wool." A good shepherd will take his sheep to the pastures, where they will find ample nourishment, and to the fresh waters, where they may quench their thirst; and so does Jesus lead those who are His own into the green pastures of His precious Gospel and to the refreshing water of life. He says to them, "Come unto me all ye that labor and are heavy laden, and I will give you rest." "If any man thirst, let him come unto me and drink." He does even more than any shepherd will do. He gives us Himself, His own body and blood, to eat and to drink in the Lord's Supper. A good shepherd will deal tenderly with his sheep. He will let the dogs bark at them and chase them from some dangerous place. But the dogs are not permitted to hurt and to harm them. And so does Jesus deal with those who are His own with the utmost caution and tenderness. His sheep know what they may expect of their Good Shepherd—nothing but love, grace, mercy, kindness. At times He does permit the Law to frighten them, so that thoughts like these will trouble them, Ah, are you not too great a sinner? can you expect to be received into heaven? But He thereby merely keeps them from carnal security, and soon again they can rejoice in His love. At times He permits trials and afflictions to harass His dear children, but they know, it is for their own eternal good, that with the unbelieving world they should not be condemned. Could any shepherd provide more lovingly for His sheep than the Good Shepherd, the Lord Jesus, provides for His flock?

III.

But He also restores those who have strayed away. Jesus says, "*And other sheep I have, which are not of this fold: them also I must bring, and they shall hear my voice; and there shall be one fold, and one Shepherd.*" The meaning of these words is obvious. The sheep of this fold are the Jews. Christ was sent to the lost sheep of the house of Israel. Here we find also who were the hirelings spoken of in the beginning of the parable. The hirelings of whom Jesus complains that they take not the proper care of the sheep, were the spiritual rulers of Israel, the chief priests and scribes, who misled the people, contending that Jesus is not the Christ. The other sheep which are not of this fold are the Gentiles. The Gentiles also Jesus promised to restore, so that there should be no more distinction before God between Jews and Gentiles, but all should constitute one fold, or, rather, one great flock under His shepherding care.

Behold the great love of our Good Shepherd to all men, to the whole fallen human race. The Gentiles in the time of the Old Testament did wrong when they did not come into the fold of Israel and did not join God's chosen people. They had strayed away from the Shepherd's care and went their own ways in superstition and idolatry. But Christ declares that from the Gentiles also He will call His sheep. There are those who are without Christ, without His Word, without His grace, roaming about in the world without a Savior. They are all His, inasmuch as He has bought them at the price of His precious blood; and not a human soul would the eternal Son of God see eternally lost. He loves even the greatest sinner, loves him because he has an immortal soul which has been redeemed with His blood. When a good shepherd misses a sheep, he will search for that lost sheep and spare no pains to find it. And when he finds the poor sheep caught in a thicket and in the hedges, or in some ravine, sore and bleeding, O how great is his joy to find it! Jesus does the same. If you are a lost sheep, He spares no pains to restore your soul. He calls you by the sweet voice of the Gospel. His voice may reach you and sound in your ears and penetrate to the very depth of your soul when you are ever so far away from Him, upon forbidden paths and in the ways of sin and shame. And when, at last, He does find you, when you answer His voice and return from the ways of sin and death to your own Good Shepherd, He will not chide with you, He will not punish you. With gladness He restores you to the fold, and even the angels in heaven take their harps and sing songs of praise when the sinner comes to repentance

May the Lord, then, grant us all His grace, that we abide
with Jesus, our Good Shepherd, and say from the depth of
our souls,

> Let me be Thine forever,
> Thou gracious God and Lord,
> Let me forsake Thee never,
> Nor wander from Thy Word.
> Lord, do not let me waver,
> But give me steadfastness,
> And for such grace forever
> Thy holy name I'll bless.
>
> Amen.

THIRD SUNDAY AFTER EASTER.

JOHN 16, 16—23.

A little while, and ye shall not see me: and again, a little while, and ye
shall see me, because I go to the Father. Then said some of his disciples
among themselves, What is this that he saith unto us, A little while, and ye
shall not see me: and again, a little while, and ye shall see me: and, Because
I go to the Father? They said therefore, What is this that he saith, A little
while? we cannot tell what he saith. Now Jesus knew that they were desirous
to ask him, and said unto them, Do ye enquire among yourselves of that I said,
A little while, and ye shall not see me: and again, a little while, and ye shall
see me? Verily, verily, I say unto you, That ye shall weep and lament, but the
world shall rejoice: and ye shall be sorrowful, but your sorrow shall be turned
into joy. A woman when she is in travail hath sorrow, because her hour is
come: but as soon as she is delivered of the child, she remembereth no more
the anguish, for joy that a man is born into the world. And ye now therefore
have sorrow: but I will see you again, and your heart shall rejoice, and your
joy no man taketh from you. And in that day ye shall ask me nothing.

BELOVED FRIENDS IN CHRIST.

The Lord Jesus spoke these words in the night in which He
was betrayed. He had already told His disciples in plain words
that He must suffer and die. Only a few days before He said to
them, "Behold, we go up to Jerusalem, and all things that are
written by the prophets concerning the Son of man shall be accomplished. For He shall be delivered unto the Gentiles, and
shall be mocked, and spitefully entreated, and spitted on: and
they shall scourge Him, and put Him to death: and the third
day He shall rise again." And now He seeks to impress on their

minds that the time is at hand. He says, "*A little while, and ye shall not see me: and again, a little while, and ye shall see me, because I go to the Father.*" But the disciples could not comprehend this matter. They understood His words. They probably knew even now that He meant to refer to His suffering, death, and resurrection. But they did not understand the things. Why? Because there was a fixed notion in their minds that, as the Messiah, Jesus must do what the children of Israel expected of their Messiah, that He must establish a glorious worldly kingdom and be the temporal ruler of God's people. The words, "*A little while,*" were especially offensive to them. How was it that Jesus would remain with them only for a little while and then go to the Father? They expected Him to remain with them a great while longer. They had escorted Him into the city of Jerusalem amid the shouts and hosannas of the multitude and had come to stay, to see their beloved Master seated upon the throne of David and Solomon, to share His glory, and to be made judges ruling the twelve tribes of Israel, and, in general, to enter upon an era of happiness and prosperity for the whole nation. And was He now about to leave them in a little while? It could not be. "*They said therefore, What is this that He saith, A little while? we cannot tell what He saith.*" But Christ does not make an attempt to explain to them the expression, "A little while." He knows, it would be of no avail in their present state. He simply tells them what will be the effect of His withdrawal and reappearance, saying to them, *Verily, verily, I say unto you, That ye shall weep and lament, but the world shall rejoice; and ye shall be sorrowful, but your sorrow shall be turned into joy.*" Sorrow and joy was in store for them: sorrow, when their beloved Lord and Master would leave them and sink into the grave, and joy, exceeding joy, when they should again behold Him in the body of His glorious resurrection.

This was not only said for the disciples of Christ at that time. Unto the end of the world Christians must expect both sorrow and joy. Let us consider with the aid of God's Holy Spirit,

THE SORROW AND THE JOY OF A CHRISTIAN,

and see

    I. *The Christian's sorrow,* and

    II. *The Christian's joy.*

I.

Many people hold that Christians should not be burdened with sorrows. They enter the Christian ranks and profess the Christian faith, and now they expect that God should so rule and govern things that their lives glide along like a smooth stream, without any trouble or hindrance. They expect of Him that He must keep away from them every calamity. When some smaller evil comes upon them, they may reconcile themselves to that and get over it, thinking that it is something which, after all, they deserve for their sins. But when they are made the victims of some great misfortune, when some great calamity has befallen them, causing immense sorrow and grief, they murmur against their divine Maker. They say, How can a gracious and merciful God send down upon us, while we are trusting in Him, such misfortunes? No; there is no Father in heaven, no divine Ruler of the universe, for if there were, we would not be in sorrow and mourning.

The fault with such people is that they expect of God something which He never promised to those who trust in Him. When and where did God promise that Christians should never be burdened with sorrows in this world? He promises you His divine protection. He promises to care for you, to provide for you, to give His holy angels charge over you, and not to tempt you above what you are able to bear. But nowhere does He promise to withhold from you all sorrows. On the contrary, Jesus says to His disciples in our text, "*Verily, verily, I say unto you, That ye shall weep and lament, but the world shall rejoice.*" Can you rightly expect greater favors from the Lord than His disciples? Can you say that they deserved more punishment than you? Does not St. Paul say distinctly, "All that will live godly in Christ Jesus shall suffer persecution"? Does he not say of himself and of all Christians, "Through much tribulation we must enter into the kingdom of God"? And look at the example of God's dear children in the Holy Scriptures. Look at men like Job, and the prophets, and the apostles. What afflictions, what griefs, what sorrows fell to their lot! No, Christians are not exempt from the common ills of mankind. They are subject to the same ailments, and diseases, and misfortunes, and calamities that the rest of the children of men must bear in this life. As a rule, they must even bear more than the unbelieving children of this world. They are the cross-bearers They must endure the reproach of the unbelieving world. They must suffer for the very reason that they are Christians. Christ says to them, "In the world ye have tribulation."

But these are not the greatest sorrows of Christians, for they are sorrows concerning only temporal things and the mortal body. The greatest sorrow of a Christian is when he is troubled about the welfare of his immortal soul. Christians must sometimes meet with the same experiences as did the disciples of Christ during the three days when Christ was taken from them, while He was lying in the grave O how must the disciples have felt then! Their hearts must have been filled with sorrow to overflowing. They still clung to Christ, they loved Him; but they felt as if all their hopes and fondest expectations were blasted. They had hoped that it was He who should redeem Israel, but what could they hope for now? Death glared from the eyes that had looked upon them so lovingly. The lips were silenced that had spoken to them words of eternal life. The tomb had received Him whom they had followed and for whom they had left everything They could see Him no more, and in their minds He was no longer the great wonder-worker, but a mangled corpse. All their comfort in life and in death was now gone Such profound sorrow they had never tasted before And to this day the greatest sorrow of Christians is when they are made to feel as if they had no Savior, when Jesus hides from them, as it were. They feel no joy. They cannot rejoice in their salvation It seems to them that they are not Christians, that they have not faith and that they have no right to appropriate to themselves the promises of eternal life. It seems to them that Jesus is dead for them, that He can do nothing for them, and that they have been trusting in Him in vain. They take their Bible and read it, and even the divine Word does not impress their soul They seek relief in prayer, and God does not seem to hear them. Their soul is shrouded in darkness They feel as if they were fast sinking to hell They must say with Job, "I cry unto Thee and Thou dost not hear me, I stand up and Thou regardest me not. Thou art become cruel to me· with Thy strong hand Thou opposest Thyself against me." and with

David, "I am troubled, I am bowed down greatly, I go mourning all the day long."

But the comforting promise given to Christians is, that their sorrow shall not long endure. How long did the disciples mourn the loss of their Master? Only a little while, only three days. And to this day God will not put heavier burdens upon His dear children than they are able to bear, and will deliver them shortly. All their troubles and sorrows must come to an end; and only for a little while must they suffer in the furnace of tribulation, that their faith may be tried and that they may be made strong in the Lord and in the power of His might. Then is their sorrow turned into joy.

II.

This is the second point of our discourse, the joy of Christians.

Which is the joy of Christians? Some people hold that to be a Christian is to be always sad and gloomy, to find fault with almost everything that is going on in the world, to find no joy whatever in earthly things, but to spend their lives in sadness and sorrow. But does not God say distinctly to the Christians, "Rejoice with them that do rejoice"? Yea, more than this, the apostle says, "Rejoice in the Lord alway, and again I say, Rejoice." The joy of the world is, at best, but an imperfect and fleeting thing.

Man's desire for happiness can never be perfectly satisfied by the joys of this life. He will always find something lacking to make his joy complete; and generally he will find a few drops of gall in the cup of pleasure. And what do worldlings say who have been tasting of nearly all the pleasures under the sun? They tell us that in the midst of their pleasures they can find no real and lasting enjoyment. All the joys of this life pass away. He that is laughing to-day may be weeping to-morrow. Finally, death comes and ends all pleasures.

A Christian, therefore, does not seek his happiness in the things of this life. For the true joy of a Christian is of a higher order. The Christian's joy is described in the words of Jesus, "*I will see you again, and your heart shall rejoice, and your joy no man taketh from you.''* The Christian's greatest joy is the possession and enjoyment of Jesus. He can say,

> Jesus, Thou art mine forever,
> Dearer far than earth to me,
> Neither life nor death shall sever
> Those sweet ties which bind to Thee

All the joys of life are as nothing compared to this joy in Jesus the Savior. He alone is truly happy who is made sure that his sins are forgiven, that God is his dear Father, and that he is God's beloved child, and that heaven is his home And of these things is every one made sure who truly believes in the Savior Jesus. Joyfully can the Christian lift up his head, even in the midst of afflictions and tribulations, and say to his heavenly Father, Thou dost love me, Thou lovest me even now, and I know that "the sufferings of this present time are not worthy to be compared with the glory which shall be revealed in me " Joyfully can the Christian face the dark future before him He knows that that future will be bright in the end, and that for him the day will come of which Jesus says, *"And in that day ye shall ask me nothing,"* an eternal day of joy and glory, a day in which he shall find all those mysterious dealings of God with him in this life explained to his perfect satisfaction.

May the Lord, then, fill our hearts with this joy which surpasses all human thought and understanding, and may we all say to our beloved Savior Jesus,

> Thou alone art all my Treasure,
> Who hast died that I may live;
> Thou conferrest noblest pleasure,
> Who dost all my sins forgive

Amen.

FOURTH SUNDAY AFTER EASTER.

JOHN 16, 5—15.

But now I go my way to him that sent me; and none of you asketh me, Whither goest thou? But because I have said these things unto you, sorrow hath filled your heart. Nevertheless I tell you the truth, It is expedient for you that I go away: for if I go not away, the Comforter will not come unto you; but if I depart, I will send him unto you. And when he is come, he will reprove the world of sin, and of righteousness, and of judgment: of sin, because they believe not on me; of righteousness, because I go to my Father, and ye see me no more; of judgment, because the prince of this world is judged. I have yet many things to say unto you, but ye cannot bear them now. Howbeit when he, the Spirit of truth, is come, he will guide you into all truth: for he shall not speak of himself; but whatsoever he shall hear, that shall he speak: and he will shew you things to come. He shall glorify me: for he shall receive of mine, and shall shew it unto you. All things that the Father hath are mine: therefore said I, that he shall take of mine, and shall shew it unto you.

BELOVED FRIENDS IN CHRIST:

In our Gospel Jesus promises to His disciples His Holy Spirit. He had informed them that He would soon leave them and go to the Father, that is, that by His death, resurrection, and ascension He would return to whence He had come, to heaven. Then they should see Him no more. He would no more be with them visibly, to guide and to teach them as He had done during the three past years. Though the disciples did not comprehend the full meaning of their Master's words, yet from His remarks they gathered so much that He was about to leave them; and this made them sad. But Jesus tells them, "*Nevertheless I tell you the truth, It is expedient for you that I go away; for if I go not away, the Comforter will not come unto you; but if I depart, I will send Him unto you.*" And then He informs them what the Comforter, the Holy Spirit, would do: that He would guide them into all truth, and show them things to come, and, above all things, that He would glorify Jesus, that is, extol and exalt Jesus in their own hearts.

And how gloriously was this promise fulfilled! On the day of Pentecost the Holy Ghost came down upon them visibly in the shape of tongues as of fire. And what a wonderful change did He produce in these men! He guided them into all truth, showed them things to come, and glorified Jesus. From the moment they were filled with the Holy Ghost, they were imbued with a profound knowledge of the great deeds of God for the salvation of man, and were enabled to proclaim those great deeds in languages which they had never learned. From the moment they were filled with the Holy Ghost they were endowed with dauntless courage and with power from on high. Boldly they stood up before Jewish and Gentile mobs, before kings and rulers, and bore witness of what they themselves had heard and seen of Jesus. From the moment they were filled with the Holy Ghost Jesus was glorified in their hearts. They saw His glory now. They no longer expected Him to establish a worldly kingdom and be a worldly ruler. They saw in Him the exalted Lord sitting at the right hand of God the Father Almighty, from whence He shall come to judge the quick and the dead, and there was not another name that sounded sweeter in their ears than the name of Jesus. Such was the operation of the Holy Ghost upon Christ's disciples. And to this day God's Holy Spirit has His divine work among Christians in particular. We know that to the Spirit of God we owe our conversion and salvation, that it is the Spirit who calls us by the Gospel, enlightens us with His gifts, sanctifies and keeps us in the true faith

But the Spirit does not only deal with the followers of Christ in particular. He "reproves the world," as Christ says in our Gospel, that is, He also addresses the children of men in general And what Christ says here about the Spirit's dealing with the world does not merely apply to unbelievers, but to Christians also, inasmuch as they are still in the world and retain their sinful flesh as long as they live upon the earth. Let us consider with the aid of God's Holy Spirit,

THE HOLY GHOST'S REPROVAL

I. *Concerning sin,*
II. *Concerning righteousness,* and
III *Concerning judgment.*

I.

Jesus says, "*And when He (the Spirit) is come, He will reprove the world of sin, and of righteousness, and of judgment.*" Here we must inquire into the meaning of the word "reprove."

The word "reprove," as used in this connection, does not mean merely to censure, but to convict. In reproving the world the Holy Ghost brings home to the children of men their errors, and makes them see that they are open to the condemnation of their conscience.

And of what does the Holy Ghost reprove the world? In the first place, of sin. I call your attention to the fact that, though the Holy Ghost is opposed to all sins, yet Jesus does not mention particular sins, He does not publish a long list of sins of which the Holy Ghost should reprove the world. No; He mentions but one sin, one particular sin. He says, "*Of sin, because they believe not on me.*" Unbelief—that is the sin of which the Holy Ghost reproves the world.

Is there a sin which is more widespread, more universal than unbelief? Like a disease, like a pestilence, this sin has seized upon the world, and there is no abatement. To this day the overwhelming majority of the inhabitants of this world is composed of heathen, Mohammedans, and Jews. And look at our own country. It has been said that this is a Christian nation. And what do our statistics say? They have disclosed the startling revelation that only one third of the number of our inhabitants are members of or attendants at Christian churches. Think of it, there are always two unbelievers to one professed believer. And if the professed believers were sifted down and only the true believers in Christ Jesus were to remain, how would the number of believers dwindle down! How many members are there of Christian churches who have never known what faith is in Christ Jesus, or have lost the faith! To this day it is true what John says of Jesus, the Light of the world, "He was in the world, and the world was made by Him, and the world knew Him not." Unbelief is the great universal sin, and, therefore, the Holy Ghost must reprove the world of sin that they do not believe on the Lord Jesus.

And unbelief is a sin which is not acknowledged to be sin by the children of this world. People will readily admit that it is a sin to lie and to steal; but tell an unbeliever that it is a sin not to believe in the Lord Jesus Christ, and he will laugh you in the face. He will say, Are not my thoughts my own? Am I responsible for my convictions? Can I be blamed for not believing as long as I am not convinced of the truth of the Gospel? On the contrary, would it not be a moral wrong for me to simulate, to pretend faith without conviction? But before the tribunal of the Holy Ghost the unbeliever's arguments in defense of his infidelity are reduced to a folly. By the Word of God the Holy Ghost can make the unbeliever tremble and perceive that unbelief is indeed *the* sin, the greatest sin in the world, the sin which makes all the rest of sins remain unforgiven, the sin which is sure to lead into eternal condemnation. He will address him and say, How dare you make light of your unbelief? It is nothing less than rebellion against your divine Maker. You have thereby been giving the lie to your God. You have discredited His divine Word and despised your own salvation. You have sinned against God and against yourself, rejecting your own eternal welfare, for "he that believeth and is baptized shall be saved, but he that believeth not shall be damned"

O my friends, let us all be on our guard against this terrible sin which is sure to hurl the unbeliever into eternal condemnation. Many a Christian believed for a while, and in the time of temptation he fell away. Many a one has made shipwreck of faith. Let us remain continually under the influence of God's Holy Spirit, hearing the Word of God and searching the Scriptures, and we shall keep the faith. It is to the Christians that St. Paul says, "Let him that thinketh he standeth take heed lest he fall," and, "Examine yourselves, whether ye be in the faith: prove your own selves."

II.

The Holy Ghost, secondly, reproves the world of righteousness. "*Of righteousness,*" says Jesus, "*because I go to my Father, and ye see me no more*" Now what righteousness is this? What has righteousness to do with Christ's going to the Father and being seen no more? We must remember that Jesus said this shortly before His suffering and death. His going to the Father led over Calvary. He did not mean simply that He must die and depart from this world, but that He must go to the Father by way of sacrificing His life for the sins of the world, that by perfect obedience unto death He must work out a spotless righteousness for all men The righteousness, then, of which

the Holy Ghost reproves the world is that righteousness which
Jesus wrought by His sinless life and vicarious suffering and
death, that righteousness of which we say,

> Jesus, Thy blood and righteousness
> My beauty are, my glorious dress.

And why does the Holy Ghost reprove the world of this
righteousness? Because the world does neither know of nor care
for this righteousness. Very many of the children of this world
never think of preparing for the hereafter. They live and die
like brutes. And those who do believe in a blessed hereafter seek
to get there by their own righteousness. By nature we all do not
know otherwise and do not think otherwise than that, if there
is another life beyond the grave, we must be good and do good
in this world, that we may obtain eternal life; we must do at
least the best we can, and rely on the mercy of a good God for
the rest: in short, we must do the work ourselves and expect
heaven as a reward for our good deeds.

Now the Holy Ghost reproves the world concerning the righteousness of Christ which He has wrought out for the whole sinful world. He addresses man by the Word of God and says to
him, How dare you expect to gain heaven by your own righteousness? You are a sinner and before God all your righteousnesses
are as filthy rags. You are born in sin, and polluted with sin,
and corrupted from head to foot. All that you are, say, and do,
is sin. Your very hope of expecting eternal life for your own
good deeds is sin, an act of disobedience. You are lost, eternally
lost, if by your own sinful righteousness you attempt to gain
heaven. But lo! God has made provision for you in His great
love. He would not have you die in your sins and be eternally
lost: He sent His beloved Son into the world to work out for
you that righteousness which you cannot afford, because you are
a sinner. He had Him lead for you, in your stead, a life without sin, and had Him atone for your transgressions by His suffering and death on the cross. And now you must appropriate to
yourself this righteousness of Jesus the Savior; you must believe
in Christ and build all your hope for a blissful hereafter on Jesus'
blood and righteousness. That is the way to eternal salvation,
and the only way; there is no other.

Let us all make sure of Christ's righteousness, then. Also Christians are sometimes tempted to forget that it is Jesus alone who has saved them, and to seek help elsewhere than in the wounds of Him who died that we might live. Let us always bear in mind that there is no salvation in any other, and that there is none other name under heaven given among men, whereby we must be saved, but the blessed name of Jesus.

III.

The Holy Ghost reproves the world, thirdly, of judgment. *"Of judgment,"* says Jesus, *"because the prince of this world is judged."* The prince of this world is the devil. He is judged. Judgment was pronounced against him when Jesus suffered and died and rose again from the dead. By sin Satan had dominion over all the children of men. He was their master. They were bound to him by the fetters of sin and could not escape from the prison of hell which he had prepared for them. But by Christ's going to the Father, by Christ's glorious work of redemption, the tie has been removed by which fallen man is bound to the prince of darkness. Sin is taken away. It is no more imputed to those who believe in the Redeemer. The old serpent's head is bruised and crushed, and he has no longer any power over man, unless man himself prefers to remain in his power and willingly serves his greatest foe. Satan has been dethroned and sentenced by our Redeemer's blessed work. The sentence will be executed on the last day, which may come upon the world at any time.

And why does the Holy Ghost reprove the world of judgment because the prince of the world is judged? That men might know whom they are really serving in sin and unbelief: the devil, from whose power they have actually been rescued by the Redeemer; the devil, who is sentenced to eternal torment. The Holy Ghost addresses man by the Word of God and says to him, What folly to serve a master whom you are not obliged to serve, a master who treats you even worse than the bloodiest tyrant, who for a short while delights you with the pleasures of sin, and then makes you suffer for it, suffer often already in this life and then suffer eternally! Behold the judgment of the prince of this world. His doom is sealed. "He is reserved in everlasting chains under darkness unto judgment of the great day." And his fate

14

shall be your fate, if you do not quit his service and commend yourself into the hands of Him who has redeemed, purchased, and won you from all sins, from death, and from the power of the devil.

O let us be careful, then, not to commit our ransomed souls to Satan's power. Let us continually pray the Lord to deliver us from temptation and not to take His Holy Spirit from us. And thus, by the grace of God, we shall conquer the devil, the world, and our own sinful flesh, and finally receive the salvation of our souls. Amen.

FIFTH SUNDAY AFTER EASTER.

JOHN 16, 23—30.

Verily, verily, I say unto you, Whatsoever ye shall ask the Father in my name, he will give it you. Hitherto have ye asked nothing in my name: ask, and ye shall receive, that your joy may be full. These things have I spoken unto you in proverbs: but the time cometh, when I shall no more speak unto you in proverbs, but I shall shew you plainly of the Father. At that day ye shall ask in my name: and I say not unto you, that I will pray the Father for you: for the Father himself loveth you, because ye have loved me, and have believed that I came out from God. I came forth from the Father, and am come into the world: again, I leave the world, and go to the Father. His disciples said unto him, Lo, now speakest thou plainly, and speakest no proverb. Now are we sure that thou knowest all things, and needest not that any man should ask thee: by this we believe that thou camest forth from God.

BELOVED FRIENDS IN CHRIST:

Our Gospel treats of prayer. We poor sinful mortals are permitted to pray, privileged to address our Creator, the great God in heaven. What an honor! Common people consider themselves highly honored when they are admitted into the presence of a mighty ruler and prince to speak to him and ask of him some favor. But how much greater is this honor, conferred upon us poor sinful creatures, that at any time and everywhere we may address the Ruler of the universe and confide to Him our troubles and cares!

Do all men make the proper use of this privilege? Do all men pray? No. Most people never pray. The unbelieving children of this world treat prayer with scorn and ridicule. At the same time, let an unbeliever get into danger of his life and, in most cases, he himself will make an attempt to pray and to call upon God to save him, as has often been witnessed in the case of shipwrecks, earthquakes, and similar calamities. Those who a short time before had blasphemed God and ridiculed prayer were seen to be among the first to fall down upon their knees, and to wring their hands, and to cry that God should help them.

Alas! it is not only the unbelieving world that neglects prayer Even faithful Christians are sometimes neglectful in their duty to pray. Satan, the old wicked foe, knows well that prayer is a bulwark against him, that there is very little chance for him to deceive and to seduce the praying Christian into misbelief, despair, and other great shame and vice. One of his old tricks is, therefore, to throw all kinds of obstacles in the Christian's way to keep him from praying.

Now in our Gospel we are told by our divine Lord Jesus how we may overcome those impediments which Satan places in our way, and with the aid of God continue in our prayers. Let me show you with the aid of God's Holy Spirit

HOW TO OVERCOME THE IMPEDIMENTS TO PRAYER.

This is done by heeding

I. *The express command of God that we should pray,*
II. *The divine assurance that God is pleased with our prayer,*
III. *The divine promise that our prayer shall be heard.*

I.

One of the main impediments by which Christians are often kept from prayer, undoubtedly, is procrastination, or a putting off of prayer for some future time. You know and feel that you ought to pray, but you think that you are not in the right mood to pray just then You are not in a suitable frame of mind to address the Almighty Your thoughts are not moving in the right channel. And so you put it off to a time when you expect to be better prepared for prayer. The appointed time comes and lo' you are no more or, perhaps, even less qualified than before You do not pray in the morning when you rise, you expect to be inspired with more devotion later in the day. The day passes, your mind is occupied with the things of this life, and you forget to pray. Or you do not pray in the evening before retiring, you

feel too tired and worn out, and make up your mind to pray the
next evening. The next evening comes, and again you feel the
same way, and prayer is neglected! My dear Christians, who
among us has not been deluded by this old trick of Satan inducing
us to put off prayer, until, by the grace of God, we found that
this procrastination was a delusion and a snare aiming at the destruction of our soul?

Now, how may Christians overcome this first and most dangerous impediment to prayer? By heeding the express command
of God that we should pray. Jesus says in our Gospel, "*Hitherto
have ye asked nothing in my name: ask, and ye shall receive, that
your joy may be full.*" This is certainly as plain a command as
there can be. Christ says to His disciples, "Ask, and ye shall
receive." He does not merely give an advice here, saying, it
were a useful thing to pray. He does not leave it to our own
judgment to determine for ourselves whether we should pray or
not. No, this is a direct and straight command, "Ask, and ye
shall receive." The same command is implied in the Second
Commandment. For when God says, "Thou shalt not take the
name of the Lord Thy God in vain," this implies that we should
make the right and proper use of the name of God, that we should
call upon Him in every time of trouble, pray, praise, and give
thanks. And the same command is also given by the words of
the holy apostle, "Pray without ceasing," and in many other
passages of the holy Scriptures, both in the Old and the New
Testament.

When, therefore, we are tempted to put off prayer, when we
hear the voice which says, You cannot pray, you are not in the
right frame of mind to converse with God, wait a while, you will
do better later on, let us remember that these suggestions come
from the devil. Let us sternly oppose the old wicked foe and
say to him, Depart from me, thou evil spirit! Shall I transgress
God's express command which bids me pray? Is not this command on the same line with all the rest of God's holy commandments? If, therefore, I should keep all the rest of God's holy
commandments and offend in this one point and not pray, I would
be guilty of all. What of it, if I deem myself unprepared and
not in a suitable frame of mind? I might also be unprepared to
hear the Word of God, and is that an excuse? No; I shall not

consider whether I am prepared or not, but deem it my duty to pray. God's command stands and remains the same, no matter how I feel about it. Aye, the less disposed I feel to pray, the more will I fear God's express command and say to Him, O God, Thou hast commanded me to pray, and I am so negligent, I have no desire and no zeal; forgive me my sins, O Lord, and fill my heart with fervency and true devotion. And, my friends, if thus we heed God's express command, we shall soon be quickened, and we shall triumphantly overcome the impediment by which Satan meant to fell us.

II.

Another impediment by which Christians are often kept from prayer is a sense of their own unworthiness. When they turn to God to address Him in prayer their own conscience will rise up against them and say, How dare you pray? How dare you say, Our Father? The holy apostles, men like Paul, John, Peter, could do that. But what are you? You are unworthy, you are a damnable sinner. And still you mean to stand up before the just and holy God, who is a consuming fire to all evil-doers? No; prayer is not a privilege for you. You must be a different creature before you can venture to pray to God. Does not the Bible say, "We know that God heareth not sinners"? Such, my friends, are Satan's darts, by which Christians are often assailed, especially when they are in some great trouble. Indifferent people, secure sinners, of course, who never feel worried about their sins, cannot understand this. Of the scribes and Pharisees, for instance, we read that they prayed a great deal, and never doubted their worthiness. The Pharisee who with the publican went up into the temple to pray, boasted of his own worthiness even in his prayer, and said, "God, I thank Thee, that I am not as other men are, extortioners, unjust, adulterers, or even as this publican." And such Pharisees are to be found to this day. They are the people who trust in themselves that they are righteous, who do not mean to receive something of God when they pray, but to give God something thereby, to enhance His glory and to make a show of their own piety. Their prayers are not true prayers, not an intercourse between the soul and the true living God, but only a mockery of prayer, mere babbling. True Christians who know how sternly God is opposed to sin, frequently are held down by their own unworthiness and are made to feel as if they must not dare to stand before the holy God and address Him in prayer.

But how may Christians overcome this second impediment to prayer? By heeding the assurance which God has given us that He is pleased with our prayer. This divine assurance is clearly stated in our Gospel, where the Lord says, "*And I say not unto you that I will pray the Father for you: for the Father Himself loveth you, because ye have loved me, and have believed that I am come out from God*" These words must be rightly understood. When Jesus says, "I say not unto you that I will pray the Father for you,' He does not mean that He will not intercede for us before the Father, or that we should not depend on His intercession for us. No; what He would say is this· Think not, my dear disciples, that I alone could pray for you, and that you were not permitted to address the Father in prayer. Know that the Father loves you for my sake; He is pleased with your prayers which you address to Him in my name Pray therefore, in spite of your own unworthiness; pray, though you feel as if you should not dare to approach the Almighty.

Let us well remember this, my dear Christians The Lord 'Jesus assured His disciples that they were God's dear children since they believed in Jesus the Savior; and so are we His dear children if we believe, for with God there is no respect of persons. And look at the disciples, how imperfect they were at the time when Christ gave them this comforting assurance They expected of Christ that He should establish a glorious worldly kingdom and make worldly rulers of them. They quarreled among themselves who should occupy the highest rank Yet they were assured that the Father loved them because they loved Jesus and believed in Jesus; yet they were assured that God was pleased with their prayers. Why, then, should we desist from prayer when Satan holds before us our unworthiness? Why should we be afraid to approach God's mercy-seat because of our sins? Let us heed the divine assurance that God is always pleased with our prayers as long as we pray in the name of Jesus, that is, in faith, with a sincere heart, in love to Jesus, and if that faith were ever so weak and frail and had dwindled down to a mere desire to believe, to a bruised reed and smoking flax.

III.

Still, there is one more, and a very frequent, impediment by which Christians are kept from prayer, and that is doubt whether our prayer shall be heard. When a Christian makes ready to pray for something Satan will say to him, What is the use of praying? Do you expect to alter the plans of the Almighty? Worm of the dust that thou art, a tiny speck in the universe, do you really expect to accomplish anything by prayer? God has arranged everything beforehand, and He will carry out His arrangements in spite of your prayer. And even if prayers are heard, your prayer will certainly not be heard, because your voice is too weak to reach to the heavenly throne. You are too insignificant a creature to be recognized by God in heaven. O how often are Christians assailed by such thoughts! And what is the result? They either pray in doubt —and then their prayer is not heard, as the holy Apostle James says, "He that wavereth is like a wave of the sea driven with the wind and tossed. For let not that man think that he shall receive anything of the Lord"—or they are kept entirely from prayer by this impediment of doubt as to the efficacy of their appeal to God.

But how is this impediment overcome? By heeding the divine promise that our prayers shall be heard. Jesus says, "*Verily, verily, I say unto you, Whatsoever ye shall ask the Father in my name, He will give it you.*" Behold, Jesus not only gives the distinct promise here that our prayers shall be heard. He even attests that promise by a double oath, saying, "Verily, verily, I say unto you." In the face of this direct promise ought not every Christian to be ashamed of himself to give room to doubts arising in his mind as to the efficacy of his prayer? Is it not a sin and a shame before God and all the world to think that your prayer will not be heard, when you know that the Son of God has attested with an oath that whatsoever we ask the Father in Jesus' name we shall receive? Do we not give God and His beloved Son Jesus the lie by such doubt? Can there be a more damnable sin? O, then, let us not pay any attention to the voice of Satan saying to us, Pray not, it is useless, you shall not be heard anyway. Let us heed the divine promise that our prayers shall be heard. Satan is a liar; Jesus tells the truth

Perhaps some one will say here, But does not God sometimes refuse to grant us our requests? Are not many prayers unheard?

The answer is, No prayer in Jesus' name will be unheard. In Jesus' name you may pray for spiritual gifts, as, the grace of God, the forgiveness of sins, and the like, and these gifts you shall always receive according to special divine promise. In Jesus' name you may also pray for temporal gifts, for which you have no special divine promise, but when you pray for these temporal gifts in Jesus' name, you cannot pray in any other way than Jesus did when He said, "Father, not my will, but Thy will be done." Though you must pray in firm faith and in no wise doubt that God will hear your prayer, yet you can never pray in Jesus' name for a temporal gift without affixing the condition, If it is Thy will, O God, for Thou alone knowest, O Lord, what is truly salutary for my immortal soul. And also this prayer for a temporal gift is always heard, either by granting the very thing for which we ask, or by granting us a still greater spiritual blessing in the place of the temporal gift which we asked and which would not have been truly beneficial had we received it.

May the Lord, then, grant us all His grace to overcome all the impediments by which Satan would keep us from our prayers: that we may heed the express command of God to pray, the divine assurance that God is pleased with our prayers, and the divine promise that our prayer in Jesus' name shall always be heard and accepted. And thus we shall be blessed with all spiritual blessings in heavenly places in Christ, until we behold the Lamb upon His throne and praise Him for ever. Amen.

ASCENSION DAY.

MARK 16, 14—20.

Afterward he appeared unto the eleven as they sat at meat, and upbraided them with their unbelief and hardness of heart, because they believed not them which had seen him after he was risen. And he said unto them, Go ye into all the world, and preach the gospel to every creature. He that believeth and is baptized shall be saved; but he that believeth not shall be damned. And these signs shall follow them that believe; In my name shall they cast out devils; they shall speak with new tongues; they shall take up serpents; and if they drink any deadly thing, it shall not hurt them; they shall lay hands on the sick, and they shall recover. So then after the Lord had spoken unto them, he was received up into heaven, and sat on the right hand of God. And they went forth, and preached everywhere, the Lord working with them, and confirming the word with signs following. Amen.

BELOVED FRIENDS IN CHRIST:

We have heard the narrative of this day's wonderful event. "God is gone up with a shout, the Lord with the sound of a trumpet. Sing praises to God, sing praises: sing praises unto our King, sing praises. For God is the King of all the earth." Thus did David rejoice in the Old Testament when God had manifested to him that the Savior would ascend into heaven and sit at the right hand of God the Father Almighty.

But is Christ's ascension into heaven really an occasion for rejoicing? Did He not thereby depart from us? Did He not leave this earth and withdraw from us His presence so that we see Him no more? He certainly did in a certain sense absent Himself by His ascension into heaven. Still, we can and must rejoice with David; for though Christ is absent in a certain sense, still, in another, in a higher and more important sense He is present with us, and that presence was brought about by His ascension. This is what I wish to impress upon your minds with the aid of God's Holy Spirit,

CHRIST ABSENT AND YET PRESENT.

Let us see

I. *In what sense He is absent from us,* and
II. *In what sense He is present with us*

I.

First, then, in what sense is Christ absent? We read, "*So then after the Lord had spoken unto them, He was received up into heaven, and sat on the right hand of God.*" And in the book of the Acts we read, "He was taken up, and a cloud received Him out of their sight." So our Lord was taken up into heaven and seen no more. After His ascension into heaven He was no more exposed to the view of men. And that is the true nature of His absence. By His ascension He permanently changed the body of His resurrection into an invisible body. Occasionally He did the same thing before this. When after His resurrection He showed Himself unto His disciples, He would suddenly appear in their midst, and then again vanish and disappear before their eyes. But now He slowly disappeared before them in such manner as to convince them that henceforth they should see Him no more, that

henceforth He would no more show Himself visibly on this earth.
His disciples should no more know Him after the flesh. The
Lord did not ascend in the manner commonly accepted; He did
not ascend into heaven in such manner as to go up higher and
higher, until He appeared to be a small speck in the blue sky,
a speck that grew so small that it could not be discerned by the
sharpest eye. No, He only went up to a certain height, where
He was plainly seen by the gazing disciples from below, and then
a cloud came, and He was enveloped in that cloud and seen no
more. He had passed from the visible into the invisible.

And "*He sat on the right hand of God,*" as our Gospel says.
Jesus Christ, we know, is God and man in one person. Now the
divine part of Jesus Christ could certainly not be seated at the
right hand of God in His ascension. According to His divine
nature He had been with God from everlasting. It was according
to His human nature that Jesus sat at the right hand of God.
And what does this mean? It means, that according to His human
nature Christ glorified assumed the full and constant exercise of
universal dominion, rule, and government over heaven and earth
and all creatures, and especially over His church on earth.

How, then, are we to look upon Christ since He ascended into
heaven, and sitteth at the right hand of God the Father Almighty?
Did Christ remove from this earth His human body and take away
from us that same body which was born of the virgin Mary, suffered under Pontius Pilate, was crucified, dead, and buried, descended into hell, and on the third day rose again from the dead?
Did He take that body away into the unlimited space above us?
Did Christ in that body go so far away from us into the skies that
now it is beyond the stars and the largest telescope cannot reach
Him? Is there a certain place there, where God, like an earthly
monarch, has a gilded throne upon which He is sitting, with Jesus
Christ, His Son, sitting at His right side? Is the body of Christ
as far away from us as the heavens are away from the earth?
No, God is a spirit. He is everywhere. He cannot be confined
to a certain spot. And did not Christ Himself say immediately
before His ascension, "Lo, I am with you alway, even unto the
end of the world"?

It is true, the earthly manifestation of Jesus Christ our Lord
closed on the Mount of Olives. In a certain sense Christ is absent

from us since the day of His ascension. That gracious countenance of our Lord is no more seen by mortal eye, that thrilling voice is no more heard. But what is it that is really absent of Christ? Is it His body? No, it is merely His visible conversation; for He was taken away in a cloud, it is merely His lowliness, His form of a servant, for He is exalted and sitteth at the right hand of God the Father Almighty, that is: unto Him is given all power in heaven and upon earth. He is withdrawn from our actual sight, and shall remain so until that great day when He shall return and come from heaven in a cloud with power and great glory to judge the quick and the dead.

II.

And now let us see in what sense He is present.

In the first place we must guard against the Calvinistic theory of Christ's spiritual presence. It is claimed that since His ascension into heaven Christ is present only spiritually, that only the divine part of Christ is present with us, but not His human part, that He is present only inasmuch as our thoughts are occupied with Him, and we believe on Him, and spiritually deal with Him in our minds while we feel and experience His gracious divine presence with us when He fills our souls with peace, comfort, and joy. This theory is wrong. It makes two Christs out of one, while there is but one God, and one Mediator between God and man. According to this theory of Christ's spiritual presence there must be one Christ far away from us, above the stars, the human Christ; and another Christ who is with us and everywhere, the divine Christ. According to this theory the two natures of Christ, His divine and His human nature, which are inseparably united in Christ's person, and like body and soul constitute and form the one Christ, are torn asunder so that there is no God-man Jesus Christ, but a man, or a human nature, which is in heaven, and a God, or a divine nature, which is upon earth, making actually two persons.

No, there is but one Christ, one person, and as little as the body of a living man can be at a certain place and his soul a thousand miles away, so little can Christ's human body be disconnected and separated from His divinity. Where His divine nature is there must be His human nature. Though Christ ascended into heaven, yet He is present with us, present not only spiritually but also bodily.

This is the very reason why we must rejoice over Christ's ascension. Had Christ withdrawn from us Himself, even His own body, what comfort would there be in His ascension? what benefit could we derive therefrom? All we could do would be to mourn over His departure as we mourn over the departure of those whom we love. But this is the true comfort and benefit of His ascension, that He no more confines His bodily presence to a certain locality, to a certain land or place, but that He is present everywhere, invisibly, but really and bodily present in heaven above and on earth below. It was His ascension that brought this about, exalting His human nature, endowing His human nature with divine glory and majesty, so that the man Jesus is just as eternal, almighty, omnipresent, omniscient, as is the God Jesus.

But though Christ is bodily present everywhere, being crowned Lord of all, to get the benefit of His presence we must seek Him in His Word and in His sacraments. We must know that we are lost and condemned sinners and that we cannot be saved in any other way but by faith in the Lord Jesus Christ, who has redeemed us poor lost and condemned sinners. We must have Christ and make Him our own that we might live. Christ is present in His Word with His saving grace. For this is what we read in our Gospel, *"Afterward He appeared unto the eleven as they sat at meat, and upbraided them with their unbelief and hardness of heart, because they believed not them which had seen Him after He was risen. And He said unto them, Go ye into all the world, and preach the Gospel to every creature. He that believeth and is baptized shall be saved; but he that believeth not shall be damned."* Here Christ institutes the office of the holy ministry to have His Gospel preached in all lands, and He promises to save all who believe the Gospel. Christ Himself is present where His Word is being preached, invisibly present, and through the Word He offers unto all who hear the preaching of His Gospel the treasures of His grace: forgiveness of sins, life, and salvation. In the early times of the Christian church Christ also gave certain signs unto them that believed. He said to His disciples, *"And these signs shall follow them that believe; In my name shall they cast out devils; they shall speak with new tongues; they shall take up serpents; and if they drink any deadly thing, it shall not hurt them; they shall lay hands on the sick, and they shall recover*   Christ promised these signs to His church. They are rarely witnessed among Christians in our days, because there is no general necessity for them. It was different with the apostles. They had to break down the ramparts of heathenism. They had to introduce the Christian religion in the world. And for this reason their preaching was supported by miracles. *"They went forth,"* as we read at the end of our Gospel, *"and preached every- where, the Lord working with them, and confirming the Word with signs following"*

Not only with His Word, the Gospel, is Christ bodily present and working with those who preach the Gospel. He is also present in His sacraments. Christ says, *"He that believeth and is bap- tized shall be saved"* When a child is being baptized Jesus is invisibly present and blesses that child. When to an adult the holy sacrament of Baptism is applied Jesus is there and imparts to the believing Christian the forgiveness of all his sins   And it is the same thing with the other sacrament, the Lord's Supper There the Lord is bodily present   In, with, and under the bread and wine He gives us His true body and blood as a token that our sins are forgiven. It is not a spiritual eating and drinking of Christ's body and blood, and the bread and wine is not merely a sign or emblem to remind us of the body He gave for us and the blood He shed for us, but therewith is connected His real, true body and blood, mysteriously connected with the bread and wine; and it is by a sacramental, incomprehensible eating and drinking that we receive the body and blood of our Lord.

Thus we have seen, my friends, though absent in a certain sense, namely inasmuch as we do not see Him, Christ is not absent from us, strictly speaking. He is present. He became even more present by His ascension than He had been before   And to this day He is making true His promise, *"Lo, I am with you alway, even unto the end of the world"*   Amen

SIXTH SUNDAY AFTER EASTER.

JOHN 15, 26—16, 4.

But when the Comforter is come, whom I will send unto you from the Father, even the Spirit of truth, which proceedeth from the Father, he shall testify of me: and ye also shall bear witness, because ye have been with me from the beginning. These things have I spoken unto you, that ye should not be offended. They shall put you out of the synagogues: yea, the time cometh, that whosoever killeth you will think that he doeth God service. And these things will they do unto you, because they have not known the Father, nor me. But these things have I told you, that when the time shall come, ye may remember that I told you of them. And these things I said not unto you at the beginning, because I was with you.

BELOVED FRIENDS IN CHRIST:

By the first words of our Gospel our attention is directed to the great festival which we shall celebrate next Sunday, the festival of Pentecost or Whitsunday. For when Jesus says, "*But when the Comforter is come, whom I will send unto you from the Father, even the Spirit of truth, which proceedeth from the Father, He shall testify of me*," He evidently refers to the wonderful effusion of the Holy Ghost, who on the day of Pentecost came down upon the disciples as they were assembled in Jerusalem, and rested upon their heads in the shape of cloven tongues as of fire, and filled their hearts, and enabled them to proclaim the great works of God, done for the salvation of man, in all the languages of the world.

But why did Jesus have the Spirit come upon His disciples in such peculiar manner and entrust them, as it were, to the Spirit, that the Spirit should take them in charge after His ascension into heaven? We have heard that in the Gospel of Sunday before last, where Christ says, "I have many things to say unto you, but ye cannot bear them now. Howbeit when He, the Spirit of truth, is come, He will guide you into all truth: for He shall not speak of Himself; but whatsoever He shall hear, that shall He speak: and He will show you things to come. He shall glorify me: for He shall receive of mine, and shall show it unto you." Behold, this is what the Holy Ghost was to do and what He did in the disciples. He was to testify of Christ, He was to endow them with a perfect understanding of Christ and His great work of redemption, He was to tell them all those things which, on account of their weakness, they could not bear while Jesus was with them.

However, Jesus says to His disciples, You must not think that testifying of me, bearing witness of me, is an exclusive work of the Holy Spirit. No, says Jesus, *"Ye also shall bear witness, because ye have been with me from the beginning."* And hereupon He discloses unto them a part of their future life. He tells them how they should be hated and persecuted of the world for bearing witness of their divine Lord and Master. This induces me to speak to you with the aid of God's Holy Spirit of

PERSECUTION FOR CHRIST'S SAKE.

I shall show you

I. *That true Christians must suffer persecution,* and
II. *Why true Christians are persecuted.*

I.

Jesus says to His disciples, *"They shall put you out of the synagogues: yea, the time cometh, that whosoever killeth you will think that he doeth God service. And these things will they do unto you, because they have not known the Father, nor me."* In the most distinct terms Jesus here predicts persecution to come upon His disciples. And the same prediction He made at different times and occasions. Shortly before our text He says, "If the world hate you, ye know that it hated me before it hated you. . . . Remember the word that I said unto you, The servant is not greater than his lord. If they have persecuted me, they will also persecute you." And at another place He says to His disciples, "Behold, I send you forth as sheep in the midst of wolves. They will deliver you up to the councils, and they will scourge you in their synagogues: and ye shall be brought before governors and kings for my sake, for a testimony against them and the Gentiles.'

Upon the disciples these predictions came true to the letter. The history of the apostles, as put down by St. Luke in the book of the Acts, contains an account of the persecutions which the disciples had to suffer at the hands of Jews and Gentiles; and the books of the early history of the Christian church are a supplement to that account. These brave witnesses of the Lord Jesus were beaten, scourged, cast into prison, placed in the stocks, stoned, tortured, killed. Stephen proclaims Jesus and is stoned to death. No sooner is Saul, the honored and distinguished Pharisee, converted to Christ than he is cast out of the synagogue. He is intensely hated by his former friends, bitterly persecuted, and finally, after enduring countless hardships, he is beheaded in the city of Rome. James is cast down from the pinnacle of the temple and killed. Each and every one of the apostles meets with a violent death excepting St. John, and he is reported to have escaped such a death by miracle.

We must not, however, think that Christ's prediction was meant for the disciples only. It was meant for all true Christians. All true Christians must expect to be hated and persecuted of the world. Jesus says expressly, "If any man will come after me, let him deny himself, and take up his cross and follow me. For whosoever will save his life shall lose it: and whosoever will lose his life for my sake shall save it." And it is of all His followers that Jesus says Matt. 10, 22, "Ye shall be hated of all men for my name's sake." And does not St. Paul say distinctly, "All that will live godly in Christ Jesus shall suffer persecution"?

If we glance over the history of the Christian church we will find that it is the history of constant persecutions, which the believers in Jesus Christ, the eternal Son of God, had to suffer, persecutions inflicted upon them by the unbelieving world. The greater the zeal with which true Christians were inspired at any period of time, the more fiercely and cruelly were they persecuted. Especially the three first centuries of the Christian era are marked by persecutions so cruel, so sickening, as to make the blood curdle when you think of it. Not only were the Christians apprehended and cast into the dungeons, they were also put to death in the most shocking manner intended to frighten the other Christians that they should deny Christ, renounce Christianity, and turn to heathen practices. They were crucified head downward, scalded with boiling oil, cast before the wild beasts in the arena, or slain with the sword. And why were the heathen so eager to shed the blood of Christians? It was, as Christ says, that by killing the Christians they thought they were doing God service. Christians were held responsible for every calamity. Did a drought occur, the common explanation was that, if God refused rain, the Christians were at fault. Did the Nile refuse its annual irrigation, or the Tiber overflow its banks, did earthquake or famine or any other calamity excite the popular mind, a ready cause was in every mouth: The anger of the gods on account of the increase of Christianity, and a ready sacrifice to propitiate the offended deities was immediately resorted to, The slaughter of the Christians.

Such were the dealings with Christians in the early times of the Christian church. And how were the true Christians treated in the time of the Reformation, four hundred years ago? Think of the horrors of the inquisition and all those instruments of torture that were invented under the papal rule to stamp out the Protestant heresy, as it was called. Think of the poor Waldenses, who dissented from the doctrines of the papacy prior to the Reformation, and who had to hide in the mountains that they might escape extermination at the hands of Rome's bloodthirsty executioners. Think of Luther, whose life was continually at stake, and whom his friends had to secrete for a time that he might escape the fate of John Huss. Think of the Huguenots in France, how they were massacred in cold blood.

And must not true Christians suffer persecution to this day? Truly, the blood of martyrs is still flowing, and though this age boasts of being an age of enlightenment and progress the Turk is permitted to massacre thousands upon thousands of Christians, and nothing is being done by the worldly powers to stay his murderous hand. Only a short time ago a letter was circulated stating that in the late Armenian massacre not less than 75,000 Christians died the death of martyrs, mostly men, and that about 100,000 Christian orphans have been left behind to be looked after, clothed, and fed by Christians in all lands. The bloody persecutions of native and foreign Christians in China are of recent occurrence. And if you are a true Christian, if you profess the faith, depend on it that you will have to suffer for it in some way. The world will hate you. Your best friends might desert you. Your own relatives, if they still cling to the world, will be against you. You will have to suffer persecution and endure the hatred, the scorn and ridicule, the antagonism, the malice of the evil world for the sake of Jesus whom you profess before them.

15

II.

And now let us see why Christians are being persecuted.

Men have often been offended in these persecutions which Christians must suffer. It has been said, Why does not God protect those whom He loves? If He is the Ruler over all, if He is almighty, if He can turn even the hearts of men, why does He not turn the hearts of those who thirst after the blood of His children and stay their murderous hands? To all questions of this kind we find a reply in our Gospel. Jesus says, *"These things have I spoken unto you, that ye should not be offended,"* and again He says, *"But these things have I told you, that when the time shall come, ye may remember that I told you of them."* Be not offended, then, says Jesus, when you see persecutions coming. Remember, I told you that they shall come and must come, and rest contented there. Do not endeavor to pry into secrets which have not been revealed, or to fathom depths which you shall never reach with the line of human understanding. *Why* God, who is and ever remains a divine Protector of all that trust in Him, will permit dire persecutions to come upon those whom He loves, *why* He will stay the hand of the persecutor in one land and not in another, *why* He will let scores of years roll on without any notable persecution and then let persecutions come in full force, *why* He will let one Christian suffer more, another less—these are mysteries which human reason will never solve. And because the faith of a Christian receives a severe shock when he must encounter persecutions, Jesus says, "Be not offended. Remember, I told you that it should come; know that I have not deserted you. I love you still. Keep the faith and endure to the end, and you shall be saved."

Our divine Lord also states the true reason why the children of this world persecute His dear Christians. He says, *"And these things will they do unto you, because they have not known the Father, nor me."* These words almost sound as if Jesus intended thereby to excuse the children of this world for persecuting the Christians, as if He would say, They are not so much to blame, they are ignorant, they know no better. But this is not the case. For to know the Father and to know Christ, in the language of the Scriptures, is the same thing as believing in and loving the Father and His Son Jesus. Not to know the

Father and Jesus is, therefore, the same thing as not to believe in, not to love, but to hate and to reject the true God and His beloved Son. So the reason why the children of this world persecute the Christians is not simply because they did not know any better and, therefore, were not to be held so much accountable for their wickedness, but because they are opposed to the true God and His beloved Son Jesus Christ, because they hate Him and instead of loving God love themselves, love sin, love the pleasures of this life and the honor and vain glory of this world. And they cannot display their hatred against God in any other way than by abusing, harassing, ill-treating, persecuting those who truly believe in Him. In the Christians they actually persecute God and the Lord Jesus. When, therefore, Saul, on his way to Damascus to persecute the Christians, was thrown to the ground and heard the voice from heaven saying, "Saul, Saul, why persecutest thou me?" and said, "Who art Thou, Lord?" the answer came, "I am Jesus whom thou persecutest." The children of this world cannot bear to see the Christians walking the narrow way that leads to eternal life, shunning the world's evil lusts, and keeping themselves from sin; for this conduct of Christians reminds them continually of their wickedness and silently condemns their evil actions. They cannot bear to hear Christians speaking of Jesus the Savior and saying that though they are sinners the blood of Jesus Christ, the Son of God, which was shed for all men on the cross, has cleansed them from all their sins; for this declaration condemns them and implies that they who refuse to believe in Christ shall be eternally lost because they do not believe in the name of the only begotten Son of God.

May the Lord, then, uphold us all in the persecutions which we must endure for His name's sake, and ours shall be the promise, "Blessed are ye when men shall revile you, and persecute you, and shall say all manner of evil against you falsely, for my sake. Rejoice and be exceeding glad: for great is your reward in heaven." Amen.

PENTECOST SUNDAY.

If a man love me, he will keep my words: and my Father will love him, and we will come unto him, and make our abode with him. He that loveth me not keepeth not my sayings: and the word which ye hear is not mine, but the Father's which sent me. These things have I spoken unto you, being yet present with you. But the Comforter, which is the Holy Ghost, whom the Father will send in my name, he shall teach you all things, and bring all things to your remembrance, whatsoever I have said unto you. Peace I leave with you, my peace I give unto you: not as the world giveth, give I unto you. Let not your heart be troubled, neither let it be afraid. Ye have heard how I said unto you, I go away, and come again unto you. If ye loved me, ye would rejoice, because I said, I go unto the Father: for my Father is greater than I. And now I have told you before it come to pass, that, when it is come to pass, ye might believe. Hereafter I will not talk much with you: for the prince of this world cometh, and hath nothing in me. But that the world may know that I love the Father; and as the Father gave me commandment, even so I do. Arise, let us go hence.

BELOVED FRIENDS IN CHRIST:

Our Gospel does not refer to the great historical fact of the day. It does not tell of the wonderful outpouring of the Holy Ghost. It goes a step farther and tells of the fruit and result of the great miracle of Pentecost. The great miracle of Pentecost is narrated in the Epistle of the day. The Lord Jesus had told His disciples, before His ascension into heaven, not to depart from the city of Jerusalem, but to remain until they should receive the Holy Ghost. It was on a Sunday morning, the tenth day after His ascension, when they were all assembled in a certain building in Jerusalem, most likely the temple. This was a festival day for the children of Israel, and that may account for the presence of the disciples in the temple. It was the fiftieth day after the feast of the Passover, called in the Greek language "Pentecost," meaning the fiftieth. On this day Jerusalem was generally filled with throngs of people coming in from the provinces, to worship the Lord in the temple and to thank Him and offer sacrifice for the first fruits of harvest. And what was done when the disciples of Christ were assembled for prayer on this day? Suddenly there was a peculiar sound from heaven as if a tornado were approaching. The noise was that of a rushing, mighty wind, which descended upon the place where the disciples were, and filled the house. The people of Jerusalem must certainly have felt alarmed and must have rushed out into the streets to find out what was the trouble. The sound led them to the temple. Perhaps they expected to find the massive structure damaged by the force of the wind. They entered and, behold, not only was the building intact, but a sight greeted them such as they had never seen. There stood the disciples of Christ, the believers in Christ, both men and women, and upon the head of each of them was to be seen a living flame in the shape of tongues as of fire, fire burning and yet not consuming Amazement seized upon the people at what they saw; but still greater was their amazement at what they heard. These simple, uneducated men, filled with the Holy Ghost, were preaching, they were proclaiming the great deeds of God. And the greatest marvel was that they spoke languages which they had never learned, so that every foreigner could hear the wonderful works of God in his own tongue.

This, my friends, is the great historical fact of the day as recorded in the Epistle. But what was the immediate fruit and result of this fact? The establishment of the Christian Church. On this day the first Christian congregation was formed in the city of Jerusalem, and not less than three thousand souls were added at once as a result of the great Pentecostal miracle. I say, therefore, that our Gospel goes a step farther, for it evidently treats of the Church of Jesus Christ. The subject of our discourse shall be, with the aid of God's Holy Spirit,

THE CHURCH OF JESUS CHRIST:

I. *Its true members.*
II. *Its undeceiving marks.*
III *Its firm foundation.*

I.

According to the divine Word the entire human family is divided into two classes of men: children of the world and children of God. The children of the world are those who walk the broad way that leads to eternal destruction, and the children of God are those who walk the narrow way that leads to eternal life. The one class is the world, and the other class is the Church of Jesus Christ; and there is no third class of men. You must either be a member of the Church of Jesus Christ or a mem-

ber of the world. You must either be walking among those who
are bound for eternal damnation, or among those who are making for eternal life.

But how may you know whether you are walking in the narrow path? How may you know whether you are a true member
of the Church of Jesus Christ? Jesus says in our Gospel, "*If a
man love me, he will keep my words: and my Father will love
him, and we will come unto him, and make our abode with him.*"
The abode, the dwelling place of Jesus Christ is His Church. And
what does He say of those with whom He will make His abode?
What does He say of the members of His Church? By what is a
man to know whether he is a true member? Jesus says, "*If a
man love me.*" Behold, then, a man may be baptized in the name
of Christ, he may be called a Christian, he may make an open
profession of the true doctrine, he may be enrolled as a church
member: and yet he may be in such a state that Jesus cannot
make His abode with him; he may not be a true member of the
Church of Jesus Christ. All is in vain, all is as nothing, if at the
same time he does not love Jesus. It is his relation to Jesus that
makes a man a true member of the church of Christ. But the
love of Jesus cannot exist without faith in Him. Love is the
first fruit of faith. The whole number of those who love Jesus
is the whole number of those who believe in Him. And these
are the Church of Christ. And of each of these Jesus says:
"*He will keep my words.*" Note well: Jesus does not merely
say, He will hear my words, or read my words, or receive my
words, but, *keep* my words. Keep them, that is, retain them as
what they are and for what they are given, the word of truth,
the word of life, the word of our salvation. For Christ's word
is properly the Word of the Gospel, the saving truth whereby
God offers us the benefits of Christ and works in us acceptance
thereof. Those who reject this Word in unbelief are not members
of the Church of Christ. But those who receive the Word of the
Gospel and keep it, believe what it teaches, confide in its promises,
follow its guidance, they, and they only love Jesus, and they are
the Church of Christ. And to emphasize this truth the Lord also
presents it in a negative form, saying, "*He that loveth me not
keepeth not my sayings.*" And if any one should say, Why must
I keep Christ's sayings in particular? Christ answers and says,

*"And the word which ye hear is not mine, but the Father's which
sent me."* The reason, then, why the keeping of Christ's words
is of such paramount importance is because His words are not
man's words, but God's words, the Father's words, the last of
God's revelation to the sinful world, containing the fulfillment of
all previous prophecies concerning the coming of the Savior and
the divine seal of His testimonies.

Who, then, are the true members of the Church of Jesus
Christ? Those who love Him and keep His words. Let a man
be ever so prominent a church member, if he does not love Jesus
and keep His words, he is *in* the Church, but not *of* the Church;
he is not a true member; he is a foreign element in the Church,
as the tares among the wheat. We call the entire assembly of
those who are baptized in the name of the Triune God and profess
the Christian faith "the Church of Jesus Christ." But properly
speaking, the Church is composed of those only who love Jesus
and keep His words, with whom the Father and the Son have
made their abode, the true believers who have been regenerated
by God's Holy Spirit and sanctified in Christ Jesus.

Consequently, the Church of Jesus Christ is an invisible institution God alone knows who are its true members Yet we
are not to think that, since the Church of Jesus Christ is an invisible Church and known to God only, it is immaterial to which
community of Christians we belong, to which church or denomi-
nation, as long as we only make sure of it that we are true members of Christ's Church. For there are undeceiving marks of the
Church, and where these marks are in a Christian community
there is the invisible Church hidden, as it were, under the outward surface.

II.

Jesus, in the words preceding our text, had told His disciples that He would soon leave them. Now when He told them
in our text that with the Father He would come and make His
abode with them, they probably thought: How can He make His
abode with us when He means to leave us? How can we in future
times be His abode, His Church? And how does He meet these
thoughts of His disciples? He says, *"These things have I spoken
unto you, being yet present with you But the Comforter, which*

is the Holy Ghost, whom the Father will send in my name, He shall teach you all things, and bring all things to your remembrance, whatsoever I have said unto you." So Jesus directs His disciples to the Comforter, the Holy Ghost, and assures them that the divine Spirit will be a most powerful agency to impart and explain to them His Word, and through them to keep His Word among men in the world, so that there should be a Church unto the end of days. Jesus declares that His words, His sayings, are the undeceiving marks of His Church.

Could it be otherwise? Did not Christ just say that His abode, His Church, are those who love Him and keep His words? Since love is something which we cannot see, but the words of Christ are perceptible to our senses, must not the words of Christ be the true, infallible marks by which we may know whether the Church is to be found in a community of men or not? The Word of Christ, His Gospel, is the power of God unto salvation. It is the incorruptible seed which has the divine promise that it shall not return void, but shall accomplish that which He pleases, and shall prosper in the thing whereto He sent it. We may be sure that where the Word of Christ is preached, there also the Holy Spirit is efficaciously active and sinners are born again, endowed with faith and the fruits of faith, love of Christ, and hope of life everlasting. And thus it is that the words of Christ are the infallible marks of the Church of Christ.

If you get into an assembly where they do not accept Christ's sayings as the Word of God, but as human traditions, then you are in a congregation of blasphemers, but not in the Church. If you get into an assembly where the words of Christ are still accepted as the divine Word in their essential parts, but, at the same time, distorted and made to conform to the dictates of human reason, then you are in a corrupted church, in a church disseminating both truth and error: truth, producing true members of Christ's invisible Church, and error, leading people astray. If you get into an assembly where the words of Christ are received and taught as they were spoken, where His Word is proclaimed in its purity and His sacraments are administered according to His institution, then you are in the true Church of Jesus Christ.

This is the glory of our dear Evangelical Lutheran Church. We know that we have the marks of Christ's true Church. We know that our doctrines are not human inferences or deductions from the Scriptures, but express statements of Christ. We know that in matters of faith our Church neither pays any attention to traditions, nor to the objections of human reason, but simply asks, What does Christ say? and then abides by His express words. Let us always abide by the letter and spirit of Christ's sayings, and His Church shall be with us, and ours shall be the promise, "If ye continue in my Word, then are ye my disciples indeed; and ye shall know the truth, and the truth shall make you free."

III.

But the question is, Can we be sure of the Church of Jesus Christ? Can we be sure that all those precious promises will come true which Christ has given to His Church? The answer is, Yes, sure beyond question and doubt For this Church also rests on a firm and solid foundation.

Jesus says, "*Peace I leave with you, my peace I give unto you · not as the world giveth, give I unto you. Let not your heart be troubled, neither let it be afraid. Ye have heard how I said unto you, I go away, and come again unto you If ye loved me, ye would rejoice, because I said, I go unto the Father for my Father is greater than I And now I have told you before it come to pass, that, when it is come to pass, ye might believe. Hereafter I will not talk much with you: for the prince of this world cometh, and hath nothing in me But that the world may know that I love the Father; and as the Father gave me commandment, even so I do Arise, let us go hence.*" What, then, is the firm and solid foundation of the Church and its glorious promises? What should make us sure and certain that it is necessary to be a member of Christ's invisible Church? that in His Church, and in His Church alone, is salvation, and that He will fulfill all His promises given to His believers? Christ's going to the Father, His victorious combat with the prince of this world, His obedience to the Father, or, in other words, His life, suffering, and death, or, in one word, His redemption. Christ our Savior "redeemed us poor lost and condemned creatures, purchased and won us not with gold or silver, but with His holy precious blood and with His innocent suffering and death " That is the immovable foundation upon which the Church of Christ is built. If Jesus Christ had not come into the world and suffered and died for the fallen human race, there never would have been such an institution as the Christian Church. What a firm foundation! It is a foundation not made by the hands of mortal man, but by the immortal God; not built in time, but reaching back into eternity, into the council of the Triune God.

The Church's eternal foundation is, in the first place, the love of the Father, who decreed from eternity to have a Church among the fallen race and to send His Son into the world to seek and to save that which was lost. The Church's foundation is, furthermore, the grace of the Son, who, in obedience to the Father, atoned for the sins of all men by the sacrifice of His life, that all who believe in Him should not perish, but have everlasting life. The Church's foundation is, finally, the communion and power of the Holy Ghost, who, on this day, came down visibly upon the disciples of Christ and ever since has His work among men, calling them by the Gospel, enlightening them with His gifts, sanctifying and keeping them in the true faith; gathering them from all nations and tongues and peoples into one fold with one Shepherd, into one holy Christian Church, the communion of saints.

May the Lord, then, grant us all His grace that every one of us be a true member of the invisible Church of Jesus Christ, that we always bear in mind the true marks of His Church and not be deceived by false prophets, and that, finally, we neither doubt our Lord's promises, nor fear for the future of the Church, because it rests upon a foundation which the world and the devil and all the powers of hell cannot overthrow.

> My Church, my Church, my dear old Church,
> My glory and my pride,
> Firm in the faith Immanuel taught,
> She holds no faith beside.
> Upon this Rock
> 'Gainst every shock,
> Though gates of hell assail,
> She stands secure
> With promise sure:
> They never shall prevail.

Amen.

PENTECOST MONDAY.

JOHN 3, 16—21

For God so loved the world, that he gave his only begotten Son, that whosoever believeth in him should not perish, but have everlasting life. For God sent not his Son into the world to condemn the world, but that the world through him might be saved. He that believeth on him is not condemned; but he that believeth not is condemned already, because he hath not believed in the name of the only begotten Son of God. And this is the condemnation, that light is come into the world, and men loved darkness rather than light, because their deeds were evil. For every one that doeth evil hateth the light, neither cometh to the light, lest his deeds should be reproved. But he that doeth truth cometh to the light, that his deeds may be made manifest, that they are wrought in God

BELOVED FRIENDS IN CHRIST·

Luther calls the first sentence of our Gospel "the little Gospel," because in it is condensed the whole Gospel truth. It is, indeed, a text which is fathomless as the depth of the sea and wider in its range than the ocean. No minister can do justice to this text in a sermon. It covers the whole field of Christian theology. Here we are told of the love of God; and who can tell all about God's love? Mention is made of the world, and that brings before our mind the history of man, his creation, his fall in sin, and his relation to the Creator. God's only begotten Son is referred to, and we are thereby reminded of the fact that there are different persons in the deity. We are told of our redemption through Christ Jesus, of faith, of heaven, and of hell. It has been said of this text that "it is so vast that it is almost impossible to do anything with it. It hampers a man into silence; it appalls him. There are some sentences that a man can walk around and walk into, and take possession of its truth. This is not such a sentence. There are sentences that are easily explained, but this is not such a sentence. There are some sentences whose meaning we may measure and take their length and breadth. No such sentence is this. It is immeasurable, infinite."

But it is in substance the very text upon which the first sermon was preached in the Christian church. It was the foundation of Peter's discourse when the first Christian congregation was being formed in the city of Jerusalem, and is, therefore, a true Pentecostal text. Since the love of God in Jesus is the keynote which sounds in our Gospel from beginning to end, I shall endeavor to make a few remarks on this inexhaustible subject. Let us consider with the aid of God's Holy Spirit,

WHAT THE LOVE OF GOD IN JESUS GIVES TO US AND ASKS OF US.

    I. *What it gives to us.*
    II. *What it asks of us.*

I.

    "God so loved the world, that He gave His only begotten Son." In the fullness of time God had His dear Son become man. This act of love is simply beyond comprehension. There is no language for it. So great is the love of God, it embraces the whole world, the world of sinners, the fallen race, and it parts with that which is dearest to Him, with His only begotten Son, for their sakes. "Through Christ heaven has come down upon the earth. He has built the bridge leading across the abyss that man's sin has made between his trembling heart and his God. He has effected the holy chain that now reaches from eternity down into time, and with which we can support ourselves in the storms of life, and by which God will in His own time draw us up to His glory above."

    For to what purpose did He give His only begotten Son? *"That whosoever believeth in Him should not perish, but have everlasting life. For God sent not His Son into the world to condemn the world; but that the world through Him might be saved."* It was the salvation of all men, of every individual, even of the greatest sinners, which God had in view when He gave His only begotten Son. In His Son He gave us a prize and a treasure which is of infinitely greater value to us than if He had given us stores of wealth and royal possessions. "You can, indeed, have many things, without Christ, such as prosperity and joy at home, honor and reputation in the world, earthly possessions and great power. But when suddenly and without warning all that of which you are proud crumbles into dust; when you are deserted by your best friends and earthly fame fades away; when you begin to feel that the deepest longings of the soul are not satisfied by that which earth can offer you—how poor and wretched must you feel without Christ!" But in Christ you have all that can make you truly happy, even when earthly happiness is turned into misery. Christ has proclaimed to us the good news that God's love is greater than our guilt; and that, when we have become rebellious and stubborn, He even then still permits His face to shine upon us. "Christ is the propitiation for our sins, and not for ours only, but also for the sins of the whole world." Christ has paid for us the ransom price and has redeemed us all with His holy precious blood and with His innocent suffering and death. Christ has successfully combated with the foes of our eternal welfare, and delivered us from death and from the power of the devil. Christ has worked out for us all a spotless righteousness, so that we should be adorned with the robe of that righteousness and, though we are and remain sinners as long as we live upon this earth, appear before the just and holy God as if we had no sin. Christ has opened for us the crystal portals of the heavenly city and gained for us all eternal life, eternal happiness and bliss, so that the sufferings of this present time are not worthy to be compared with the glory that shall be revealed in us.

Behold, this is what the love of God in Jesus gives to us, offers to us, presents to us: forgiveness of all our sins, life, salvation, peace, happiness without end. When God gave His only begotten Son, was not this the greatest deed of love the world ever witnessed?

II.

And now, in the second place, let us consider what this love of God in Jesus asks of us.

Does God ask of us that we perform certain acts and do certain things to show that we are worthy of His love? Does He affix certain conditions and say, I will love you and give you life and salvation, if you pray to me, worship me, and walk in my commandments? Many think that they must gain God's favor by their own deeds. They think that they must pray and be good, and then God will love them. No; God loved us first; He loved us before we were born; He loved us in all our misery and sin. From eternity He loved us and decreed to give us His Son, and did actually give us His Son, when the time was fulfilled. How can we induce God to love us when He has already manifested His love to us in His only begotten Son?

All that the love of God in Jesus asks of us is that we accept the gift which of His boundless grace and mercy He has bestowed upon us, that we accept His Son and, with His Son, all those heavenly treasures conveyed to us by His Son's work. Our Gospel therefore says, "*He that believeth on Him is not condemned; but he that believeth not is condemned already, because he hath not believed in the name of the only begotten Son of God.*" By faith we must accept the great gift of God. Hence it is by faith alone that we are saved, not by our own deeds and works of righteousness. If we do not believe in the only begotten Son of God we thereby openly despise God's love to us and reject the gift of eternal salvation which He extends to us in His Son. Hence it is that he that does not believe is condemned. His condemnation follows as a matter of course. He is not condemned because God did not love him. God loved him as much as all the rest of the world, and gave His Son for him as well as for the rest of men. Condemnation is his own choice, as our Gospel says, "*And this is the condemnation, that light is come into the world, and men loved darkness rather than light, because their deeds were evil. For every one that doeth evil hateth the light, neither cometh to the light, lest his deeds should be reproved. But he that doeth truth cometh to the light, that his deeds may be made manifest, that they are wrought in God.*" Much has been said and written in defense of unbelievers to make it appear as if, in some cases at least, there were a good moral excuse for man's unbelief. But the Word of God finds no excuse whatever for unbelievers. It says, "They love darkness rather than light, and their deeds are evil." If the love of God, which has been made manifest in Christ, and which supports and sustains us, and gives us the best that we could wish for ourselves; if the love of God which promises heaven to us as the place where our souls can rest in peace; if the love of God, which on the first day of the Christian Pentecost so wondrously manifested itself in the coming of the Spirit — if this love of God does not awaken a responsive love in man's heart, there must be an obstinate aversion in such a heart to that which is good and a preference to that which is evil.

O let us love Him, then, for He hath first loved us! Let us believe in God's only begotten Son and thereby accept the gift of our salvation! Let us "not be of them who draw back unto perdition, but of them that believe to the saving of the soul."

And now it remains to be said that this acceptance of the benefits of Christ is not a condition that man must fulfill, but again a free gift of God to man. The same means of divine grace by which God offers all the spiritual blessings prepared for us, is also the power of God which works in us the acceptance of what is earnestly offered to all. Natural man, as described in our text, is only capable of rejecting the grace of God in Christ, loving darkness rather than light, yea, being himself darkness, dead in sin, an enemy of God, unable and unwilling to accept the salvation which is in Christ Jesus. But God so loved the world that He also provided the means whereby sinners may be led forth from the thraldom of sin, the power of darkness, to His marvelous light. It is the Gospel of Christ whereby faith is engendered in the sinner's heart, and whereby the Holy Spirit preserves us with Jesus Christ in the one true faith. Thus it is God who not only enacted the wondrous works of Christmas, and Good Friday, and Easter, but who also works the miracle of Pentecost through all ages and to the end of time. And hereof we, too, are witnesses. And hence, to the end of our lives, our prayer shall be. —

> Lord God, Thou Holy Spirit,
> My Comforter and Guide,
> Grant that in Jesus' merit
> I always may confide,
> Him to the end confessing,
> Whom I have known by faith
> Give me Thy constant blessing,
> And grant a Christian death
>   Amen.

CPSIA information can be obtained at www.ICGtesting.com
Printed in the USA
BVOW07s1041240314

348580BV00010B/332/P